Still the Big News

Still
the Big News,

*Racial Oppression
in America*

BOB BLAUNER

TEMPLE UNIVERSITY PRESS
Philadelphia

Temple University Press, Philadelphia 19122
Copyright © 2001 by Bob Blauner
All rights reserved
Published 2001
Printed in the United States of America

A revised and expanded edition of *Racial Oppression in America,*
this book was previously published by Prentice-Hall, Inc. ©1972 Prentice-Hall, Inc.

♾ The paper used in this publication meets the requirements of the
American National Standard for Information Sciences—Permanence
of Paper for Printed Library Materials, ANSI Z39.48-1984.

Library of Congress Cataloging-in-Publication Data
Blauner, Bob.
    Still the big news : racial oppression in America / Bob Blauner.
        p. cm.
    Includes bibliographical references.
    ISBN 1-56639-873-8 (cloth : alk. paper) — ISBN 1-56639-874-6
        (pbk. : alk. paper)
        1. Racism—United States. 2. Race discrimination—United States.
        3. United States—Race relations. 4. Afro-Americans—Social conditions—
        1975–   . I. Title.

E184.A1 B556 2001
305.8'00973—dc21   00-051155

Contents

Preface

IN RUSSELL Banks's great novel *Cloudsplitter,* Owen Brown summed up the views of his father, the abolitionist martyr John Brown, as follows: "Father took race to be the central and inescapable fact of American life and character, and thus he did not apologize for its being the central fact of his own life and character." This "inability to forget" about race explained why Negroes, both slave and free, trusted John Brown; they responded to "his insistence on seeing [race] as a factor in every dealing, every relationship, every conflict between any two Americans."[1]

The point that the novelist has so well expressed—that race is the central reality of the American experience, that it inhabits every aspect of our social institutions, as well as our personal lives—was also the primary thesis of my 1972 book *Racial Oppression in America.* And although thirty years have passed since the essays collected in that book were written, race remains a central and pervasive force in American life, as the recent *New York Times* series "How Race Is Lived in America" abundantly documents.[2] Indeed, in American life and history, race is like a gritty old boxer who just won't stay down. Every time an over-optimistic social commentator celebrates the eclipse of race and heralds the arrival of the colorblind society, racial divisions and the tensions they breed rise up phoenix-like from the ashes.

As the philosopher Charles Mills argues, American society was founded on the basis of a "racial contract" through which power and privilege were reserved primarily for white men.[3] Given our country's slavery past and its usurpation of the lands of the Indians and the Mexicans, it should come as no surprise that we continue to be haunted by the poisonous demons of racial division and hatred. Much more surprising is the way that European societies in the recent past have been ravaged by differences of ethnicity, nationality, and religion, which have been at the center of the political struggles that have led to secession, war, and even genocide. Sociologists were not prepared for these developments, in large part because the great European pioneers of social theory believed that racial, ethnic, national, and religious loyalties would eventually disappear in modern industrial societies, because capitalist societies are organized into classes and therefore have no room in the long run for such parochial bonds of allegiance. However, such bonds proved more durable than predicted, so that in both Europe and the United States, race and ethnicity are still the big news.

My title, *Still the Big News,* is borrowed from Robert Ezra Park, an early-twentieth-century pioneer of American sociology. Park encouraged his students at the University of Chicago to study that city's ethnic and racial minorities, as well as urban issues in general. By the time I became a student there in the late 1940s, Park had retired, but for my introduction to sociology I am indebted to his colleagues Ernest W. Burgess, Everett Hughes, Louis Wirth, and, above all, Herbert Blumer. Park's conception of sociology influenced my own approach to the field. Before he entered academia and pioneered the sociology of race and ethnic relations, Park had been Booker T. Washington's personal secretary, as well as a journalist. In high school I had been a newspaper reporter and editor, which is perhaps why I identified, not only with Park's jargon-free writing style, but also with his dictum that sociologists were "superjournalists" whose mission was to tell and to interpret "the big news" of social change.

The second half of the 1960s was a period of rapid and bewildering social change in America, especially with regard to race relations. To try to make sociological sense of what was happening, I used the great events of that era—the riots in South Central Los Angeles ("Watts") and other urban centers, the renaissance of black and Chicano culture, the rise of the Black Panthers, the growth of a "third world movement," and the struggles for black and ethnic studies programs—as starting points for a series of essays later collected in *Racial Oppression in America.* At the outset of that book I expressed the fear that these essays would soon become outdated, since they were so much a product of the unusually volatile historical era in which they were written. To offset this possibility I tried to uncover the "deep structure" of American race relations and analyze these persisting patterns in my discussions of internal colonialism, institutionalized racism, and the paradoxical connection between racial oppression and culture.

That I succeeded, even beyond my own expectations, first became apparent during the 1970s, when the book sold extremely well. After a brief period in the late 1970s and early 1980s, when interest in race receded in academia, the persistence of the patterns I had identified was again demonstrated, when the theory of internal colonialism came back into fashion. To my surprise, my essays were cited once again by other scholars, reprinted in new anthologies on America and its race relations, and included (most often without permission) in course readers. As always, race had refused to be knocked out, and for more than a decade now it has been a central preoccupation in a wide variety of fields besides sociology. Indeed the demand for the present volume may have something to do with the fact that, without any conscious intent, my old essays, in particular those on internal colonialism and institutionalized racism, presaged a number of contemporary schools of analysis in cultural studies, law, and the social sciences, including critical race theory and whiteness studies. That's the good news.

The bad news is that so many experts in these areas seem to think that my essays, written to describe and explain the American system of racial oppression in the late 1960s, apply just as well to America at the beginning of the new millennium. The question of racial change—what the 1960s accomplished and failed to accomplish—is a complex one that I've addressed in *Black Lives, White Lives: Three Decades of Race Relations in America* (1989). But it is a theme that also underlies almost every essay in the present book, above all the concluding one.

In the more than fifty years that I've been fascinated by the literature on what Gunnar Myrdal called "the American dilemma," I have read no single work that gets to the heart of race in America as well and as profoundly as Russell Banks's novel *Cloudsplitter*. So I end this preface with an additional quote by Banks's fictionalized John Brown. Whites, John Brown believed, had to separate themselves from "the luxurious unconsciousness" that characterized their race, because "in America whites are as much stuck with their skin color and bannered by it as the Negroes, and the Indians and Orientals, too. . . . Paradoxically then, it is when a white person *resists* the privilege of turning colorless that he frees himself, at least partially, from the sickness of racialism. It's the only way for a white man to finally clamber up and out of the pit of Negro slavery wherein this nation was unnaturally conceived."[4]

If the essays in this book emphasize race and racism more than is comfortable for many of my readers, it is my hope that, by challenging such "luxurious unconsciousness," more of us can begin to "clamber up" and out of the pits and potholes of a society that, again in Banks's/Brown's words, is "poisoned at the root."

I have divided this volume into three parts. Part One contains material from *Racial Oppression* as well as the essay "Almost a Race War: The Climate of the Late 1960s," written for *Black Lives, White Lives*. My goal in this opening chapter is to give those readers who did not experience that extraordinary period of social conflict and racial polarization a feeling for the times in which the essays that follow it were written. Whereas Part One is largely concerned with theoretical matters, Part Two is concerned with how the ferment in sociological thinking about race helped to uncover the racist frameworks within social institutions, such as law and higher education. Part Two also draws from *Racial Oppression* but ends with a 1970 article, "Toward the Decolonization of Social Research." Part Three consists of essays written in the 1990s that reflect my current views on the sociology and politics of race; the more recent work can be read as a kind of a dialogue with the earlier formulations.

When I read the essays in Parts One and Two of this book again in the year 2000, I was most struck by the tone of utter certainty that marked my writing thirty years ago. This confidence would be shattered only a year after *Racial Oppression* was published, when the first in a series of midlife crises brought doubt and uncertainty to the forefront of my mind. I never regained that early sense of certainty, which is one of the reasons why the essays in Part Three, all written in the 1990s, differ in tone from their earlier counterparts. Other factors include changes in the historical period and changes brought on by my own development, including growing older. All of these developments combined to modulate the anger, intensity, and impatience with which I had addressed America's racial injustices in the late 1960s and early 1970s. And today, with many more miles remaining on the road to equality, I no longer even harbor the idea that I might witness a society in which, as we said in a pre-feminist era, all men would be brothers. Being forced to give up the dream that inspired me in my youth has been one of the most painful experiences of my life.

Readers may also note that I no longer use the idea of internal colonialism in these more recent writings. The reasons for giving up that concept are discussed in the conclusion to this volume. It wasn't just that I saw too many problems with colonial theory. Even more important, I became disaffected with, even distrustful of, *all* sociological theory. The "theory" that I use in more recent essays emerges from real-life situations that I've been a part of, above all the classroom debates that I discuss in the essay "Talking Past One Another: Black and White Languages of Race."

The 1980s and 1990s saw an explosion of interest in language and discourse in virtually every academic field. In the essays in Part Three I participate in that trend by analyzing the idea of racism, the master concept in the language of race. I explore how this critical term is used by different groups and the consequences of their varying usage. Rather than using institutional racism to explain American social realities, as I did in Part One of this book, I now put the spotlight on the word itself.

But with all these differences, the essay form remains my most comfortable vehicle of expression, especially as that form has become more personal (once again mirroring the times). And just as with the earlier essays, most of the more recent ones were inspired by the big news of race in America, for example, the Rodney King case (see Chapter 13) or the upsurge in tension between Jewish and black Americans (see Chapter 15).

One notable exception: I wrote nary a word about the racially charged O. J. Simpson trial of 1995. There were moments, I must admit, when I was tempted to sell my soul for the big money I might have made as an expert witness on one side or the other, or, much more speculatively, to parlay my credentials as an authority on race into a bestselling book on the case. But I must confess why I pursued neither of these ventures: I never watched a minute of the trial on television; I turned the channel whenever it came up on a network newscast; and although I am a great newspaper reader, I did not read a single item about one of the biggest news stories of the decade. My avoidance is best explained by a contrary—perhaps even ornery—streak in my character, a revulsion against hype and what I see as the worst excesses of mass culture, above all America's undue concentration on celebrities.[5]

Finally, a few words about how I have edited my work. The brief introductory remarks to each chapter attempt to situate the essay in the larger social-political context, as well as the personal context, in which it was first written. I have eliminated most of the original notes and some of the references that no longer seemed necessary. With two exceptions, I have made only minor cuts in the text of the original essays. In a few cases I have changed a chapter's title in order to better describe its contents.

Acknowledgments

WHEN I was younger the circle of friends among whom I circulated drafts of my writing was much larger. Acknowledging them all might take up several pages in my earlier books. Fortunately I have already thanked many of the people whose criticisms helped so much in preparing these essays when they first appeared. But several friends, above all David Wellman and Stephen Steinberg, merit my gratitude for encouraging, even insisting, that I get this book into print. Steinberg's publicly avowed support for my early work has meant a lot to me, and I have also enjoyed the exchange of letters in which we have aired some of our disagreements on the classic studies of race in America. He, Wellman, and Michael Omi also provided excellent feedback on an early version of the conclusion. I also appreciated the fine comments of Charles Henry on an essay on Martin Luther King, Jr., which didn't make the book, as well as the suggestions of Russ Ellis for improving my discussion of the 2000 elections in the final chapter.

It has been a special pleasure to work with Janet Francendese, Temple University Press's editor-in-chief. Her enthusiasm and intelligence have made a big difference in my getting the job done. In addition, her assistant, Margaret Weinstein, was always most helpful, and in the last stages of production, the manuscript was improved by the absolutely first-rate copyediting of David Updike.

And finally, I thank the two people who most consistently have supported my various writing projects: my agent, Andrew Blauner of Blauner Books, even though he was not directly involved in my arrangements with Temple University Press; and Karina Epperlein, who has been telling me to get this out almost as long as we've been married, and to whom I am indebted for daily doses of love and creative stimulation.

PART ONE

THE EMERGENCE OF A CRITICAL RACE THEORY

1   Almost a Race War

The Climate of the Late 1960s

The conflict between an increasingly militant black movement and a society whose white majority resisted most of its demands had escalated throughout the 1960s. Black–white relations and attitudes were already polarized in April 1968, when the rioting that followed the assassination of Martin Luther King, Jr., led many Americans to believe that the long-feared racial civil war had finally arrived.

At the time of the assassination I was carrying out research based on depth interviews with black and white Americans that encompassed the life histories of our subjects, as well as their attitudes toward contemporary social problems, particularly race relations. No topic revealed such a chasm between the races as the death of King. For Afro-Americans, the loss was a personal one, like a death in the family. But many of the whites we talked to were indifferent to the assassination, as well as highly critical of the civil rights martyr. And even some of the people who were shocked or saddened by King's death told us that if that civil war did come to pass, they were prepared to shoot and kill blacks, including their black friends.

The spring and summer of 1968 saw an ever-growing sense of crisis, but the issues that divided the nation transcended race. The success of the North Vietnamese Tet offensive, coupled with the increasing mass support for the antiwar movement, caused President Lyndon Johnson to announce that he would not seek re-election that year. America seemed to be dividing into two camps: those who were for "the system" and those who were against it.

Two years earlier, during the summer of 1966, Stokely Carmichael of the Student Nonviolent Coordinating Committee (SNCC) had first raised the call for "Black Power" during a march for civil rights in Mississippi. The idea of Black Power would help further radicalize the black movement and polarize the races. The media contributed to this polarization. Instead of emphasizing the straightforward meanings of Black Power—self-determination for Afro-Americans in controlling their own communities and defining their cultural realities—the press, as well as many white politicians, played up (and even manufactured) sinister undertones of violence, racial revenge, and black domination.

Black Power played an important role in the Afro-American quest for a positive sense of identity, which in turn forced members of the majority to confront their "whiteness" and to think long and hard about their personal responsibility for the system of racial inequality.

IF THE call for "Freedom Now!" epitomized the first decade of the modern civil rights movement that began with the Montgomery, Alabama bus boycott of 1955–56, the racial politics of the late 1960s centered on the demand for "Black Power." First articulated in 1966 by SNCC leader Stokely Carmichael an other young militants, Black Power stressed self-determination, the right of ethnic minorities to define their group identity and to make the decisions that affected their lives. Since the rules of the "system" were biased, the advocates of Black Power would invent their own rules, use "any means necessary," in the words of Malcolm X, the militants' theoretician and martyred hero.

In the black community this new mood provoked an intense debate about priorities and strategies for change. Should Afro-Americans continue to demand their right to participate fully in every aspect of American life, in essence following the white middle-class model for mobility and success? Or, since they would never be accepted as equal citizens in a racist society, would always be a group apart, should they instead turn inward and develop the strengths and potential of the black community as an economic, political, and cultural force that could stand on its own? "A decade of racial dialectics—of the cut and thrust of white racism and Black Power," as Thomas Blair explains, had touched the emotional roots of an ethnic ambivalence.[1] As the promise of America seemed to wither in violent conflicts—a divisive war, disruptions on college campuses, and political assassinations—blacks pondered James Baldwin's rhetorical question: "Would you want to integrate into a burning house?"

Integration versus separatism (or black nationalism)—a "choice" that proved to be oversimplified when posed as mutually exclusive alternatives—emerged as the central issue in the black politics of the late 1960s. This controversy had, of course, dominated black political thought for more than a century, but, except for the Garvey movement in the 1920s, the integrationist-separatist debate had been confined to a small circle of intellectuals. In the sixties the discussion moved out onto the streets—and onto television, which played a critical role in defining and publicizing what had been a private in-group debate. Television focused on the most extreme positions, playing up, even exaggerating, the differences between them. The media coverage emphasized personalities and turned leaders into symbols: Martin Luther King versus Malcolm X and the Black Muslims; later, King versus Stokely Carmichael.

Though some of the people we interviewed stressed the complementarity of the moderate and the militant strategies, the pendulum was clearly swinging to the younger generation of nationalists, especially in the North and West. Pro-integration leaders like Whitney Young of the Urban League and Roy Wilkins of the NAACP seemed outmoded compared to Carmichael or the Black Panthers. And even Martin Luther King was called a "has-been."

BLACK POWER, VIOLENCE, AND THE POLICE

In 1968 almost all the blacks we interviewed, including the moderates, favored some form of Black Power. The slogan had stimulated wide interest, but it was too ambiguous a term to be a focal point for developing a unified political strategy. To moderate blacks, Black Power meant building up black business; to liberals, it denoted greater electoral participation and more educational and employment opportunities. To cultural nationalists and many intellectuals, Black Power signified the right of black people to define their own group realities, choose their priorities, write their history, create a culture. Political nationalists stressed the importance of building autonomous all-black institutions—schools, businesses, police—in their communities. Militants of various tendencies equated Black Power with fighting back against racist provocations. In the vehemence of militant rhetoric, many whites—and not a few blacks—sensed undertones of violence.

The shift from integration to Black Power confused whites. They wondered what blacks really wanted, what they would do next. Schooled by traditions of racist thought to view blacks categorically, whites expected them to speak with one voice and had difficulty appreciating their personal, philosophical, and political diversity. If blacks wanted to build their own separate communities, whites asked, why are they still demanding special treatment in the system—at work or at school?

In the separatist rhetoric of the Black Power advocates, whites also saw a rejection of consensual values, particularly the national myth of the melting pot. And by tirelessly pointing the finger at America's racist structure, black militants challenged the commonly held idea that a minority group could find equality and justice through the normal workings of the American way. Further, the militants were no longer willing to wait for the fate of their people to slowly improve as the result of aggregate personal efforts and sacrifices made by specific individuals; they wanted immediate equality for all blacks.

In challenging basic American values and myths, Black Power advocates antagonized virtually every strand of white opinion. The greatest opposition came from liberals, whose integrationist credo was offended by Black Power's separatist emphasis. "Colorblind" liberals especially objected to the idea that power blocs should be based on race. Conservatives tended to be more comfortable than liberals with frank talk about power, but few welcomed its association with people of color. More explicit racists insisted that power should remain with whites. Even most white radicals, otherwise sympathetic to black militancy, expressed skepticism, seeing Black Power as a threat to the fragile bonds among the sixties' anti-establishment movements or as an obstacle to the Marxist dream of working-class unity or the counterculture's vision of universal love.

The idea of Black Power also tapped into deep-seated fears and anxieties, highly emotional associations between race and violence. Whites had difficulty accepting that Black Power was what blacks said it was: community control, economic autonomy, and political self-determination. Though some learned to appreciate these meanings, most suspected that Black Power was a disguised call to use violence to achieve black domination. Black rioting in the cities, the appearance of nationalist groups "taking up the gun," and the pervasive talk—as well as the reality—of political and personal violence gave shape to racist fears. In such a highly charged atmosphere, most whites did not make a sharp distinction between a principled adherence to nonviolence and a more open-ended political strategy. They saw instead the aggressive potential in any militant action, sensed the threat of violence even in nonviolent civil disobedience.

At the same time, many blacks were hard pressed to maintain their own commitment to nonviolence. The strategy of "turning the other cheek" appealed to religious ideals and to an Afro-American redemptive humanism that had been a strikingly successful tactic in the early stages of the civil rights movement. But temperateness was increasingly seen as ineffective, cowardly, even unmanly. Nonviolence had not prevented civil rights workers in the South from being beaten and killed; in the North nonviolence had little to offer the younger generation of low-income blacks, particularly the street youth who saw in groups like the Black Panthers a more appropriate vehicle for their rebellious mentality.

When "riots"—more often termed "rebellions" or "revolts" by politically conscious militants—first erupted in 1964 and 1965, even moderate blacks were sympathetic, understanding the depth of the anger that lay behind the outbursts. Many of these blacks were hopeful that such extreme measures would spur fundamental reforms. By the time we began our interviews, however, people were very critical of the violence. Their objections were not based on a moral condemnation so much as a cost-benefit analysis: what was the political payoff of rioting, when only their own communities were being destroyed, their own people dominating the list of dead and wounded?

This may explain why the summer of 1967 was the last of the "long hot summers." Although some of the decade's heaviest rioting followed the assassination of Dr. King in April 1968, there were no major ghetto revolts during the summers of 1968 or 1969, years when racial tension was otherwise at its peak. Rather, riotlike actions in the late sixties moved away from the "Watts model" toward more focused settings: high schools, colleges, and especially prisons. There were also organized actions by black nationalist groups against the police in a number of cities. Many blacks to whom we talked in 1968 were moving toward an acceptance of this kind of controlled, focused violence—but not without conflict. They searched their souls to find ways to reconcile their ethical values with the growing feeling that desperate measures were necessary, especially in dealing with the police.

The police were major actors in the racial drama. Because they were on the front lines, trying to contain riots, seeing that civil rights and other demonstrations operated within the law, and making arrests in racially sensitive situations, their role was often controversial. Blacks and whites viewed them quite differently. Most blacks saw law enforcement as the country's most racist institution. Though they appreciated the need for public safety and deterring criminals, they resented being harassed by white cops and were disturbed by widespread allegations of brutality. As law enforcement became more politicized, targeting militant organizations such as the Black Panthers, many blacks began to view white police forces as colonial armies of occupation.

For many whites, in contrast, the police were the "thin blue line" protecting them from anarchy, revolution, and black violence. Often with friends or relatives on the local force, whites tended to identify with police officers, seeing them as workers with a job to do, decent men besieged by belligerent blacks, overzealous antiwar activists, and rebellious college students. A solid majority of whites approved the actions of the Chicago police in suppressing radical antiwar demonstrators at the Democratic Convention in 1968; blacks overwhelmingly disapproved.[2] A year earlier, after the decade's worst riots in Detroit and Newark, a Harris poll showed that whites had supported, by a ratio of 2.5 to 1, the police's shooting of looters; blacks had disapproved by the same ratio.[3] And unlike black people, most whites did not agree with the Kerner Commission's premise that urban riots were spontaneous manifestations of discontent arising from discrimination and prejudice. Instead, whites suspected that the violence was the result of agitation by communists or by leaders such as King and Carmichael—to many whites the political differences between moderate and militant black leadership seemed unimportant.

BLACK IDENTITY AND WHITE CONSCIOUSNESS

Throughout the 1960s blacks were becoming more aware of their systematic oppression, of the institutional character of the racism that marked the parameters of their existence—their present lives as well as past histories. It was common then to say that no black person had to learn this, for each had lived it directly, his or her consciousness of oppression forged in the pain of survival. The interviews we conducted suggest that this was more true for the older southern-reared generation, which had experienced the clearcut lines of traditional segregation. But there were quite a few others, mostly northern-raised youth or Californians, who told us that they had never been discriminated against, never really knew what "all the fuss was about" until the movements and the mood of the sixties began their education in race relations, giving them for the first time a sense of racial grievance.

Along with an intensifying awareness of racism came a new attitude toward black ethnic identity. Many of our interviews capture the still-fresh excitement of this discovery, as positive feelings like pride and identification replace negative ones like self-doubt and alienation. Pride in blackness and the new identification with "black culture" also suggested a solution to the dilemma of integration. On the one hand, to get one's fair share of society's benefits, it was necessary to participate, at least to a certain extent, in the mainstream, which was, after all, "the only game in town." On the other hand, if integration meant "becoming white," compromising one's ethnicity and deepest self, it seemed less and less worth the price. During the late sixties, black pride, black culture, and Black Power promised to give Afro-Americans a way to negotiate this dilemma, to feel that they were setting some of the terms of the assimilation bargain.

Many blacks we talked to remained skeptical about the existence of a black culture—until the 1960s the standard view had been that slavery and assimilation had eliminated most vestiges of distinctive ethnicity—but others celebrated its growing recognition. They searched for their culture's themes and essential features and inventoried its strengths and weaknesses. Black Power with its separatist overtones was appealing because it promised to nourish and preserve the uniqueness of the black experience. This fear that the communal solidarity of black life would be lost in the American melting pot also contributed to the widespread ambivalence toward integration in the late 1960s.

The word *black* itself symbolized this new outlook, and its rapid acceptance showed the power of this "cultural revolution." In our earliest interviews, everyone—black and white alike—referred to people of Afro-

American descent primarily as *Negroes*. By late 1968 (for blacks) and by the summer of 1969 (for whites) the dominant, almost exclusive, usage was *black* people.

In emphasizing race and racism so markedly, in flaunting their blackness so aggressively, the black militants forced many whites to confront the fatefulness of skin color and its social implications. Living in a multiracial society with democratic ideals and a colorblind ideology, whites as the dominant group had not experienced race and racism as pressing realities in their everyday lives. Especially since de facto segregation limited regular contacts with racial minorities, American whites had been able to confine their "whiteness" to remote corners of their consciousness, identifying themselves primarily as Americans, or as Irish or Italians, Catholics or Baptists. Outside the South (and the minds of transplanted southerners), whiteness per se was rarely a significant component of personal identity. (The very phrase "white identity" seems strange and jarring.) In the 1960s, however, blacks made it harder for whites to keep their racial identities so conveniently compartmentalized. Black actions impinged on white lives directly: at work, in the community, above all in politics and public life. The black demand that Euro-Americans own up to their whiteness met resistance. People who saw themselves as fairminded and committed to equality and individual responsibility did not want to face the possibility that their social position might be, even in part, the product of racial privilege.

This issue of who was responsible for racial inequality was not an abstract one, because it was tied to the practical matter of who would pay the costs of social change. In broad terms, whites addressed the question in one of three ways. First, they could accept personal responsibility for racism, viewing themselves and their families, friends, and fellow workers as personally implicated in the problems of black Americans. Having acknowledged their own racist bias, they could decide how best to act on this new self-understanding. And a few whites did wrestle with these agonies, sometimes in affecting ways, like the hippies we talked to who considered themselves racists just because they *noticed* differences of color.

But other whites didn't feel like racists. They thought of themselves as decent human beings, as people deserving what little they had achieved in their lives, not as oppressors or exploiters. Some adopted a sociological explanation of racism, condemning the society itself as a racially oppressive one. Among the people we interviewed, the liberals and the radicals in particular took this position and supported, if only ambivalently, fundamental social change to create racial justice.

Fundamental social change, however, threatened whites' own interests, and most whites found the analysis of racism as an impersonal force, an attribute of a system rather than of individuals, too abstract, too removed from their personal experience, or just plain wrong. So the majority took a third view. They neutralized the reality of racism by minimizing their own color privileges and denying their personal prejudices. Rather than indicting themselves or the social system, they "blamed the victim," locating the barriers to racial equality in the characteristics of the minority group. With traditional racism discredited as an ideology, few people now blamed the "deficits" of blacks on biology or genetics. More fashionable was some version of "cultural deprivation." Blacks were not able to advance like other groups because they lacked the critical attributes necessary for success: education, motivation, good work habits, discipline, and family cohesiveness.[4]

WHY THERE WAS NO RACE WAR

Underlying and facilitating racial and social ferment in the 1960s was an unprecedented economic boom. Employers' needs for more workers dovetailed with civil rights pressures to bring down discriminatory barriers, and blacks entered new industries and occupations. Paradoxically, these changes were too slow for the excluded minorities, whose expectations had been raised throughout the decade, and at the same time too fast for the white majority, whose interests seemed threatened by the prospect of racial change. As the nation moved slowly toward greater equality, conflict increased rather than lessened.

Conflict particularly intensified in day-to-day personal encounters. In every sphere of life, blacks challenged the spoken and unspoken assumptions that had governed race relations for generations. No longer were they accepting an inferior position, especially in the racial struggle itself. Those sympathetic whites who had once played important, even leading, roles in racial politics found themselves unwelcome in civil rights organizations.

For centuries blacks had lived in fear of whites. Now whites were afraid of blacks, their political militancy, their new aggressiveness, their potential violence. Whereas whites, as the "superior race," had long rejected blacks, now black people—especially the separatists—were rejecting whites, as political allies, as carriers of values, as models to be emulated. Instead of taking racial insults, blacks were calling the names "whitey," "honky," "racist"—and whites were learning how it felt to be the object of racial hatred, to be viewed categorically rather than as individuals. To many, it seemed as if the customary relationship between the races was being turned on its head.

Still, communication between blacks and whites was not closed. In the workplace, whites were hearing from black co-workers viewpoints on Black Power and other issues that countered the more alarming ideas they picked up from television and other whites. But whites sensed a change in black attitudes and demeanor, an anger and a withdrawal that were hard to deal with. Their most common complaint was that blacks were becoming too "touchy."

In other places where the races met—in high schools and the streets of mixed neighborhoods—racial tension was even more pronounced. In San Francisco's Haight-Ashbury white hippies complained of the frequent street hassles provoked by blacks. As one very pro-black hippy put it, poignantly but without a trace of irony: "It's so hard to be white these days." For their part, blacks, even moderates still committed to racial harmony, integration, and nonviolence, took some measure of delight in these reversals.

The great fear of whites was that blacks would go all the way and turn the tables. They thought blacks wanted to dominate them, just as blacks had been dominated. On both sides fear and paranoia were rife. Many blacks talked of genocidal plots, of concentration camps being readied. Whites thought that black militants were organizing armed insurrection, that their goal was to seize power through violent revolution. Especially after the assassination of Martin Luther King, people of both races worried that a civil war between whites and blacks might break out. One white man we talked to regretted the prospect of having to shoot some of his Negro friends; other whites contemplated going over to the black side; interracial couples agonized over their special predicament. At bottom, most people really didn't think it would come to a civil war, but the specter of racial holocaust aggravated the despair and pessimism of many blacks and intensified the fear of many whites.

Despite the widening color gap, racial division was never total, even during the polarized year of 1968. Though the polls found blacks consistently more opposed than whites to the war in Vietnam, some black conservatives sounded very much like white backlashers, supporting both the war and the actions of the Chicago police. And some whites were highly critical of the police and supportive of black militancy. Thus the forces that seemed to be dividing the society into two camps—either for or against "the system"—were not simply racial. The division was based rather on a collision between differing political priorities and philosophical assumptions about American society and social change.

On one side were those whose sense of urgency about racial problems transcended other concerns and values. Viewing racism and racial inequality as American democracy's most vital unfinished business, this group wanted to take advantage of the unique opportunity for a fundamental breakthrough that had been opened by the civil rights movement and, later, by the black militants. For those who held this position, the goal of incorporating blacks in the system was so paramount that it justified drastic changes in institutions and values to accommodate the special needs and interests of the previously excluded minorities. If such changes threatened an already fragile social order, the risk was worth taking, since it was these very institutions and values—whatever their democratic presumptions or "positive functioning"—that maintained a racially stratified society. Not surprisingly, this position was held by many (though not necessarily most) blacks, along with a small (though not necessarily insignificant) segment of the white population.

The "other side" had different priorities. Whether or not they supported the goal of racial equality, their major concern was the defense of a society whose integrity and stability seemed threatened by the divisiveness, the widespread violence, and the near anarchy of the time. For this group what was at stake was the democratic process itself. And because black militants insisted on setting their own rules and procedures and refused to accept conventional understandings of how to effect change, they were perceived as a threat to basic precepts of America's political culture. If black demands had merit, they must be accommodated to the consensual values of the society; racial minorities could not expect privileges unavailable to other groups. Most whites probably agreed with this point of view, and so did more than a few blacks and other minorities. Of course, there were people of both races who would not have subscribed to either position. They were somewhere in the middle, politically apathetic or uninterested in racial issues.

The events of the late 1960s challenged many people's assumptions and made them think about America and its social problems, especially race, on a deeper level. Ordinary people, not just intellectuals, struggled to make sense of the racial crisis, advancing theories to explain racial inequality, the urban riots, and the differences among minority groups. They approached a gamut of social issues with sophisticated critical perspectives; they drew generalizations from the conflicts and the public discourse of the time; and many of them experienced for the first time the excitement of participating in historically significant social movements and contributing to social change. Above all, people of every ethnic background debated issues of race and racism with the kind of urgency that the nation had not witnessed since the debates over slavery and Reconstruction a hundred years earlier.

2   Theoretical Perspectives

I first taught the sociology of race and ethnic relations at the University of Chicago in 1963. Two years later this specialty became the focus of my research and writing. As I read the literature I was struck by the weakness of the theoretical frameworks purporting to explain the most important division in American society. Even though I was learning from these theories, they had an ad hoc quality and seemed unconnected to the great traditions of social thought—unlike theories about social class, work and organizations, and political sociology I had studied.

It would have been unfair to expect race relations theory to predict the big news of the era: the eruption of a modern civil rights movement in the 1950s and that movement's turn from the goal of integration to that of Black Power and nationalism in the late 1960s. Almost everyone had been caught short by these historic events. But something had to be seriously wrong with theories whose logic pointed in a direction diametrically opposed to the drift of social change. The idea that I might be able to develop a better theoretical framework for the sociology of racial and ethnic relations inspired much of my writing during the late 1960s.

This chapter traces the failure of race theory to the fact that the giants of social thought whose ideas had shaped American sociology—Karl Marx, Max Weber, Emile Durkheim, Ferdinand Toennies, and Georg Simmel—all believed, despite their many differences, that racial and ethnic allegiances were primordial bonds that were destined to disappear as traditional societies gave way to modern ones. But just the opposite had happened; in the United States, race remained *at least* as central as class to our social order, pervasive and powerful in its impact on every area of existence.

I also take a critical look at the five perspectives on race in America that dominated the literature during the 1950s and 1960s. My shorthand labels for these "theories" are the *assimilation approach,* the *immigrant analogy, caste and class,* the focus on *prejudice and discrimination,* and *economic class reductionism.* During the 1970s and 1980s these theories would be critiqued by other scholars, with the result that they have been largely replaced by newer and more satisfactory frameworks (for example, the "racial formation" theory developed by Howard Winant and Michael Omi). But these old ideas still live in the minds of ordinary Americans. The immigrant analogy may no longer be popular among social scientists, but who has not heard a third-generation descendant of a European ethnic group voice words like, "My grandparents were poor and they made it, so why can't the blacks?"

THE PRESENT crisis in American life has led to the questioning of long-accepted frameworks. The pressure of events has forced intellectuals and social scientists to reexamine old definitions of the character of our society, the role of racism, and the workings of basic institutions. The depth and volatility of contemporary racial conflict challenge sociologists in particular to assess the adequacy of the theoretical models by which we have explained American race relations in the past.

In my view social theory should identify the significant social forces and trends of a historical period and, at the least, illuminate the relations among them. As a sociologist who was attempting to analyze the big news of the 1960s, I found that general sociological theory, as well as the more specific "theories" in the race relations field, was pointing in the wrong direction. These theories failed to predict and illuminate new developments—the shift from civil rights to group power strategies, the outbreak of rebellions in the urban ghettos, the growth of militant nationalism and ethnic consciousness—in short, the deepening of racial awareness and conflict in America. Furthermore, the "theories" actually obscured the meaning of these issues, making them more difficult to comprehend.

THE SOCIOLOGY OF RACE: AN ALTERNATIVE FRAMEWORK NEEDED

The present work parts company with the leading ideas and implicit assumptions that until recently, at least, have guided most American social scientists in their study of (or reluctance to consider) our racial order: First, the view that racial and ethnic groups are neither central nor persistent elements of modern societies. Second, the idea that racism and racial oppression are not independent dynamic forces but are ultimately reducible to other causal determinants, usually economic or psychological. Third, the position that the most important aspects of racism are the attitudes and prejudices of white Americans. And, finally, the so-called *immigrant analogy,* the assumption, critical in contemporary thought, that there are no essential long-term differences—in relation to the larger society—between the *third world* or racial minorities and the European ethnic groups.

In his *Crisis of the Negro Intellectual* Harold Cruse describes how Marxist interpretations of race and nationality came to dominate the perspectives of leading Afro-American theorists and political figures, even though this framework of analysis arose out of specific European conditions, which varied considerably from American realities.[1] In my view, sociology in the United States experienced a somewhat similar distortion, which had profound consequences for its outlook on race—although in this case it was not only Marxism but the larger structure of European social thought that steered American scholars off course. Despite the fact that the young discipline of sociology was not theory conscious before World War II, the limited and pragmatic concepts it utilized were predominantly home-grown.

Therefore, the leading figures of its developing years—such men as Albion Small, William Graham Sumner, W. I. Thomas, Charles Cooley, and Robert Park—gave major attention to race relations in their writings.[2] The life conditions and problems of immigrant groups and racial minorities were perhaps the predominant research emphasis. After the war the prestige of European social theory overpowered the contributions of the indigenous American sociologists and provided the basis for the conceptual schemes that today inform social science analysis of modern societies, including the United States.

For my purpose the most important assumption in this body of social theory is the idea that as industrial societies develop and mature, race and ethnicity become increasingly irrelevant as principles of group formation, collective identity, and political action. This assumption, so strikingly at odds with contemporary realities in the modern world as a whole as well as in the United States, can be traced directly to the impact of European social analysis.[3]

Karl Marx, Max Weber, Emile Durkheim, Ferdinand Toennies, and Georg Simmel stand as the great pioneers of sociology. Diverse as their theories were, a concern with interpreting the new bourgeois industrial order that had replaced a more traditional feudal society was a central intellectual priority for each of these scholars. In analyzing the modern world and the social forces that gave rise to it, they devoted relatively scant attention to ethnic and racial division and conflict. They saw such social bonds as essentially parochial survivals from preindustrial societies, and fundamentally opposed to the logic of modernity. Marx assumed that national differences would dissolve as the world proletariat developed a vision and practice based on class consciousness; he saw the more complex social differentiation of the past giving way to a dynamic of simplification and polarization that was leading to the predominance of only two classes as significant social forces. Durkheim and Toennies developed ideal types of traditional and modern social structures: *mechanical solidarity* versus *organic solidarity,* and the *gemeinschaft-gesellschaft* dichotomy, respectively. Ethnic solidarity belonged to the earlier social forms. Their conceptions of modern social arrangements precluded sentimental attachments based on race or ethnicity, or at least the likelihood that men would act on them consistently and frequently. Simmel saw in the city a metropolitan way of life in which such primordial bonds (to use Edward Shils's term) must lose their power and persistence.[4] And for Weber, perhaps the least disposed among them to an evolutionary perspective (and, incidentally, the theorist whose constructs are potentially the most fruitful for analyzing race and ethnicity), the basic historical dynamic—the movement from tradition to rationality—also appeared to indicate a weakening of these ties.[5] Thus the general conceptual frame of European theory implicitly assumed the decline and disappearance of ethnicity in the modern world; it offered no hints in the other direction. Without significant alteration, American sociology synthesized this framework into its models of social structure and change.

Rather than race, ethnicity, and nationality, the characteristic features of modern industrial societies were the centrality of classes and social stratification (Marx, Weber), the growth and ubiquity of large-scale bureaucratic organizations (Weber, Robert Michels), the trend toward occupational and professional specialization (Durkheim), and the dominance of the metropolis and its distinctive patterns and problems over less urban areas and concerns (Simmel, Toennies, and Durkheim). After World War II the subfields of sociology devoted to these phenomena were favored by the overall logic of social theory; specialties such as stratification, organizations, politics, urban studies, and so on, were thereby linked to the major theoretical paradigms and fertilized with the seminal ideas and conceptual schemes that were the European legacy to the American discipline. These fields also attracted the most talented scholars because their concerns penetrated the heart of modern society and its dynamics. After a promising start in the early period, the study of race and ethnic relations suffered correspondingly. With little room for ethnic and racial phenomena in the macroscopic models of social structure and process, the field was isolated from general sociological theory and particularly from those leading conceptual themes that might have provided coherence and useful lines of inquiry: stratification, culture, community. The study of race relations developed in a kind of vacuum; no overall theoretical framework guided its research and development. Not surprisingly, it has failed to attract leading social scientists, particularly during the past twenty-five to thirty years. While the fields of organization and bureaucracy, industry and occupation, interaction and deviance, have grown in depth and sophistication during the past generation, the same has not been true of the study of race relations, especially in terms of theoretical advancement.[6]

Without support from a general social theory, the study of race relations in sociology became organized around a variety of disparate approaches or foci of analysis. The leading approaches developed in ad hoc fashion. They were not well integrated with one another; of particular significance, none of them was able to articulate racial and ethnic phenomena to the structure and dynamics of the larger society satisfactorily. These approaches—with perhaps one exception that I discuss below—shared the key assumption of general sociology that racial groups and racial conflict were epiphenomenal and ephemeral. Thus the dominant perspectives within the subfield of race—among which the most representative have been Robert Park's theory of the race relations cycle and its present-day expression in the study of assimilation and ethnic groups, the caste-class model, the analysis of prejudice and discrimination, and the immigrant analogy—made it inevitable that sociological experts would miss the thrust of social change and movement during the 1950s and 1960s. A closer look at some of their key assumptions might help us understand why sociologists (not unlike other Americans) were caught napping by the intensity and scale of civil rights protest, the furor of ghetto revolt, and the rapidity with which Black Power, cultural nationalism, and other militant third world perspectives emerged and spread.

THE ASSIMILATIONIST BIAS

The most influential theory within the sociology of American racial studies has been that of the *race relations cycle* advanced by Robert Park. According to Park, when dominant and minority groups come into contact, they enter a series of relationships that he characterizes in terms of successive stages of competition, accommodation, and assimilation. Though Park and his students never clarified the dynamics that would inevitably lead from one stage to the next, the assumption that assimilation and integration were the likely end-products of ethnic and racial diversity has dominated American sociology. On the question of black people, Park was ambivalent and ambiguous. At times he saw them as a group in the process of being assimilated, at other times as an exception to the cyclical scheme.[7]

In addition to supporting the idea that American society is based on a dynamic of integration, the "assimilationist bias" distorted the analysis of the attitudes and movements of minority groups. Louis Wirth, a student and colleague of Park, granted the possibility that minorities could have other goals—separation, cultural pluralism, militant dominance. However, his view that in America the assimilationist goal was the only viable one became standard.[8] Afro-Americans were considered even more assimilation oriented than the European immigrants because it was believed that they had no ethnic culture of their own. In recent years third world nationalists have pointed out the ideological repressiveness implicit in the assumption that the cultural traditions of people of color are either nonexistent or less valuable than those of the dominant society. They have noted how social scientists have tended to ignore or distort the experiences and values of such groups as Indians and Mexicans, who have long histories of resistance to assimilation. Although some sociologists have developed the concept of assimilation in less dogmatic directions and qualified the rigid assumption of a *melting* pot solution (Milton Gordon and Nathan Glazer, especially),[9] most scholars did not seriously consider the possibility that racial minorities might prefer to build their own cultures and community institutions rather than choose absorption into the mainstream.

CASTE AND CLASS

The idea that assimilation and integration are the most probable outcomes of racial as well as ethnic heterogeneity rests on the assumption that racial oppression is an aberration rather than a fundamental principle of American society. The only major challenge to this premise within academic sociology has come from a group led by W. Lloyd Warner known as the *caste-class school.* Warner suggested that Negroes might be an exception to the general tendency toward ethnic assimilation because of the special power of color prejudice among white Americans.[10] In a series of studies of southern towns undertaken by his associates, John Dollard, Allison Davis, Burleigh Gardner, and Mary Gardner, the researchers were impressed by the similarity between the racial order they discovered and the historic caste system of India. They oriented their investigations around the castelike nature of the color line separating white and black, the class structure of each racial group, and the relations between these two principles of stratification.[11] This theoretical approach was useful for analyzing small communities over a limited period, and the idea of color caste had the special virtue of treating race and racial oppression as independent realities. But lacking the capacity to account for changes in racial patterns generated from within the system, it was a static conception. The only possibilities the caste-class school envisioned for obliterating the color line were southern industrialization and black migration to northern cities, processes that would thrust blacks and southern whites alike into the overall class system. Furthermore, this approach, like all the others, assumed, first, that a rigid racial order was a peculiarly rural phenomenon; second, that there was a fundamental disparity between northern and southern social structure; and third; that the North would be the spearhead of democratic racial change.

THE FOCUS ON PREJUDICE

Each of these three assumptions has been shattered by recent history. Although the emergence of the civil rights movement, and particularly its southern provenience, took sociology by surprise, the movement of the 1950s did not at first call into question the assimilationist premise. The predominant goal of southern blacks was integration and equality in institutional treatment. In a few years, however, massive white resistance and a growing realization of the limits of the movement's very success began to shake up prevailing thought about race in America. Most critically, the civil rights period exposed the depth and pervasiveness of racism in a society that appeared, on the surface, to be moving toward equality.[12]

Social science experts assumed that this movement toward equality depended primarily on the reduction of prejudice in the white majority, rather than upon the collective actions of the oppressed groups themselves or upon basic transformations in the society. Here sociologists were reflecting the general ethos of American culture, which minimizes a consciousness of, and concern with, group power—with the structure of institutions and their constraints—emphasizing in their stead the ideas and attitudes of individuals. Gunnar Myrdal had written in 1944 that all major transformations in American race relations would stem from determinants on the white side of the color line.[13] Sociologists and psychologists began to focus their research on racial attitudes (a development that was also furthered by a fascination with the unparalleled power of anti Semitism in Nazi Germany), and public opinion surveys noted that from the thirties through the fifties and sixties there was a consistent decline in racial prejudice and stereotypic thinking.[14] The 1954 *Brown* decision by the Supreme Court appeared to confirm the idea that powerful white institutions would respond in time to these changes in attitudes. Yet very soon afterwards, with the Montgomery bus boycott and subsequent civil rights actions, the initiative toward change in race relations passed out of white hands. The continuing deepening of racial crisis and conflict made it more and more apparent that white attitudes were peripheral rather than primary determinants of racial arrangements. There were still sociologists celebrating the impressive decline in racial prejudice at the very moment that Watts burst into flames.

I would not deny that ideas of white superiority are powerful in their impact, and that stereotypes of racial minorities have a tenacious hold on the conscious and unconscious mind. But prejudiced attitudes are not the essence of racism. Racism is unfortunately too often equated with intense prejudice and hatred of the racially different—thus with people of evil intent. This kind of racial extremism—while all too prevalent and very likely on the upswing among some segments of the American people today—is not necessary for the maintenance of a racist social structure. Virulent prejudice tends to be reduced, and crude stereotypes changed, by education and by exposure to more sophisticated environments. The people of goodwill and tolerance who identify racism with prejudice can therefore exempt themselves from responsibility and involvement in our system of racial injustice and inequality by taking comfort in their own "favorable" attitudes toward minority groups.

The error in this point of view is revealed by the fact that such people of goodwill help maintain the racism of American society and in some cases even profit from it. This takes place because racism is institutionalized. The processes that maintain domination—control of whites over nonwhites—are built into the major social institutions. These institutions either exclude or restrict the participation of racial groups by procedures that have become conventional, part of the bureaucratic system of rules and regulations. Thus there is little need for prejudice as a motivating force. Because this is true, the distinction between racism as an objective phenomenon, located in the actual existence of domination and hierarchy, and racism's subjective concomitants of prejudice and other motivations and feelings is a basic one.

THE IMMIGRANT ANALOGY AND ECONOMIC REDUCTIONISM

The perspective that has become most widely accepted recently is the immigrant analogy. It is based on an alleged similarity between the historical experience of European ethnic groups and the contemporary situation of racial minorities, who have become predominantly urban as a result of migrations from more rural areas of the South and Southwest. The analogy posits a common dynamic in the American experience through which lower-class and ethnically diverse outsiders become incorporated into the national consensus. Thus it may be viewed as an updated and perhaps sophisticated version of the assimilationist position. Although the immigrant analogy need not deny the special impact of racism, in practice its advocates tend to discount or minimize the pervasiveness of racial oppression, especially as a reality of the present period. In their view racism tends to be located in our past heritage of slavery, segregation, and discrimination. These historical forces and their present-day effects on the racially oppressed have slowed the assimilation and social mobility of people of color, maintaining minority groups in lower-class status for a longer period than was the case for the European ethnics. But for the common man who subscribes to this folk sociology, as well as for its academic exponents, racism is now largely a thing of the past. Therefore, those who hold this perspective are not pessimistic, despite the massive economic imbalances and social problems correlated with race. They assume that blacks, Chicanos, and even Native Americans will eventually follow the path of acculturation and "Americanization" marked out by the white immigrants. Thus the immigrant analogy serves to bolster a desperate need of many Americans to believe that our society can solve its internal problems; it is a contemporary version of the myth of progress and opportunity.

A variant of this perspective is the common view that the social position, life styles, and social problems of urban racial minorities in the North are predominantly reflections of poverty and economic class status, since a racial hierarchy has not been officially sanctioned. If "racial" problems are essentially problems of a recent arrival into urban lower-class position, then acclimation to city life and economic mobility will in time reduce the salience of race itself. This tendency to reduce race to class has been practiced by radical theorists as well as liberal policy-makers. Marxists have expected that a developing class consciousness cutting across ethnic and racial lines would eliminate national and racial considerations and lead to the collective solidarity of oppressed groups. Liberal sociologists expected race and ethnic concerns to recede as large numbers of individuals from the minority groups began to move into the middle class. Curiously enough, in the recent period it has more often been the mobile and middle-class elements from third world groups who have asserted their racial identities most aggressively.

The most important spokesman for economic class reductionism has been Daniel Patrick Moynihan. As President Nixon's chief advisor on urban social problems, Moynihan suggested that the nation stop thinking and acting in terms of race and focus instead on the common problems associated with poverty and class. Moynihan and the Nixon administration assumed that racial groups and racial oppression would disappear as social forces if third world people and "liberal-radical" whites (to use Spiro Agnew's fine expression) ceased talking about them. Thus the economic class reductionism inherent in the conservative doctrine of *benign neglect* merges with the *colorblind approach* to social reality that many white liberals have long favored. These approaches are of course ostrich-like. Race and racism are not figments of demented imaginations, but are central to the economics, politics, and culture of this nation.

COLONIALISM AND RACIAL OPPRESSION

Racial oppression occupies a central and independent role in American life. Unfortunately, social science lacks a model of American society and its social structure in which racial division and conflict are basic elements rather than phenomena to be explained (or explained away) in terms of other forces and determinants. To close this theoretical gap, in part, I rely on the framework of colonialism.

The connections between the American racial experience and the imperialism of Western societies have been blurred by the standard usage of the term "colonial America" in general parlance and in the field of history. In emphasizing the relations between the emerging nation of white settlers and the English mother country rather than the consolidation of white European control, the conventional usage separates the American experience from the matrix of Western European expansion. When we Americans think about European colonialism, it is the domination of Asia and Africa, which reached its peak in the late nineteenth century, that comes to mind. Yet American society has always been a part of this Western colonial dynamic, however isolated we were from the European center. Our own development proceeded on the basis of Indian conquests and land seizures, on the enslavement of African peoples, and in terms of a westward expansion that involved war with Mexico and the incorporation of half that nation's territory. Our economic and political power penetrates the entire non-Communist world, a new American empire, basing its control on neocolonial methods, having supplanted the hegemony of the European nations. The democratic and liberal self-image of our national ethos has deeply repressed these realities of our heritage. But revolutions in the third world and the stirrings of colonized populations in our own society have brought into the foreground a new consciousness of both domestic colonialism and empire abroad.

A focus on colonialism is essential for a theory that can integrate race and racial oppression into a larger view of American social structure. The colonial order in the modern world has been based on the dominance of white Westerners over non-Western people of color; racial oppression and the racial conflict to which it gives rise are endemic to it, much as class exploitation and conflict are fundamental to capitalist societies. Western colonialism brought into existence the present-day patterns of racial stratification; in the United States, as elsewhere, it was a colonial experience that generated the lineup of ethnic and racial division. Just as developing capitalism in Europe produced social classes out of a medley of rural and urban strata and status groups, the colonial system brought into being races, from an array of distinct tribes and ethnic peoples. It was European conquest and colonial wardship that created "the Indian," an identity irrelevant to men who lived their lives as Crow, Sioux, or Iroquois. And as a result of slavery the "Negro race" emerged from the heterogeneity of African ethnicity.

Yet the colonial perspective cannot by itself provide the theoretical framework necessary to grasp the complexities of race relations and social change in America. When the colonial model is transferred from the overseas situation to the United States without substantial alteration, it tends to miss the total structure, the context of advanced industrial capitalism in which our racial arrangements are embedded—a context that produces group politics and social movements that differ markedly from the traditional colonial society. Not enough work has gone into elaborating the main dimensions of the overall context and pursuing their implications for the social transformations of the future.

The new theoretical model needed to analyze and interpret American society might be based on the combined existence, historical interaction, and mutual interpenetration of the colonial-racial and the capitalist class realities. For America is clearly a mixed society that might be termed colonial capitalist or racial capitalist. Neither the explanatory framework of colonial theory nor conventional Marxist models of capitalism can adequately capture the complexity and paradoxes of racial oppression in relation to other compelling social forces.

3 White Privilege

The Key to Racial Oppression

> *He was a white man, with all the inescapable powers, privileges, and prerogatives of his race and sex: he could vote, own property, move about the land and settle wherever he chose; he could belong to any institution or church or attend any school he could afford; he could borrow money and loan it; he could invest his money in land or livestock and grow rich or become a bankrupt; he could own firearms; he could go to sleep at night and not fear that he would be wakened by slave-catchers and bounty-hunters come to sell him down the river; he knew who his parents, grandparents, and great-grandparents were and where they were buried; his children and wife would never be taken from him by another man; he was a white man, and he knew it.*
> —RUSSELL BANKS (DESCRIBING JOHN BROWN), CLOUDSPLITTER

In 1971 when I laid out my essays for the book that would be published as *Racial Oppression in America*, I had two articles on internal colonialism for its opening theoretical section. What I needed was a more general, less charged treatment of America's racial order, one that would highlight through clear documentation the systematic privileges enjoyed by white Americans in every sphere of social life. The chapter that follows was written to accomplish that, and though much of the data (for example, census statistics on wage differences between whites and blacks) have become outdated, the larger issues of privilege, control, and exploitation are still part of today's racial drama.

The term "racial oppression" in the subtitle of this essay (and the title of my 1972 book) needs some explanation. Then and now the generic term for my subspecialty of sociology is racial and ethnic *relations*. But as one of the field's leading experts, Stephen Steinberg, likes to remind me, "race relations" is an insipid term that misleads us by downplaying the systematic inequalities that are the essence of racial stratification. That is why I chose instead racial oppression, a term and an idea that makes much clearer the reality of domination and inequality.

THE PROBLEM OF RACIAL PRIVILEGE

Oppression is usually studied for what it does to the oppressed; even in dictionary definitions the role of the oppressor is a shadowy one. Yet all forms of social oppression, whatever their motivation, confer certain privileges on the individuals and groups that oppress or are able to benefit from the resultant inequalities. It is the creation and defense of group privileges that underlie the domination of one sex over the other, as well as the emergence of slavery, caste, and economic classes. Privilege is the heart of racial oppression also—for Albert Memmi the colonizer's privilege was the essence of the colonial relationship.[1] The various forms of social oppression all involve exploitation and control. To generate privilege, certain people have to be exploited, and to be exploited they must be controlled—directly or indirectly. The mechanisms of control, ranging from force and violence to legal restrictions to cultural beliefs, ideologies, and modes of socioeconomic integration, are therefore central to an understanding of oppression. Social oppression is a dynamic process by which one segment of society achieves power and privilege through the control and exploitation of other groups, which are *literally* oppressed, that is, burdened and pushed down into the lower levels of the social order.

There is much that is unique and special about racial oppression, but it shares the common elements and dynamics that make up social oppression as a generic phenomenon. In a racial order a dominant group, which thinks of itself as distinct and superior, raises its social position by exploiting, controlling, and keeping down others who are categorized in racial or ethnic terms. When one or more groups are excluded from equal participation in society and from a fair share of its values, other groups not so excluded and dominated are correspondingly elevated in position. The racist restrictions that strike at people of color in America result in a system of special privilege for the white majority. Whether or not particular racist practices are followed *consciously* in order to benefit whites is not the issue. Whatever the intent, the system benefits all strata of the white population, at least in the short run—the lower and working classes as well as the middle and upper classes.

I define privilege in terms of unfair advantage, a preferential situation or systematic "headstart" in the pursuit of social values (whether they be money, power, position, learning, or whatnot). Social privilege is not unique to racist societies. Like hierarchy and exploitation, it is a universal feature of all class societies, including those in which ethnic and racial division are insignificant. The values that people seek are never distributed equally; in the struggle for subsistence and social rewards there are always obstacles that impede some groups more than others. Thus systematic inequality and systematic injustice are built into the very nature of stratified societies. But when these inequities and injustices fall most heavily upon people who differ in color or national origin because race and ethnicity are primary principles upon which people are excluded or blocked in the pursuit of their goals, such a society is in addition racist.

White Americans enjoy special privilege in all areas of existence where racial minorities are systematically excluded or disadvantaged: housing and neighborhoods, education, income, and life style. Privilege is a relative matter, of course, but in racial and colonial systems it cannot be avoided, even by those who consciously reject the society and its privileges.[2] The iron law of white privilege gives rise to truly ironic situations. The children of the middle class who have "dropped out" to live in near-poverty conditions always hold in reserve their racial prerogatives when and if they decide to re-enter the mainstream. Many of these young cultural rebels have chosen the post office as an occasional means of subsistence, and in doing so they have threatened what has been a relatively protected sanctuary of black employment. And from the civil rights movement to the more recent student demonstrations, the white radicals have received a relatively more benign treatment from the police and the courts than have their third world counterparts.

Though racial privilege pervades all institutions, it is expressed most strategically in the labor market and the structure of occupations. In industrial capitalism economic institutions are central, and occupational role is the major determinant of social status and life style. If there is any one key to the systematic privilege that undergirds a racial capitalist society, it is the special advantage of the white population in the labor market.

As I emphasize in the next chapter, the white immigrants entered the labor force under considerably more favorable conditions than did the racial minorities. As the European ethnics and their children have moved up in the class structure, the casual, unskilled, low-paying jobs in the economy have been filled in good part through a new form of migration from rural to urban centers within the American continent. The lower stratum of the working class has become predominantly Afro-American, Mexican-American, and Puerto Rican. Suffering high rates of unemployment and marginal employment, third world workers fit Marx's conception of an industrial reserve army, which meets the system's need for an elastic labor pool. When working they tend to be concentrated in jobs that are insecure, dirty, unskilled, and at the bottom of the hierarchy of authority where there is little possibility for advancement. The result is that white workers have a monopoly or a near monopoly on jobs that are secure, clean, highly skilled, involve authority, and provide the possibilities of promotion. This pattern is so consistent that some economists argue that a *dual labor market* exists in many cities, one for whites and one for racial minorities.[3] Moreover, a number of studies summarized recently by Harold Baron show that black workers tend to be concentrated in old industries that are economically stagnant and declining in labor requirements.[4] The most advanced and progressive industries like oil and chemicals typically have all-white labor forces.

The white avoidance of dirty and servile work is a linchpin of colonial labor systems. As of 1960 more Negro men worked as janitors or porters than in any other detailed occupational category in the United States; more black women were employed as private household domestics than in any other line of work.[5] Blacks are either the majority or strikingly overrepresented in the work of cleaning floors and toilets, washing dishes and clothes, shining shoes, and handling the messes of sick people in hospitals and dead bodies in morgues.[6] The white working class elevates its status by protecting itself from the contamination of such unpleasant work and in the bargain increases its share of "good, clean jobs."

White monopoly over the skilled trades has, of course, become a national scandal; the unions have put up the most effective resistance to the general movement against racism. In 1960 only 5 percent of craftsmen and foremen were nonwhite. By 1970 this figure had increased to only 7 percent. In the union-dominated construction industry, where blacks have been concentrated in the laborer and other lower-paying trades, there was no increase in the proportion of craftsmen who were nonwhite between 1960 and 1970.[7] A vast number of studies have documented the slowness of employers, public and private, to promote people of color. Although in 1970 blacks made up 15 percent of all federal government employees, they held only 3 percent of the higher grade jobs under the Federal Classification Act, 4 percent of the higher grade positions in the postal service, and less than 10 percent of those blue-collar government jobs paying more than $8,000 a year.[8] In 1960 only 1.5 percent of industrial foremen were nonwhite;[9] by 1970 the proportion had risen to 5 percent.[10] The fact that for Afro-Americans going to work has almost always meant being bossed by whites is one reason why many independent personalities have preferred hustling within the ghetto to conventional employment.

I do not believe that the generally high living standards of white America can be attributed *in toto* to racial oppression and privilege, as the rhetoric of many radicals suggests. Of course, there would be no United States at all without the original colonial conquest. And the contribution of slavery to our economic development was immense. Yet today's widespread affluence is due primarily to the organizational and technological capacities of American capitalism and the historically high productivity of our rural and urban work force. We do not know precisely how much racial privilege has contributed to white living standards. In part because of the multiple variables involved and the lack of satisfactory data, in part because social scientists, like other Americans, do not face squarely their racial privileges, the problem has only recently begun to receive serious attention. In the most careful analysis to date, based on 1960 census data, Lester Thurow calculates a figure of $15.5 billion as the gain in overall white income that is derived from five areas of racial discrimination: more steady employment, higher wages, more lucrative occupations, greater investment in human capital (that is, education), and labor union monopoly. This averages out to a bonus of $248 a year for every white member of the labor force, and a corresponding loss of $2,100 for each nonwhite worker or job-seeker.[11]

Although the figure of $250 per capita appears to be too low, Thurow's findings suggest that a comparative study of racist societies would show an impressive contrast between the traditional colonial situation and that in advanced capitalist societies, like our own. Racial privilege varies from society to society, in both absolute amount and relative degree. In overseas colonialism, Europeans were a minority, either a tiny clique of officials or a more sizable settler population, as in South Africa and Algeria. The impact of racial privilege on white life styles in these colonial situations is suggested by the fact that every European who went overseas to a colonial station in Asia or Africa could afford, and was expected to have, one or more "native" servants. By contrast, in the antebellum South this was generally possible only for plantation owners, and in contemporary urban America only for the upper middle classes. In European colonies white income typically averaged *ten to twenty times* that of the colonized; even for the same work, white employees were paid four to ten times as much in the mines of Rhodesia and South Africa.[12] By contrast again, when racial wage differentials for the same job were common in American industry, they rarely surpassed 10 to 20 cents an hour. And in recent years the income of blacks has ranged between 50 and 60 percent of that of whites. These impressionistic indicators suggest the likelihood that white privilege, while real and significant, is not as inherently crucial to our economic system and social life styles as it was in classical colonialism. A numerical minority can live off a majority population in a more or less parasitical fashion; it is not possible for a numerical majority to do so. Nevertheless, white Americans tend to be very tenacious in resisting any threats to such privilege, whatever its absolute or relative level.

This may be because the salience of racial privilege is not identical for every segment of the colonizing population. Since white working-class people tend to have little formal education and specialized training, their occupational possibilities are few and tend to overlap with those of the racial minorities, especially when the latter are beginning to move and are

challenging their subordination. With relatively low income, white workers have few housing choices and therefore compete more directly with
people of color in the effort to improve residential situations. The same
point holds for education. Thus the marginal increment that racial privilege contributes to overall life chances may be higher for the white working class than it is for the middle and upper classes. Needless to say, the
class privileges of the latter are immeasurably greater.

Racial privilege is not simply economic. It is a matter of status also. Jef-
ferson Davis understood this when he said that Negro slavery "raises
white men to the same general level, that it dignifies and exalts every white
man by the presence of a lower race."[13] One hundred years later James
Baldwin put the same notion into a more sophisticated analysis when he
reasoned that the fluidity and insecurity of the American status order
required the Negro—so that white people would know where the bottom
is, a fixed point in the system to which they could not sink.[14]

Deplorable and despicable as these ideas are, they are real in terms of
social dynamics, the ways in which most white Americans orient their
actions. Although race has been a central organizing principle of our class
system, racial groups are not economic classes. In Max Weber's terms,
they are "status groups," collectivities based on an attempt to monopolize
social honor as well as economic advantage. All kinds of social forma-
tions—aristocratic and military elites, new religions, ethnic groups—have
striven to maximize their relative prestige. The ability of white Europeans
to command status in every racially mixed society on the basis of color
alone has certainly been the most fateful case of this tendency in modern
history.[15] The relevance of race to status illuminates the particular aggressiveness with which whites have defended segregated residential communities and, today, the schools that are rooted in them. The average person
in our society has a very limited opportunity to achieve status through the
social recognition of her or his work or income. The concern with status,
aggravated by the mass media and the competitive value system of capitalism, centers around home ownership and the quality and image of the
neighborhood in which the home is located. The sense of community
integrity among both white suburbanites and white ethnic groups in the
cities is threatened by the presence of nonwhite people.[16] The other status
concern of Middle America, the upward mobility of its children, appears
endangered by integrated schools.

Because economic and status privileges are bulwarks of racial stratification, racism cannot simply be viewed as a set of subjective irrational
beliefs that might be overcome through more and better contact, communication, and understanding. When such a focus on prejudice forms
the dominant approach to racial conflict—as it does in America today,

even among social scientists—then the fact that whites, blacks, Chicanos, and other third world groups have distinct objective interests is overlooked. Ethnic and racial groups are first and foremost interest groups. The Marxian view that "false consciousness" explains the failure of white workers to support racial movements and the nonwhite poor only illuminates one part of a complex reality. Since racial groups are real in America, the status concerns of race have a basis in social life. White workers know that they have something to lose by the elimination of racial privilege.

The fact of racial interest does not belie the importance of divergent and conflicting interests among different segments of the same racial groups, divisions that might widen with changing economic and political circumstances. In American society races and classes interpenetrate one another. Race affects class formation and class influences racial dynamics in ways that have not yet been adequately investigated. The entire relation between racial and class interest (and racial and class privilege) is an exceedingly complicated one that social theorists might well explore in a deeper fashion. It is the most important question that must be faced in constructing a theoretical model of racial capitalist society. But it is by no means only an academic problem, since the relation between class and race in contemporary America has bedeviled radical theorists and movement organizers seeking a strategy for revolutionary politics, as well as liberal policy-makers attempting to promote change within education, welfare, employment, and other urban institutions.

EXPLOITATION AND CONTROL

Modern race relations ultimately owe their origins to the exploitative dynamic and expansionist thrust of Western Europe that exploded in the late fifteenth century, ushering in the so-called "Age of Discovery." Purely economic motives predominated in the institution of new systems of domination through which whites appropriated the land, labor, and resources of various non-Western and nonwhite people. Most crucial was the racial division of labor that was established on slave plantations, in the haciendas of Indo-America, and later in the colonies of Asia and Africa. Labor and its exploitation must be viewed as the first cause of modern race relations; as we have seen, the main outlines of this division of labor are still reflected in the privileged position of whites within the occupational distribution and economic stratification of present-day multiracial societies.

All forms of labor exploitation—the factory as well as the plantation—require discipline and control. When unpleasant tasks are not integrated into kinship networks or traditional rituals, people have to be induced to do them for a minimal remuneration—especially when others determine the conditions of work and appropriate its results.

The discipline and control over the young proletariat in the early stages of English industry was brutal and heavy handed, as Marx's *Capital* attests. However the problems associated with the control of a working class in capitalist societies are of a lesser order than those generated by a colonial labor system.

The young proletariat under early capitalism resisted exploitation aggressively, through on-the-job actions and wider social movements. As a relatively unassimilated and restive class, the proletariat posed threats to the new economic arrangements and the stability of the larger social order. The capitalists therefore had to institutionalize factory discipline and at the same time contain the specters of anarchy, revolution, and the undermining of culture evoked by the working class and its movements. Both control problems were largely resolved in Western Europe, as well as the United States, through a long period of economic and political conflict. The working classes gained what T. H. Marshall has called *citizenship* in the larger society, with substantive rights and privileges.[17] Mass education, the assimilation of ethnic groups, voting and political parties, and economic mobility contributed to this process. Along with the institutionalization of labor unions, which have been strategic regulators of plant discipline, these developments have brought about the political integration of white working classes in Western capitalist societies. Such citizenship and political integration, made possible by new technology and increasing wealth, characterize the stage of advanced capitalism. Since the white worker no longer threatens the social order, industrial control has become specific to the factory. It is only a means to the ends of more efficient exploitation, stable profits, and the maintenance of the factory system as a paying enterprise. It is not an end in itself.

Crucial to industrial citizenship was the fact that Western proletariats were indigenous, of the same race and bearers of the same traditions as the ruling elites. The existing cultural gap was a product of poverty and economic position—or sometimes national origin, as with the Irish workers in England. But, as variations within European culture, these cultural differences were much smaller than those between Western and non-Western ways of life that racial labor systems institutionalized. Perhaps for this reason the proletariat, although typically stigmatized and deemed inferior, was not viewed as wholly outside the pale of humanity, as irrevocably "the other."

The problem of control was different in racial systems. Originating out of conquest or other forms of physical coercion, the labor force was recruited from societies and cultural traditions that were considered alien.

Because of this origin in force and social dislocation, the possibility of resistance and revolt, or at least the fear of them, was greater. Because of the cultural disparities and the colonizer's belief in his racial and cultural superiority, the society had no place for people of color to fit into the system in the long run as free citizens and equal competitors. Once such a labor system was established and white supremacy and its packet of privilege became valued in themselves, people of color had to be controlled and dominated because they were black, Mexican, Indians, or natives—not only because they were convenient resources for exploitation.[18] Since the kind of citizenship that integrated workers into an advanced capitalism was not a possibility, racial control became an end in itself, despite its original limited purpose as a means to exploitation and privilege.

Cultural domination may be the most significant mechanism of such racial control. The expansion of Europe and European peoples (including white Americans) over the world was motored by economic forces *and* by deeply held convictions that Christianity and other core Western values were superior to non-Western ways of life. In the course of conquest and consolidating control, the imperial powers attacked, disrupted, and violated in a thousand ways the original cultures of the colonized. The depth of white race feeling is intimately connected with this Western cultural arrogance, the seeming incapacity to appreciate and coexist in a nonaggressive fashion with diverging modes of organizing society and living in the world.

The United States was founded on the principle that it was and would be a white man's country. Nowhere was this insistence expressed more clearly than in the hegemony of Western European values in the national consciousness and in the symbolic forms that have expressed this cultural hegemony—institutionalized rituals (such as the ceremonies of patriotism and holidays), written history, the curriculum of the schools, and today the mass media. Indian, African, Asian, and Latin American groups had to adapt to what Harold Cruse has called "the cultural imperatives" of the white ethnic groups;[19] in the process their own cultural contributions were absorbed, obliterated, or ignored. Even the promise of assimilation to those individuals whose adaptations were deemed successful was at bottom a control device, since assimilation weakened the communities of the oppressed and implicitly sanctioned the idea of white cultural superiority. Cultural control over third world minorities has been particularly significant in intellectual life. The very characterization of their existence and group realities and the interpretation of their history and social experience have been dominated by the analyses of white thinkers and writers.

Racial control pervades every institution of American life today. This does not mean that all white people have power, all people of color none.

In a bureaucratic capitalist society, even most whites are without effective power, their lives controlled by the decisions of distant bureaucratic structures and the operations of the market. At the same time many individual third world people control some aspects of their own lives and command power over others of their group, as political leaders, employers, professionals, and so on, despite the persistence of the organizational norm that they must not wield authority over whites. Thus I am not making the argument that each person of color is completely powerless, nothing but the pawn of whites who direct and command. The systematic racial control that I am stressing operates on the collective level. Third world communities lack autonomy and self-determination; they are controlled by white economic and political structures. Perhaps the ghetto best illustrates this point.

Today's urban ghettos and barrios, like the legal segregation of the past, are devices for racial control. They reflect the basic contradiction of racial systems, which bring nonwhites into a society to appropriate their land or labor and not to associate with whites as free and equal citizens. The ghettos are the modern "solution" to this insoluble dilemma. They provide walls between the racially oppressed and the mainstream, shield the white majority from the anger and hostility of the confined, and permit the middle class to go about its daily business with a minimal awareness of how basic is racial division to American life. The modern ghetto is not the product of "blind" economic or market forces as many suppose. Rather, it is produced and maintained by deliberate policies of the real estate industry, supported by powerful segments of federal and local government and, unfortunately, buttressed by majority sentiments of the white population.[20] The police and the national guard are key factors in this equation. They channel the individual and collective violence that stems from racial colonialism, keeping it within the ghetto's own boundaries and containing sporadic tendencies for it to spill over into "white" areas.

Moreover, the black ghetto and other third world equivalents further the economic exploitation of the racial minorities. As Reich summarizes the situation: "Blacks pay higher rents for inferior housing, higher prices in ghetto stores, higher insurance premiums, higher interest rates in banks and lending companies, travel longer distances at greater expense to their jobs, suffer from inferior garbage collection and less access to public recreational facilities, and are assessed at higher property tax rates when they own housing."[21] Racial exploitation is more than economic, however. It is not necessary to argue that the labor of third world people has become dispensable in an automating technology and that economic exploitation is no longer a central underpinning of racism[22] to appreciate Cruse's insight that cultural exploitation of the Afro-American population takes on a special importance in the contemporary period. As Cruse emphasizes, the cultural, economic, and political aspects of oppression are intimately intertwined.[23] Cultural exploitation furthers political control, which serves to maintain economic subordination. The importance of subtle cultural manipulation as well as the dialectic between racial control and exploitation were vividly dramatized in the official national response to the assassination of Martin Luther King.

The death of a national leader is always disorienting. King's death was particularly disruptive to the precarious racial order of America, since he was the one black leader who combined a sizable following among his own people with high status in the country as a whole. His death was threatening because he was the major spokesman of the traditional civil rights movement and its philosophy of integration through nonviolence (values shared, at least in principle, by the liberal establishment)—a bulwark against the developing storms of nationalism and violence.

For a few days on the symbolic level, the death of King ironically brought about that integration of black people into American life that the assassinated leader had striven for. The young minister was lionized and elevated into the position of a national hero; it was clear that he would be the first Afro-American for whom schools, streets, and projects in white neighborhoods were to be named-unlike Booker T. Washington, George Washington Carver, Paul Laurence Dunbar, Frederick Douglass, and others, whose symbolic immortality is confined to segregated ghettos. During the period of national mourning, the mass media, which is virtually the bloodstream of America's body cultural, concentrated almost exclusively on the life and death of King and the problems of his people. It was a concerted attempt to incorporate Afro-American realities as part of the national experience through the creation of a hero and a legend.

Yet, with all the tribute to the fallen leader, the control and exploitation of black America remained the primary imperatives underlying the official reaction, which under close inspection revealed the classic motifs of racism. National leaders and the mass media made a bid to *appropriate* Martin Luther King—just as white America has historically ripped off the economic and cultural products of black life. King was a product of the southern Negro experience, his viability as a national figure related to the close ties he had maintained with his people. But in his death white establishment power, through the speeches of politicians and the work of television, claimed King as its own, as someone with whom it had always identified, someone it had supported. This did not come from any deep belief that the black leader had been speaking as their leader. Instead it was motivated by a desire to control the black population, to restrain its angry masses from riots and demonstrations, by incorporating them into a national pseudoconsensus of grief and dedication to King's principles. Thus placated by the outpouring of national respect, the black community, through its identification with King, was expected to feel integrated into American society, even though the economic and power arrangements of that society had not changed one whit and were still based on racial oppression. (This strategy was advanced by the attendance at the funeral, and its style. With all major politicians present except the President, it became a ceremony for national celebrities rather than a funeral made up of the poor and the blacks who were the murdered man's real constituency.)

But the most important way in which King was exploited in his death was through the distortion of his values and beliefs. Part of the mentality of racism seems to be an unconscious process of distorting the messages of minority people, particularly when individually or collectively they are acting "out of place," that is, not in accord with conventional stereotypes. This same thing took place with fateful effect as a response to the Black Power movement. Despite the efforts of black spokesmen to explain the ideas of cultural self-definition and economic and political control, it was only the threat of violence, usually at most only implicit in the tone of the militant's rhetoric, that white journalists and politicians seized upon. In the case of King the distortion may have been more conscious and calculated. His social philosophy was presented to the nation as centering almost exclusively on nonviolence as an end in itself. Politicians and commentators invoked his strictures against violence and hatred in an attempt to use him to keep the ghettos quiet. Virtually nothing was said about the three major enemies of King's wrath, to which he had devoted his recent efforts and speeches—racism, poverty, and war. Thus the living exploit the dead, and white power exploits black leaders and their philosophies.

The depth of white privilege was revealed by the strange spectacle of television reveling in the life and death of an Afro-American. The commentators and newscasters who introduced us to the dense geography and culture of King's formative years, explained his roots in the southern Negro religious tradition, and traced his emergence as a civil rights leader were in almost all cases white men. If ever there was an assignment appropriate for a black reporter, this was it. The programs dramatized the fact that the black experience had become a major industry in this country. During the 1960s, racial revolution, protest, and ghetto life with its social, economic, and human problems provided the major news that filled the space on television between the westerns, the ball games, and the old movies. Although many local stations have hired blacks, and many more must be looking for that qualified Negro, the reportage of the King assassination underlined how systematically black men and women have been excluded, on the national level, from profitable careers with the mass media. Exclusion from the desirable values of the society—the best jobs, the best homes and neighborhoods, the best schools—is a basic mechanism of racial domination. The other side of black exclusion is white privilege. This digression into the death of Martin Luther King is intended to illustrate the interconnection of privilege, exploitation, and control in the dynamics of racial oppression.

CONTROL OF MOBILITY AND THE IDEA OF PLACE

> If me want for go in a Ebo, Me can't go there!
> Since them tief me from a Guinea, Me can't go there!
>
> If me want to go to a congo, Me can't go there!
> Since them tief me from my tatta, Me can't go there!
>
> If me want for go in a Kingston, Me can't go there!
> Since massa go in a England, Me can't go there!
>
> — A JAMAICAN SLAVE SONG[24]

In order to control a racially defined people systematically, and so maintain special privilege for the dominant group, limits must be placed on the mobility of the oppressed minority. I refer both to the mobility of individuals in physical space and to collective mobility in socioeconomic status. Restrictions on the freedom of movement, part of the logic of all forms of oppression, are particularly strategic in racial systems. Perhaps this is because the modern racial order emerged from international movements of people, movements that were color patterned.

Exploration, trade, slavery, the settlement of colonies, and industrial development in the capitalist nations were processes that set in motion mass movements of population, which drastically altered the racial ecology of the world. Because expansion was a project of Western Europe and involved to an important extent the land, labor, and resources of non-Western people, this historical transformation intensified the salience of race and color. In the migrations, both voluntary and forced, that brought about the modern era, the primary movers were whites; people of color were, in the main, the moved.

The very essence of slavery is its rigid control over the human impulse to move about, as the Jamaican song expresses so poignantly. In the United States, the decision to maintain the racial order after Emancipation required new devices to constrain the movement and mobility of the freedmen. This was accomplished by ensuring their economic dependency, in most cases through tenant farming and sharecropping; by such "legal" devices as vagrancy statutes, pass laws, and jim crow ordinances; and by political intimidation practiced by the Klan and similar groups. For many years the North attracted Afro-Americans because it promised a greater degree of personal freedom; but even in the North restriction of mobility was commonplace.[25]

Other third world groups in the United States experienced limits on individual and collective movement, in large part because they entered as laborers in work situations that were particularly binding: debt servitude, peonage, and agricultural gang systems. Native Americans were, of course, a special and extreme case: their territory was continually constricted; their movements were more and more constrained by federal laws, broken treaties, and settler aggression. The special restrictions that were placed on the immigration of Asian and Latin American groups, including obstacles to attaining citizenship, also contributed to this dynamic. Many Chinese and Mexicans, for example, were able to enter this country only through unofficial or illegal channels, which prevented the possibility of naturalization. The activities of immigration officials in these ethnic communities intimidated citizen and noncitizen alike. European immigrants were favored because they started out as free laborers in industry, were less affected by discriminatory immigration and naturalization laws, and had the advantage of being white. One role of color is to serve as a visible badge of group membership that facilitates this blockage of mobility.

Thus, systems of racial domination depend ultimately on control over the movements of the oppressed and restriction of their full participation in society. Although this control may be secured by laws, or by violence or the threat of violence, the most common and more stable mechanisms reside in cultural beliefs and psychological adaptations. Here the notion of place is central. The idea that there is an appropriate place—or set of roles and activities—for people of color, and that other places and possibilities are not proper or acceptable, is a universal element of the racist dynamic. In America, as in the European colonies, white people used to say (and many still do): "The Negro (or native) is all right as long as he stays in his place."

The idea of place has had an infinite variety of expressions. Its classic form was the old-fashioned southern "etiquette of race relations," patterns of deference and demeanor in interpersonal interaction between the races. Occupationally, it meant that certain jobs were reserved for blacks and, to a degree, for other racial minorities. Its physical manifestation has been the Indian reservation, the Mexican section of town (or barrio), and the ghetto. Because blacks, for example, are supposed to "belong" only in their own neighborhoods, Negroes found in white areas—when they cannot easily be categorized in terms of a conventional racial role—are objects of suspicion and alarm, no matter how legitimate their business. Since police in our society are legally sanctioned to stop people "on suspicion," the practice of law enforcement confines Afro-Americans within the white man's idea of his place.

Central to this dynamic of place is the assumption, at times subconscious, that people of color should be subservient to whites. In the political sphere whites neither expect nor desire to see third world groups acting autonomously, defining their own goals, and controlling the pace of their social movements. The stricture to operate "within the system" along individualistic American lines rather than moving collectively "against" the society reflects the white imperative of overall control. Thus, civil rights activity commanded the support of white liberals as long as blacks were working within the framework of national leadership and accepting the rules and procedures of political decision making in America. The autonomous and aggressive character of the Black Power thrust was a rejection of this traditional Negro followership role, and many whites therefore cried "unfair."

Within the national culture, people of color have been prescribed distinctive roles. Indians are either romantic figures or the noble savages of our past—or, like the Mexicans, they are ignored, particularly in the contemporary urban condition. Blacks have usually been the group most central to pressing political issues and national obsessions. In the cultural sphere their major role assignment has been that of entertainer. As vaudeville comic, singer, dancer, musician, or athlete, they could make people laugh, cry, or wonder at their exploits; however, they were not to make people think or question their lives, because the roles of intellectual, cultural critic, creator, and political statesman were out of place.

Of course there have always been those who refused to accept "their place" in society. Various Native American tribes carried on armed struggle over a period of three hundred years. In the Southwest the Mexicans who fought Anglocolonialism and racial arrogance were labeled bandits and outlaws. Similarly, the black man who rebelled against white dominance became the "bad nigger," a term that invoked some respect within the Afro-American group. For generations, lynching was the prescribed punishment meted out to "uppity" Negroes who violated the norms of the racial order. It is a general law of colonial racial systems that the oppressing group has a license to kill members of the "inferior" race without serious likelihood of punishment.[26] Legitimizing this ultimate sanction assures control of the oppressed group, because emerging protest movements are checked in their early stages. Even in the recent period, when protest and even rebellion have become commonplace and "bad niggerism" almost an accepted style in race relations, many if not most of the important leaders of the black movement have met violent deaths, and a group such as the Panthers has seen much of its leadership imprisoned or otherwise harassed.

The importance of place and the dynamics of accommodation and resistance explain why racism modifies the forms of social stratification and the processes of social mobility in a racial capitalist society like America. The collective mobility of the racial minorities is reduced because of discrimination in the labor market and at the work place. Some economic gains have taken place, resulting primarily from the movements from rural regions to industrial urban centers and the cyclical swings of the economy. But the pervasiveness of white privilege and blocked movement distorts even this form of individual mobility. Improvements in income and occupation are not easily translated into an overall raising of social status and increase in political effectiveness, as they are for white groups. The symbols and prerequisites by which status is validated—improved residence, neighborhood, and life style—are not available, because the housing market is racist. And political power and the general respect of society lag far behind improvements in group economic position. Finally, the conversion of parental gains into family (intergenerational) mobility is limited by the institutional racism of the schools, which thwarts the aspirations and educational achievements of minority children.

In still another way, racial oppression negates the general sorting and sifting processes of social mobility, by which class redistribution takes place in advanced capitalist societies. Studies based on the white population suggest that there is some truth to the old saying, "talent rises to the top." According to this research, the children of the poor and working classes who are above average in intelligence and energy are the ones most likely to attend college and move into the middle classes.[27] But because the institutions that serve as gateways to class placement express the racial oppressiveness of the society, the most sensitive, creative, and energetic youth from minority communities are those most likely to come into conflict with these institutions, challenging the authority of the mediocre functionaries—schoolteachers, policemen, and others—who personally maintain the colonial relationship. The explosion of creative talent and political leadership that has emerged from the prisons and the street corners suggests that the rebellious spirits whose careers have been a cycle of difficulties in school, entanglements with the law, and dropping from the mainstream might have fed the political, economic, and cultural elites of the society had they been born into a nonracist order. The foremost example is Malcolm X, who achieved greatness through the schools of street hustling, prison, and the Black Muslim movement. Eldridge Cleaver and the late George Jackson exemplify the creative talents locked up in prisons; but these two successful writers and revolutionary thinkers are only the tip of the iceberg, as the recent political and cultural ferment in state penitentiaries suggests. It is significant that Harold Cruse, perhaps the outstanding theoretician of the black movement in America, developed his scholarship through twenty years in the marginal world of bohemian radicalism rather than in the universities where the leading white social theorists are found. Examples could be multiplied.

One virtue of the poverty program and related special opportunity projects in education and industry is that they have provided a second chance for many of these talented men whom racism had brought to despair or forced to operate outside the system. The demand that poverty organizations hire only indigenous leaders and workers has created a new avenue for the recognition, the use, and the development of these potentials. Even the colleges and the universities, now that they are opening some doors to minority students, are finding that many of the most able are those whom the lower schools had once labeled as unfit for academic pursuits.

In summary, the logic of racial oppression denies members of the subjugated group the full range of human possibility that exists within a society and culture. From this standpoint racism is a historical and social project aimed at reducing or diminishing the humanity or manhood (in the universal, nonrestrictive meaning of the word) of the racially oppressed. All the roles, places, and stereotypes that are forced upon the dominated share a common feature: they function to define the person of color within frameworks that are less than, or opposed to, the status of full adult manhood. The tendency of racism is to convert the colonized into objects or things to be used for the pleasure and profit of the colonizer; the stereotypes and mental imagery of the white population then depict them as animals or children, the better to justify such less-than-human patterns of relatedness. This dynamic of racial colonialism has been eloquently expressed by Toynbee:

> When we Westerners call people "Natives," we implicitly take the cultural colour out of our perceptions of them. We see them as trees walking, or as wild animals infesting the country in which we happen to come across them. In fact, we see them as part of the local flora and fauna, and not as men of like passions with ourselves, and seeing them thus as something infrahuman, we feel entitled to treat them as though they did not possess ordinary human rights. They are merely natives of the lands which they occupy; and no term of occupancy can be long enough to confer any prescriptive rights. Their tenure is as provisional and precarious as that of the forest trees which the Western pioneer fells or that of the big game which he shoots down. And how shall the "civilized" Lords of Creation treat the human game,

when in their own good time they come to take possession of the land which, by right of eminent domain, is indefeasibly their own? Shall they treat these "Natives" as vermin to be exterminated, or as domesticable animals to be turned into hewers of wood and drawers of water? No other alternative need be considered, if "niggers have no souls." All this is implicit in the word "Natives" as we have come to use it in the English language in our time.[28]

THE REFUSAL OF RACISM AND THE AMBIGUOUS FUTURE

The dehumanization inherent in racial oppression explains why a concern with personal dignity and manhood is central to anticolonial and antiracist movements. The insistence on affirming these principles lies at the heart of present-day racial conflict in the United States. What is new among third world people today, particularly the youth, is a stubborn unwillingness to compromise the principle of personal dignity. It is difficult for whites to comprehend how the major institutions in our society (as in others based on a history of racial colonialism)—the schools, the labor market, welfare, police and the courts—consistently belittle and diminish the sense of personal worth and dignity of nonwhite people. In the past the majority of the oppressed adapted to this situation in one way or another; those who could not or would not came into open conflict with institutional authority. Today this numerical balance is shifting.

Therefore the big news in America today is not really racism, the pervasiveness of white domination. Rather, it is the consistent challenge to patterns of racial control that the oppressed are mounting in every area of society. Perhaps the deepest refusal of racial norms has come in the cultural sphere, where entire third world generations are rapidly discarding assumptions about the superiority of white people and Euro-American values.

People are talking about racism today because race relations are up for grabs. Not since Reconstruction has there been such an extended period of volatility in our racial order. The traditional norms have lost their force as the colonized minorities refuse to be controlled by oppressive institutions. As more and more people of color refuse to play the part of victim of racism, the contradiction between their shifting orientations and white-dominated institutions intensifies. The refusal of racism forces change in education, in employment, in politics, and in other institutions. But because of white privilege and organizational inertia, the changes are too slow for the excluded groups and at the same time too fast for the dominant majority, many of whom have become frightened and confused.

Thus, racial awareness and conflict escalate, even if "things are getting better" for at least important segments of nonwhite populations.

Today many of the specific notions of place operate only weakly. Firms hire blacks as door-to-door salesmen in white neighborhoods, and even Wall Street has welcomed its first black-owned brokerage firm. Many institutions have been forced to accept the independent political role of third world caucuses and communities. Television has accelerated the widening of cultural roles, especially for blacks. But breaks in the racial order do not portend its imminent collapse, although they permit the observer to see its outlines more clearly. The specific constellations of the roles reserved for people of color in our society undergoes change, generally in a less restrictive direction, but the underlying themes reappear in new and unexpected ways.

The thesis that informs this essay—that racial division and oppression are leading elements (and probably indispensable ones) in American society and culture as they are presently constituted—is not an optimistic one. Theorists who interpret race within a framework of economic and social class are less pessimistic because they see more explicit promise of progressive social change. The liberal can look forward to eventual integration of, and citizenship for, the racial minorities, like the industrial working class and the ethnic immigrants; the radical Marxist can hold up the prospect of future class-based revolution. But in a racial or colonial capitalist society where the racially oppressed are a numerical minority, how can racism be overcome when the majority of the population gains from it and presumably will defend these privileges as rational and objective interests? Here even the solution reached by victims of classical colonialism, the ejection of the colonizer and the achievement of national independence, does not seem to be a realistic possibility.

If my analysis is correct, the situation is unique and the problems are real and difficult. Yet race is not the only reality of American society, nor its only principle of human oppression. Although I have emphasized in this essay that the racial privileges of the white majority are rooted in objective interests, it is equally important to stress that racial domination is not the only significant interest of white people. The various axes along which people are exploited, manipulated, or, otherwise controlled in a capitalist society create potential group interests within the wider population. Workers, employees, consumers, women, old people, youth, and students have specific needs that are not satisfied, and problems that are not resolved, simply by favored position in the racial order. Furthermore, there are interests shared by all people to which racial inequality—and the civil conflict it breeds—is antithetical. These include membership in a social order with at least a minimum of solidarity and community, and a system of cultural values with a modicum of integrity, not one shot through with falsity and contradiction. The political and cultural rebellion of white youth is a symptom of the fact that these crucial human needs are not met by the larger society.[29]

In the long run, the movements of third world people against racial oppression may play a strategic role in creating the conditions for the conversion of these latent nonracial interests into overt challenges to the system. As the civil rights movement made clear, racial protest exposes the contradictions of the larger society and the limits of the possibilities inherent in its political and economic arrangements. In its first stages, such exposure contributes very little to basic social transformation. The majority group responds by resisting change, digging in to maintain its privileges. The so-called "backlash" may represent a more explicit awareness of racial position, a new white consciousness, defensive and reactionary in nature, but, as with all racial consciousness, in large part rational and based on a partial grasp of social reality. As the racial minorities step up the momentum of their demands and white consciousness and racial privilege reveal their limitations as answers to group conflicts, a more complex awareness of the social forces underlying the contemporary crisis should emerge. Third world militancy may play an essential role in the development of a more widespread political consciousness of the oppressive dynamics of racial capitalism. Such a consciousness is a prerequisite for effective mass movements of social transformation.

4　Colonized and Immigrant Minorities

In the early years of the Cold War the whole world seemed divided between the Western capitalist countries led by the United States and the Communist societies of Eastern Europe and Asia who followed the Soviet model. In order to better resist the persistent pressures to join one of these two great camps, a number of nonaligned nations came together in 1955 at a conference in Bandung, Indonesia. They would be called *le tiers monde,* a "third world" destined to become a force in international politics independent of the first world of capitalism and the second of communism. The term caught on and by the end of the 1960s when most of the former colonies of Africa and Asia had achieved independence, the aggregate of nations and peoples in the less economically developed parts of the globe was routinely referred to as the "third world."

The success of the anticolonial movements was an inspiration to people of color in America, who began to define their struggles for equality in the context of national liberation. In the past, America's racial minorities—Native Americans, Chicanos, Asians, and blacks—had pursued their own political agendas, only rarely working together. But that changed in the 1960s. During the 1968 student strikes at San Francisco State and Berkeley for the creation of ethnic studies curricula, the four groups came together as a "third world movement," using that appellation both to point out their shared oppression within the United States and to underscore their identifications with people of color in Asia, Africa, and Latin America.

At this time I was working with a number of other social scientists on a book devoted to the experiences of America's four major racial minorities. My task was to assemble materials for a general section on colonialism. The essay that follows was first written as an introduction to the section of that book, which we were calling *The Third World Within.*

The rationale for classifying the four nonwhite groups into one sociological category is that each underwent experiences of colonization that were not shared with the white ethnic groups who had immigrated from Europe. There is some overlap between the discussions of "the colonization complex" in this essay and what follows in Chapter 5. Since the latter essay was written three years earlier, I had time to refine the arguments of the present chapter, to make it stronger and more compelling, and to add a new dimension to the colonization complex: the colonial labor principle.

As for *The Third World Within,* our editor dropped out of publishing to become a hippy, so the book never appeared. I revised the draft in 1971 for my book *Racial Oppression in America.* The essay remains one of my favorites, even though I now feel that I went too far in pushing the contrast between the colonized and the immigrants, with some potentially negative consequences (see Chapter 12).

DURING THE late 1960s a new movement emerged on the Pacific Coast. Beginning at San Francisco State College and spreading across the

44

bay to Berkeley and other campuses, black, Chicano, Asian, and Native American student organizations formed alliances and pressed for ethnic studies curricula and for greater control over the programs that concerned them. Rejecting the implicit condescension in the label "minority students" and the negative afterthought of "nonwhite," these coalitions proclaimed themselves a "third world movement."[1] Later, in the East and Midwest, the third world umbrella was spread over other alliances, primarily those urging unity of Puerto Ricans and blacks. In radical circles the term has become the dominant metaphor referring to the nation's racially oppressed people.

As the term *third world* has been increasingly applied to people of color in the United States, a question has disturbed many observers. Is the third world idea essentially a rhetorical expression of the aspirations and political ideology of the young militants in the black, brown, red, and yellow power movements, or does the concept reflect actual sociological realities? Posed this way, the question may be drawn too sharply; neither possibility excludes the other. Life is complex, so we might expect some truth in both positions. Furthermore, social relationships are not static. The rhetoric and ideology of social movements, if they succeed in altering the ways in which groups define their situations, can significantly shape and change social reality. Ultimately, the validity of the third world perspective will be tested in social and political practice. The future is open.

Still, we cannot evade the question, to what extent—in its application to domestic race relations—is the third world idea grounded in firm historical and contemporary actualities? To assess this issue we need to examine the assumptions upon which the concept rests. There are three that seem to me central. The first assumption is that racial groups in America are, and have been, colonized peoples; therefore their social realities cannot be understood in the framework of immigration and assimilation that is applied to European ethnic groups. The second assumption is that the racial minorities share a common situation of oppression, from which a potential political unity is inferred. The final assumption is that there is a historical connection between the third world abroad and the third world within. In placing American realities within the framework of international colonialism, similarities in patterns of racial domination and exploitation are stressed and a common political fate is implied—at least for the long run. I begin by looking at the first assumption since it sets the stage for the main task of this chapter, a comparison and contrast between immigrant and third world experience. I return to the other points at the end of the essay.

The fundamental issue is historical. People of color have never been an integral part of the Anglo-American political community and culture because they did not enter the dominant society in the same way as did the European ethnics. The third world notion points to *a basic distinction between immigration and colonization as the two major processes through which new population groups are incorporated into a nation.* Immigrant groups enter a new territory or society voluntarily, though they may be pushed out of their old country by dire economic or political oppression. Colonized groups become part of a new society through force or violence; they are conquered, enslaved, or pressured into movement. Thus, the third world formulation is a bold attack on the myth that America is the land of the free, or, more specifically, a nation whose population has been built up through successive waves of immigration. The third world perspective returns us to the origins of the American experience, reminding us that this nation owes its very existence to colonialism, and that along with settlers and immigrants there have always been conquered Indians and black slaves, and later defeated Mexicans—that is, colonial subjects—on the national soil. Such a reminder is not pleasant to a society that represses those aspects of its history that do not fit the collective self-image of democracy for all men.

The idea that third world people are colonial subjects is gaining in acceptance today; at the same time it is not at all convincing to those who do not recognize a fundamental similarity between American race relations and Europe's historic domination of Asia and Africa. (I discuss how U.S. colonialism differs from the traditional or classical versions toward the end of the chapter.) Yet the experience of people of color in this country does include a number of circumstances that are universal to the colonial situation, and these are the very circumstances that differentiate third world realities from those of the European immigrants. The first condition, already touched upon, is that of a forced entry into the larger society or metropolitan domain. The second is subjection to various forms of unfree labor that greatly restrict the physical and social mobility of the group and its participation in the political arena. The third is a cultural policy of the colonizer that constrains, transforms, or destroys original values, orientations, and ways of life. These three points organize the comparison of colonized and immigrant minorities that follows.

GROUP ENTRY AND FREEDOM OF MOVEMENT

Colonialism and immigration are the two major means by which heterogeneous or plural societies, with ethnically diverse populations, develop. In the case of colonialism, metropolitan nations incorporate new territories or peoples through processes that are essentially involuntary, such as war, conquest, capture, and other forms of force or manipulation. Through immigration, new peoples or ethnic groups enter a host society more or less freely. These are ideal-types, the polar ends of a continuum; many historical cases fall in between. In the case of America's racial minorities, some groups clearly fit the criterion for colonial entry; others exemplify mixed types.

Native Americans, Chicanos, and blacks are the third world groups whose entry was unequivocally forced and whose subsequent histories best fit the colonial model. Critics of the colonial interpretation usually focus on the black experience, emphasizing how it has differed from those of traditional colonialism. Rather than being conquered and controlled in their native land, African people were captured, transported, and enslaved in the southern states and other regions of the Western hemisphere. Whether oppression takes place at home in the oppressed's native land or in the heart of the colonizer's mother country, colonization remains colonization. However, the term *internal colonialism* is useful for emphasizing the differences in setting and in the consequences that arise from it.[2] The conquest and virtual elimination of the original Americans, a process that took three hundred years to complete, is an example of classical colonialism, no different in essential features from Europe's imperial control over Asia, Africa, and Latin America. The same is true of the conquest of the Mexican Southwest and the annexation of its Spanish-speaking population.

Other third world groups have undergone an experience that can be seen as part colonial and part immigrant. Puerto Rico has been a colony exploited by the mainland, while, at the same time, the islanders have had relative freedom to move back and forth and to work and settle in the States. Of the Asian-American groups, the situation of the Filipinos has been the most colonial. The islands were colonies of Spain and the United States, and the male population was recruited for agricultural serfdom both in Hawaii and in the States. In the more recent period, however, movement to the States has been largely voluntary.

In the case of the Chinese, we do not have sufficient historical evidence to be able to assess the balance between free and involuntary entry in the nineteenth century. The majority came to work in the mines and fields for an extended period of debt servitude; many individuals were "shanghaied" or pressed into service; many others evidently signed up voluntarily for serflike labor.[3] A similar pattern held for the Japanese who came toward the end of the century, except that the voluntary element in the Japanese entry appears to have been considerably more significant.[4] Thus, for the two largest Asian groups, we have an original entry into American society that might be termed semicolonial, followed in the twentieth century by immigration. Yet the exclusion of Asian immigrants and the restriction acts that followed were unique blows, which marked off the status of the Chinese and Japanese in America, limiting their numbers and potential power. For this reason it is misleading to equate the Asian experience with the European immigrant pattern. Despite the fact that some individuals and families have been able to immigrate freely, the status and size of these ethnic groups have been rigidly controlled.

There is a somewhat parallel ambiguity in the twentieth-century movement from Mexico, which has contributed a majority of the present Mexican-American group. Although the migration of individuals and families in search of work and better living conditions has been largely voluntary, classifying this process as immigration misses the point that the Southwest is historically and culturally a Mexican, Spanish-speaking region. Moreover, from the perspective of conquest that many Mexicans have retained, the movement has been to a land that is still seen as their own. Perhaps the entry of other Latin Americans approaches more nearly the immigrant model; however, in their case, too, there is a colonial element, arising from the Yankee neocolonial domination of much of South and Central America; for this reason, along with that of racism in the States, many young Latinos are third world oriented.

Thus the relation between third world groups and a colonial-type entry into American society is impressive, though not perfect or precise. Differences between people of color and Europeans are shown most clearly in the ways the groups first entered. The colonized became ethnic minorities *en bloc,* collectively, through conquest, slavery, annexation, or a racial labor policy. The European immigrant peoples became ethnic groups and minorities within the United States by the essentially voluntary movements of individuals and families. Even when, later on, some third world peoples were able to immigrate, the circumstances of the earlier entry affected their situation and the attitudes of the dominant culture toward them.

The essentially voluntary entry of the immigrants was a function of their status in the labor market. The European groups were responding to the industrial needs of a free capitalist market. Economic development in other societies with labor shortages—for example, Australia, Brazil, and Argentina—meant that many people could at least envision alternative destinations for their emigration. Though the Irish were colonized at home, and poverty, potato famine, and other disasters made their exodus more of a flight than that of other Europeans, they still had some choice of where to flee.[5] Thus, people of Irish descent are found today in the West Indies, Oceania, and other former British colonies. Germans and Italians moved in large numbers to South America; Eastern Europeans immigrated to Canada as well as to the United States.

Because the Europeans moved on their own, they had a degree of autonomy that was denied those whose entry followed upon conquest, capture, or involuntary labor contracts. They expected to move freely within the society to the extent that they acquired the economic and cultural means. Though they faced great hardships and even prejudice and discrimination on a scale that must have been disillusioning, the Irish, Italians, Jews, and other groups had the advantage of European ancestry and white skins. When living in New York became too difficult, Jewish families moved on to Chicago. Irish trapped in Boston could get land and farm in the Midwest, or search for gold in California. It is obvious that parallel alternatives were not available to the early generations of Afro-Americans, Asians, and Mexican-Americans, because they were not part of the free labor force. Furthermore, limitations on physical movement followed from the purely racial aspect of their oppression, as I stressed in the previous chapter.

Thus, the entrance of the European into the American order involved a degree of choice and self-direction that was for the most part denied people of color. Voluntary immigration made it more likely that individual Europeans and entire ethnic groups would identify with America and see the host culture as a positive opportunity rather than an alien and dominating value system. It is my assessment that this element of choice, though it can be overestimated and romanticized, must have been crucial in influencing the different careers and perspectives of immigrants and colonized in America, because choice is a necessary condition for commitment to any group, from social club to national society.

Sociologists interpreting race relations in the United States have rarely faced the full implications of these differences. The *immigrant model* became the main focus of analysis, and the experiences of all groups were viewed through its lens. It suited the cultural mythology to see everyone in America as an original immigrant, a later immigrant, a quasi-immigrant, or a potential immigrant. Though the black situation long posed problems for this framework, recent developments have made it possible for scholars and ordinary citizens alike to force Afro-American realities into this comfortable schema. Migration from rural South to urban North became an analog of European immigration, blacks became the latest newcomers to the cities, facing parallel problems of assimilation. In the no-nonsense language of Irving Kristol, "The Negro Today Is Like the Immigrant of Yesterday."[6]

The Colonial Labor Principle in the United States

European immigrants and third world people have faced some similar conditions, of course. The overwhelming majority of both groups were poor, and their early generations worked primarily as unskilled laborers. The question of how, where, and why newcomers worked in the United States is central, for the differences in the labor systems that introduced people of color and immigrants to America may be the fundamental reason why their histories have followed disparate paths.

The labor forces that built up the Western hemisphere were structured on the principle of race and color. The European conquest of the Native Americans and the introduction of plantation slavery were crucial beginning points for the emergence of a worldwide colonial order. These "New World" events established the pattern for labor practices in the colonial regimes of Asia, Africa, and Oceania during the centuries that followed. The key equation was the association of free labor with people of white European stock and the association of unfree labor with non-Western people of color, a correlation that did not develop all at once; it took time for it to become a more or less fixed pattern.

North American colonists made several attempts to force Indians into dependent labor relationships, including slavery.[7] But the native North American tribes, many of which were mobile hunters and warrior peoples, resisted agricultural peonage and directly fought the theft of their lands. In addition, the relative sparsity of Indian populations north of the Rio Grande limited their potential utility for colonial labor requirements. Therefore Native American peoples were either massacred or pushed out of the areas of European settlement and enterprise. South of the Rio Grande, where the majority of Native Americans lived in more fixed agricultural societies, they were too numerous to be killed off or pushed aside, though they suffered drastic losses through disease and massacre.[8] In most of Spanish America, the white man wanted both the land and the labor of the Indian. Agricultural peonage was established and entire communities were subjugated economically and politically. Either directly or indirectly, the Indian worked for the white man.

In the Caribbean region (which may be considered to include the American South),[9] neither Indian nor white labor was available in sufficient supply to meet the demands of large-scale plantation agriculture. African slaves were imported to the West Indies, Brazil, and the colonies that were to become the United States to labor in those industries that promised and produced the greatest profit: indigo, sugar, coffee, and cotton. Whereas. many lower-class Britishers submitted to debt servitude in the 1600s, by 1700 slavery had crystallized into a condition thought of as natural and appropriate only to people of African descent.[10] White men, even if from lowly origins and serflike pasts, were able to own land and property, and to sell their labor in the free market. Though there were always anomalous exceptions, such as free and even slave-owning

Negroes, people of color within the Americas had become essentially a class of unfree laborers. Afro-Americans were overwhelmingly bondsmen; Native Americans were serfs and peons in most of the continent.

Colonial conquest and control has been the cutting edge of Western capitalism in its expansion and penetration throughout the world. Yet capitalism and free labor as Western institutions were not developed for people of color; they were reserved for white people and white societies. In the colonies European powers organized other systems of work that were noncapitalist and unfree: slavery, serfdom, peonage. Forced labor in a myriad of forms became the province of the colonized and "native" peoples. European whites managed these forced labor systems and dominated the segments of the economy based on free labor. This has been the general situation in the Western hemisphere (including the United States) for more than three out of the four centuries of European settlement. It was the pattern in the more classical colonial societies also. But from the point of view of labor, the colonial dynamic developed more completely within the United States. Only here emerged a correlation between color and work status that was almost perfect. In Asia and Africa, as well as in much of Central and South America, many if not most of the indigenous peoples remained formally free in their daily work, engaging in traditional subsistence economies rather than working in the plantations, fields, and mines established by European capital. The economies in these areas came within the orbit of imperial control, yet they helped maintain communities and group life and thus countered the uprooting tendencies and the cultural and psychic penetration of colonialism. Because such traditional forms of social existence were viable and preferred, labor could only be moved into the arenas of Western enterprise through some form of coercion. Although the association of color and labor status was not perfect in the classical colonial regimes, as a general rule the racial principle kept white Europeans from becoming slaves, coolies, or peons.

Emancipation in the United States was followed by a period of rapid industrialization in the last third of the nineteenth century. The Civil War and its temporary resolution of sectional division greatly stimulated the economy. With industrialization there was an historic opportunity to transform the nation's racial labor principle. Low as were the condition and income of the factory laborer, his status was that of a free worker. The manpower needs in the new factories and mines of the East and Midwest could have been met by the proletarianization of the freedmen along with some immigration from Europe. But the resurgent southern ruling class blocked the political and economic democratization movements of Reconstruction, and the mass of blacks became sharecroppers and tenant farmers, agricultural serfs little removed from formal slavery. American captains of industry and the native white proletariat preferred to employ despised, unlettered European peasants rather than the emancipated Negro population of the South, or for that matter than the many poor white southern farmers whose labor mobility was also blocked as the entire region became a semi-colony of the North.

The nineteenth century was the time of "manifest destiny," the ideology that justified Anglo expansionism in its sweep to the Pacific. The Texan War of 1836 was followed by the full-scale imperialist conquest of 1846–1848 through which Mexico lost half its territory. By 1900 Anglo-Americans had assumed economic as well as political dominance over most of the Southwest. As white colonists and speculators gained control (often illegally) over the land and livelihood of the independent Hispano farming and ranching villages, a new pool of dependent labor was produced to work the fields and build the railroads of the region. Leonard Pitt sums up the seizure of California in terms applicable to the whole Southwest:

> In the final analysis the Californios were the victims of an imperial conquest. . . . The United States, which had long coveted California for its trade potential and strategic location, finally provoked a war to bring about the desired ownership. At the conclusion of fighting, it arranged to "purchase" the territory outright, and set about to colonize, by throwing open the gates to all comers. Yankee settlers then swept in by the tens of thousands, and in a matter of months and years overturned the old institutional framework, expropriated the land, imposed a new body of law, a new language, a new economy, and a new culture, and in the process exploited the labor of the local population whenever necessary. To certain members of the old ruling class these settlers awarded a token and symbolic prestige, at least temporarily; yet with that status went very little genuine authority. In the long run Americans simply pushed aside the earlier ruling elite as being irrelevant.[11]

Later, the United States' economic hegemony over a semicolonial Mexico and the upheavals that followed the 1910 revolution brought additional mass migrations of brown workers to the croplands of the region. The Mexicans and Mexican-Americans who created the rich agricultural industries of the Southwest were as a rule bound to contractors, owners, and officials in a status little above peonage. Beginning in the 1850s, shipments of Chinese workmen—who had sold themselves or had been forced into debt servitude—were imported to build railroads and to mine gold and other metals. Later other colonized Asian populations, Filipinos and East Indians, were used as gang laborers for Western farm factories.[12] Among the third world groups that contributed to this labor stream, only the Japanese came from a nation that had successfully resisted Western domination. This may be one important reason why the Japanese entry into American life and much of the group's subsequent development show some striking parallels to the European immigrant pattern. But the racial labor principle confined this Asian people too; they were viewed as fit only for subservient field employment. When they began to buy land, set up businesses, and enter occupations "reserved" for whites, the outcry led to immigration restriction and to exclusion acts.[13]

A tenet central to Marxian theory is that work and systems of labor are crucial in shaping larger social forces and relations. The orthodox Marxist criticism of capitalism, however, often obscures the significance of patterns of labor status. Since, by definition, capitalism is a system of wage slavery and the proletariat are "wage slaves," the varied degrees of freedom within industry and among the working class have not been given enough theoretical attention. Max Weber's treatment of capitalism, though based essentially on Marx's framework, is useful for its emphasis on the unique status of the free mobile proletariat in contrast to the status of those traditional forms of labor more bound to particular masters and work situations. Weber saw "formally free" labor as an essential condition for modern capitalism.[14] Of course, freedom of labor is always a relative matter, and formal freedoms are often limited by informal constraint and the absence of choice. For this reason, the different labor situations of third world and of European newcomers to American capitalism cannot be seen as polar opposites. Many European groups entered as contract laborers,[15] and an ethnic stratification (as well as a racial one) prevailed in industry. Particular immigrant groups dominated certain industries and occupations: the Irish built the canal system that linked the East with the Great Lakes in the early nineteenth century; Italians were concentrated in roadbuilding and other construction; Slavs and East Europeans made up a large segment of the labor force in steel and heavy metals; the garment trades were for many years a Jewish enclave. Yet this ethnic stratification had different consequences than the racial labor principle had, since the white immigrants worked within the wage system whereas the third world groups tended to be clustered in precapitalist employment sectors.

The differences in labor placement for third world and immigrant can be further broken down. Like European overseas colonialism, America has used African, Asian, Mexican and, to a lesser degree, Indian workers for the cheapest labor, concentrating people of color in the most unskilled jobs, the least advanced sectors of the economy, and the most industrially backward regions of the nation. In a historical sense, people of color provided much of the hard labor (and the technical skills) that built up the agricultural base and the mineral-transport-communication infrastructure necessary for industrialization and modernization, whereas the Europeans worked primarily within the industrialized, modern sectors.[16] The initial position of European ethnics, while low, was therefore strategic for movement up the economic and social pyramid. The placement of nonwhite groups, however, imposed barrier upon barrier on such mobility, freezing them for long periods of time in the least favorable segments of the economy.

Rural versus Urban

European immigrants were clustered in the cities, whereas the colonized minorities were predominantly agricultural laborers in rural areas. In the United States, family farming and corporate agriculture have been primarily white industries. Some immigrants, notably German, Scandinavian, Italian, and Portuguese, have prospered through farming. But most immigrant groups did not contribute to the most exploited sector of our industrial economy, that with the lowest status: agricultural labor. Curiously, the white rural proletariat of the South and West was chiefly native born.

Industry: Exclusion from Manufacturing

The rate of occupational mobility was by no means the same for all ethnics. Among the early immigrants, the stigmatized Irish occupied a quasicolonial status, and their ascent into a predominantly middle-class position took at least a generation longer than that of the Germans. Among later immigrants, Jews, Greeks, and Armenians—urban people in Europe—have achieved higher social and economic status than Italians and Poles, most of whom were peasants in the old country. But despite these differences, the immigrants as a whole had a key advantage over third world Americans. As unskilled laborers, they worked within manufacturing enterprises or close to centers of industry. Therefore they had a foot in the most dynamic centers of the economy and could, with time, rise to semiskilled and skilled positions.

Except for a handful of industrial slaves and free Negroes, Afro-Americans did not gain substantial entry into manufacturing industry until World War I,[17] and the stereotype has long existed that Asians and Indians were not fit for factory work. For the most part then, third world groups have been relegated to labor in preindustrial sectors of the nonagricultural economy. Chinese and Mexicans, for example, were used extensively in mining and building railroads, industries that were essential to the early development of a national capitalist economy, but which were primarily prerequisites of industrial development rather than industries with any dynamic future.[18]

Geography: Concentration in Peripheral Regions

Even geographically the Europeans were in more fortunate positions. The dynamic and modern centers of the nation have been the Northeast and the Midwest, the predominant areas of white immigration. The third world groups were located away from these centers: Africans in the South, Mexicans in their own Southwest, Asians on the Pacific Coast, the Indians pushed relentlessly "across the frontier" toward the margins of the society. Thus Irish, Italians, and Jews went directly to the northern cities and their unskilled labor markets, whereas Afro-Americans had to take two extra "giant steps," rather than the immigrants' one, before their large-scale arrival in the same place in the present century: the emancipation from slavery and migration from the underdeveloped semicolonial southern region. Another result of colonized entry and labor placement is that the racial groups had to go through major historical dislocations within this country before they could arrive at the point in the economy where the immigrants began! When finally they did arrive in northern cities, that economy had changed to their disadvantage. Technological trends in industry had drastically reduced the number of unskilled jobs available for people with little formal education.

Racial Discrimination

To these "structural" factors must be added the factor of racial discrimination. The argument that Jews, Italians, and Irish also faced prejudice in hiring misses the point. Herman Bloch's historical study of Afro-Americans in New York provides clear evidence that immigrant groups benefited from racism. When blacks began to consolidate in skilled and unskilled jobs that yielded relatively decent wages and some security, Germans, Irish, and Italians came along to usurp occupation after occupation, forcing blacks out and down into the least skilled, marginal reaches of the economy.[19] Although European immigrants were only struggling to better their lot, the irony is that their relative success helped to block the upward economic mobility of northern blacks. Without such a combination of immigration and white racism, the Harlems and the South Chicagos might have become solid working-class and middle-class communities with the economic and social resources to absorb and aid the incoming masses of southerners, much as European ethnic groups have been able to do for their newcomers. The mobility of Asians, Mexicans, and Indians has been contained by similar discrimination and expulsion from hard-won occupational bases.[20]

Our look at the labor situation of the colonized and the immigrant minorities calls into question the popular sociological idea that there is no fundamental difference in condition and history between the nonwhite poor today and the ethnic poor of past generations. This dangerous myth is used by the children of the immigrants to rationalize racial oppression and to oppose the demands of third world people for special group recognition and economic policies—thus the folk beliefs that all Americans "started at the bottom" and most have been able to "work themselves up through their own efforts." But the racial labor principle has meant, in effect, that "the bottom" has by no means been the same for all groups. In addition, the cultural experiences of third world and immigrant groups have diverged in America, a matter I take up in the next section.

CULTURE AND SOCIAL ORGANIZATION

Labor status and the quality of entry had their most significant impact on the cultural dynamics of minority people. Every new group that entered America experienced cultural conflict, the degree depending on the newcomers' distance from the Western European, Anglo-Saxon Protestant norm. Since the cultures of people of color in America, as much as they differed from one another, were non-European and non-Western, their encounters with dominant institutions have resulted in a more intense conflict of ethos and world view than was the case for the various Western elements that fed into the American nation. The divergent situations of colonization and immigration were fateful in determining the ability of minorities to develop group integrity and autonomous community life in the face of WASP ethnocentrism and cultural hegemony.

Voluntary immigration and free labor status made it possible for European minorities to establish new social relationships and cultural forms after a period of adjustment to the American scene. One feature of the modern labor relationship is the separation of the place of work from the place of residence or community. European ethnics were exploited on the job, but in the urban ghettos where they lived they had the insulation and freedom to carry on many aspects of their old country cultures—to speak their languages, establish their religions and build institutions such as schools, newspapers, welfare societies, and political organizations. In fact, because they had been oppressed in Europe—by such imperial powers as England, Tsarist Russia, and the Hapsburg Monarchy—the Irish, Poles, Jews, and other East Europeans actually had more autonomy in the New World for their cultural and political development. In the case of the Italians, many of their immigrant institutions had no counterpart in Italy, and a sense of nationality, overriding parochial and regional identities, developed only in the United States.[21]

But there were pressures toward assimilation; the norm of "Anglo-conformity" has been a dynamic of domination central to American life.[22]

The early immigrants were primarily from Western Europe. Therefore, their institutions were close to the dominant pattern, and assimilation for them did not involve great conflict. Among later newcomers from Eastern and Southern Europe, however, the disparity in values and institutions made the goal of cultural pluralism attractive for a time; to many of the first generation, America's assimilation dynamic must have appeared oppressive. The majority of their children, on the other hand, apparently welcomed Americanization, for with the passage of time many, if not most, European ethnics have merged into the larger society, and the distinctive Euro-American communities have taken on more and more of the characteristics of the dominant culture.

The cultural experience of third world people in America has been different. The labor systems through which people of color became Americans tended to destroy or weaken their cultures and communal ties. Regrouping and new institutional forms developed, but in situations with extremely limited possibilities. The transformation of group life that is central to the colonial cultural dynamic took place most completely on the plantation. Slavery in the United States appears to have gone the farthest in eliminating African social and cultural forms; the plantation system provided the most restricted context for the development of new kinds of group integrity.

In New York City, Jews were able to reconstruct their East European family system, with its distinctive sex roles and interlocking sets of religious rituals and customs. Some of these patterns broke down or changed in response, primarily, to economic conditions, but the changes took time and occurred within a community of fellow ethnics with considerable cultural autonomy. The family systems of West Africans, however, could not be reconstructed under plantation slavery, since in this labor system the "community" of workers was subordinated to the imperatives of the production process. Africans of the same ethnic group could not gather together because their assignment to plantations and subsequent movements were controlled by slaveholders who endeavored to eliminate any basis for group solidarity. Even assimilation to American kinship forms was denied as an alternative, since masters freely broke up families when it suited their economic or other interests.[23] In the nonplantation context, the disruption of culture and suppression of the regrouping dynamic was less extreme. But systems of debt servitude and semifree agricultural labor had similar, if less drastic, effects. The first generations of Chinese in the United States were recruited for gang labor; they therefore entered without women and children. Had they been free immigrants, most of whom also were male initially, the group composition would have normalized in time with the arrival of wives and families. But as bonded laborers without even the legal rights of immigrants, the Chinese were powerless to fight the exclusion acts of the late nineteenth century, which left predominantly male communities in America's Chinatowns for many decades. In such a skewed social structure, leading features of Chinese culture could not be reconstructed. A similar male-predominant group emerged among mainland Filipinos. In the twentieth century the migrant work situation of Mexican-American farm laborers has operated against stable community life and the building of new institutional forms in politics and education. However, Mexican culture as a whole has retained considerable strength in the Southwest because Chicanos have remained close to their original territory, language, and religion.

Yet the colonial attack on culture is more than a matter of economic factors such as labor recruitment and special exploitation. The colonial situation differs from the class situation of capitalism precisely in the importance of culture as an instrument of domination. Colonialism depends on conquest, control, and the imposition of new institutions and ways of thought. Culture and social organization are important as vessels of a people's autonomy and integrity; when cultures are whole and vigorous, conquest, penetration, and certain modes of control are more readily resisted. Therefore, imperial regimes attempt, consciously or unwittingly, either to destroy the cultures of colonized people or, when it is more convenient, to exploit them for the purposes of more efficient control and economic profit. Among America's third world groups, Africans, Indians, and Mexicans are all conquered peoples whose cultures have been in various degrees destroyed, exploited, and controlled. One key function of racism, defined here as the assumption of the superiority of white Westerners and their cultures and the concomitant denial of the humanity of people of color, is that it "legitimates" cultural oppression in the colonial situation.

The present-day inclination to equate racism against third world groups with the ethnic prejudice and persecution that immigrant groups have experienced is mistaken. Compare, for example, intolerance and discrimination in the sphere of religion. European Jews who followed their orthodox religion were mocked and scorned, but they never lost the freedom to worship in their own way. Bigotry certainly contributed to the Americanization of contemporary Judaism, but the Jewish religious transformation has been a slow and predominantly voluntary adaptation to the group's social and economic mobility. In contrast, the U.S. policy against Native American religion in the nineteenth century was one of all-out attack; the goal was cultural genocide. Various tribal rituals and beliefs were legally proscribed and new religious movements were met by military force and physical extermination. The largest twentieth-century movement, the Native American Church, was outlawed for years because of its peyote ceremony.[24] Other third world groups experienced similar, if perhaps less concerted, attacks on their cultural institutions. In the decade following the conquest, California prohibited bullfighting and severely restricted other popular Mexican sports.[25] In the same state various aspects of Chinese culture, dress, pigtails, and traditional forms of recreation were outlawed. Although it was tolerated in Brazil and the Caribbean, the use of the drum, the instrument that was the central means of communication among African peoples, was successfully repressed in the North American slave states.[26]

American capitalism has been partially successful in absorbing third world groups into its economic system and culture. Because of the colonial experience and the prevalence of racism, this integration has been much less complete than in the case of the ethnic groups. The white ethnics who entered the class system at its lowest point were exploited, but not colonized. Because their group realities were not systematically violated in the course of immigration, adaptation, and integration, the white newcomers could become Americans more or less at their own pace and on their own terms. They have moved up, though slowly in the case of some groups, into working-class and middle-class positions. Their cultural dynamic has moved from an initial stage of group consciousness and ethnic pluralism to a present strategy of individual mobility and assimilation. The immigrants have become part of the white majority, partaking of the racial privilege in a colonizing society; their assimilation into the dominant culture is now relatively complete, even though ethnic identity is by no means dead among them. In the postwar period it has asserted itself in a third-generation reaction to "overassimilation"[27] and more recently as a response to third world movements. But the ethnic groups have basically accepted the overall culture's rules of "making it" within the system, including the norms of racial oppression that benefit them directly or indirectly.

The situation and outlook of the racial minorities are more ambiguous. From the moment of their entry into the Anglo-American system, the third world peoples have been oppressed as groups, and their group realities have been under continuing attack. Unfree and semifree labor relations as well as the undermining of non-Western cultures have deprived the colonized of the autonomy to regroup their social forms according to their own needs and rhythms. During certain periods in the past, individual assimilation into the dominant society was seen as both a political and a personal solution to this dilemma. As an individual answer it has soured for many facing the continuing power of racism at all levels of the society. As a collective strategy, assimilation is compromised by the recognition that thus far only a minority have been able to improve their lot in this way, as well as by the feeling that it weakens group integrity and denies their cultural heritage. At the same time the vast majority of third world people in America "want in." Since the racial colonialism of the United States is embedded in a context of industrial capitalism, the colonized must look to the economy, division of labor, and politics of the larger society for their individual and group aspirations. Both integration into the division of labor and the class system of American capitalism as well as the "separatist" culture building and nationalist politics of third world groups reflect the complex realities of a colonial capitalist society.

The colonial interpretation of American race relations helps illuminate the present-day shift in emphasis toward cultural pluralism and ethnic nationalism on the part of an increasing segment of third world people. The building of social solidarity and group culture is an attempt to complete the long historical project that colonial domination made so critical and so problematic. It involves a de-emphasis on individual mobility and assimilation, since these approaches cannot speak to the condition of the most economically oppressed, nor fundamentally affect the realities of colonization. Such issues require group action and political struggle. Collective consciousness is growing among third world people, and their efforts to advance economically have a political character that challenges longstanding patterns of racial and cultural subordination.

CONCLUSION: THE THIRD WORLD PERSPECTIVE

Let us return to the basic assumptions of the third world perspective and examine the idea that a common oppression has created the conditions for effective unity among the constituent racial groups. The third world ideology attempts to promote the consciousness of such common circumstances by emphasizing that the similarities in situation among America's people of color are the essential matter, the differences less relevant. I would like to suggest some problems in this position.

Each third world people has undergone distinctive, indeed cataclysmic, experiences on the American continent that separate its history from the others, as well as from whites. Only Native Americans waged a 300-year war against white encroachment; only they were subject to genocide and removal. Only Chicanos were severed from an ongoing modern nation; only they remain concentrated in the area of their original land base, close to Mexico. Only blacks went through a 250-year period of slavery. The Chinese were the first people whose presence was interdicted by exclusion acts. The Japanese were the one group declared an internal enemy and rounded up in concentration camps. Though the notion of colonized minorities points to a similarity of situation, it should not imply that black, red, yellow, and brown Americans are all in the same bag. Colonization has taken different forms in the histories of the individual groups. Each people is strikingly heterogeneous, and the variables of time, place, and manner have affected the forms of colonialism, the character of racial domination, and the responses of the group.

Because the colonized groups have been concentrated in different regions, geographical isolation has heretofore limited the possibilities of cooperation. When they have inhabited the same area, competition for jobs has fed ethnic antagonisms. Today, as relatively powerless groups, the racial minorities often find themselves fighting one another for the modicum of political power and material resources involved in antipoverty, model-cities, and educational reform projects. Differences in culture and political style exacerbate these conflicts.

The third world movement will have to deal with the situational differences that are obstacles to coalition and coordinated politics. One of these is the great variation in size between the populous black and Chicano groups and the much smaller Indian and Asian minorities. Numbers affect potential political power as well as an ethnic group's visibility and the possibilities of an assimilative strategy. Economic differentiation may be accelerating both between and within third world groups. The racial minorities are not all poor. The Japanese and, to a lesser extent, the Chinese have moved toward middle-class status. The black middle class also is growing. The ultimate barrier to effective third world alliance is the pervasive racism of the society, which affects people of color as well as whites, furthering division between all groups in America. Colonialism brings into its orbit a variety of groups, which it oppresses and exploits in differing degrees and fashions; the result is a complex structure of racial and ethnic division.[28]

The final assumption of the third world idea remains to be considered. The new perspective represents more than a negation of the immigrant analogy. By its very language the concept assumes an essential connection between the colonized people within the United States and the peoples of Africa, Asia, and Latin America, with respect to whom the idea of *le tiers monde* originated. The communities of color in America share essential conditions with third world nations abroad: economic underdevelopment, a heritage of colonialism and neocolonialism, and a lack of real political autonomy and power.[29]

This insistence on viewing American race relations from an international perspective is an important corrective to the parochial and ahistorical outlook of our national consciousness. The economic, social, and political subordination of third world groups in America is a microcosm of the position of all peoples of color in the world order of stratification.

This is neither an accident nor the result of some essential racial genius. Racial domination in the United States is part of a world historical drama in which the culture, economic system, and political power of the white West has spread throughout virtually the entire globe. The expansion of the West, particularly Europe's domination over non-Western people of color, was the major theme in the almost five hundred years that followed the onset of "The Age of Discovery." The European conquest of Native American peoples, leading to the white settlement of the Western hemisphere, and the African slave trade were the two leading historical events that ushered in the age of colonialism. (The other major event was instituting trade with India.) Colonial subjugation and racial domination began much earlier and have lasted much longer in North America than in Asia and Africa, the continents usually thought of as colonial prototypes. The oppression of racial colonies within our national borders cannot be understood without considering worldwide patterns of white European hegemony.

The present movement goes further than simply drawing historical and contemporary parallels between the third world within and the third world external to the United States. The new ideology implies that the fate of colonized Americans is tied up with that of the colonial and former colonial peoples of the world. There is at least impressionistic evidence to support this idea. If one looks at the place of the various racial minorities in America's stratified economic and social order, one finds a rough correlation between relative internal status and the international position of the original fatherland. According to most indicators of income, education, and occupation, Native Americans are at the bottom. The Indians alone lack an independent nation, a center of power in the world community to which they might look for political aid and psychic identification. At the other pole, Japanese-Americans are the most successful nonwhite group by conventional criteria, and Japan has been the most economically developed and politically potent non-Western nation during most of the twentieth century. The transformation of African societies from colonial dependency to independent statehood, with new authority and prestige in the international arena, has had an undoubted impact on Afro-Americans in the United States; it has contributed both to civil rights movements and to a developing black consciousness.

What is not clear is whether an international strategy can in itself be the principle of third world liberation within this country. Since the oppression, the struggle, and the survival of the colonized groups have taken place within our society, it is to be expected that their people will orient their daily lives and their political aspirations to the domestic scene. The racial minorities have been able to wrest some material advantages from American capitalism and empire at the same time that they have been denied real citizenship in the society. Average levels of income, education, and health for the third world in the United States are far above their counterparts overseas; this gap will affect the possibility of internationalism. Besides which, group alliances that transcend national borders have been difficult to sustain in the modern era because of the power of nationalism.

Thus, the situation of the colonized minorities in the United States is by no means identical with that of Algerians, Kenyans, Indonesians, and other nations who suffered under white European rule. Though there are many parallels in cultural and political developments, the differences in land, economy, population composition, and power relations make it impossible to transport wholesale sociopolitical analyses or strategies of liberation from one context to another. The colonial analogy has gained great vogue recently among militant nationalists—partly because it is largely valid, partly because its rhetoric so aggressively condemns white America, past and present. Yet it may be that the comparison with English, French, and Dutch overseas rule lets our nation off too easily! In many ways the special versions of colonialism practiced against Americans of color have been more pernicious in quality and more profound in consequences than the European overseas varieties.

In traditional colonialism, the colonized "natives" have usually been the majority of the population, and their culture, while less prestigious than that of the white Europeans, still pervaded the landscape. Members of the third world within the United States are individually and collectively outnumbered by whites, and Anglo-American cultural imperatives dominate the society—although this has been less true historically in the Southwest where the Mexican-American population has never been a true cultural minority. The oppressed masses of Asia and Africa had the relative "advantage" of being colonized in their own land. In the United States, the more total cultural domination, the alienation of most third world people from a land base, and the numerical minority factor have weakened the group integrity of the colonized and their possibilities for cultural and political self-determination.

Many critics of the third world perspective seize on these differences to question the value of viewing America's racial dynamics within the colonial framework. But all the differences demonstrate is that colonialisms vary greatly in structure and that political power and group liberation are more problematic in our society than in the overseas situation. The fact that we have no historical models for decolonization in the American context does not alter the objective realities. Decolonization is an insistent and irreversible project of the third world groups, although its contents and forms are at present unclear and will be worked out only in the course of an extended period of political and social conflict.

5   Internal Colonialism and Ghetto Revolt

In April 1968, shortly after the assassination of Martin Luther King, Jr., Paul Jacobs, a radical journalist and Ralph Greenson, a socially minded psychoanalyst whose patients had included such celebrities as Marilyn Monroe, organized a June conference at UCLA on "Violence and Social Change," where I presented the first draft of "Internal Colonialism and Ghetto Revolt."

At least in my lifetime, America had never been as polarized or as close to cataclysm as it was in the first half of 1968. On March 1, the Kerner Commission had stated that America was now divided into two nations, one white and one black. A month later, President Lyndon Johnson announced that he would not seek re-election, the mounting protests against his escalation of the war in Vietnam having divided the nation even further. And then in the wake of Dr. King's assassination came another wave of urban riots.

With such a backdrop, this essay was more radical than the one on black culture written a year earlier (see Chapter 6). In it I offer a more complete statement of the colonial analysis I first introduced in "Whitewash over Watts" (see Chapter 8). The new paper was extremely well received, the applause and admiring comments suggesting how deeply the radical mood had penetrated academic and psychoanalytic circles. But one panelist, the famous Bruno Bettelheim, livid with rage, accused me of justifying violence and opening the door to fascism. Margaret Mead was kinder and gentler, but adamant in her belief that race relations in America were not at all parallel to what she had witnessed in colonial situations around the world.

With only minor revisions I published my talk in the spring 1969 issue of *Social Problems*. Reprinted sixty times, it would become a staple in anthologies for the next two decades, by far the most influential of all my writings on race. For my own critique, written in the 1990s, of the formulation of internal colonialism, see Chapter 12.

DURING THE late 1950s identification with African nations and other colonial or formerly colonized peoples grew in importance among black militants. As a result the United States was increasingly seen as a colonial power, and the concept of domestic colonialism was introduced into the political analysis and rhetoric of militant nationalists. During the same period Afro-American theorists began developing this frame of reference for American realities. As early as 1962, Harold Cruse characterized race relations in this country as *domestic colonialism*.[1] Two years later in *Youth in the Ghetto* Kenneth Clark demonstrated how the political, economic, and social structure of Harlem was essentially that of a colony.[2] Finally, in 1967 a comprehensive discussion of *internal colonialism* provided the theoretical framework for Stokely Carmichael and

Charles Hamilton's widely read *Black Power*.[3] The following year the colonial analogy gained currency and new "respectability" when Eugene McCarthy habitually referred to black Americans as a colonized people during his campaign. While the rhetoric of internal colonialism was catching on, other social scientists began to raise questions about its appropriateness as a scheme of analysis.

The colonial interpretation has been rejected as obscurantist and misleading by scholars who point to the significant differences in history and sociopolitical conditions between our domestic patterns and what took place in Africa and Asia. Colonialism, traditionally refers to the establishment of domination over a geographically external political unit, most often inhabited by people of a different race and culture, where this domination is political and economic and the colony exists subordinated to and dependent upon the mother country. Typically, the colonizers exploit the land, the raw materials, the labor, and other resources of the colonized nation; a formal recognition is given to the difference in power, autonomy, and political status, and various agencies are set up to maintain this subordination. Seemingly the model must be stretched beyond utility if the American case is to be forced into its mold. For here we are talking about group relations within a society; the geographical separation between mother country and colony is absent. Although whites certainly colonized the territory of the original Americans, internal colonization of Afro-Americans did not involve the settlement of whites in a land that was unequivocally black. Unlike the classical situation, there has been no formal recognition of differences in power, outside the South, since slavery was abolished. Traditional colonialism involves the control and exploitation of the majority of a nation by a minority of outsiders, whereas in America the oppressed black population is a numerical minority and was, originally, the "outside" group.

This conventional critique of internal colonialism is useful in pointing to the differences between our domestic patterns and the overseas situation. At the same time its bold attack tends to lose sight of common experiences that have historically been shared by the subjugated racial minorities in America and nonwhite peoples in other parts of the world. These common core elements—which make up a complex I shall call *colonization*—may be more important for understanding the most significant developments in the recent racial scene than the undeniable divergences between the two contexts.

The common features ultimately relate to the fact that classical colonialism of the imperialist era and American racism both developed out of the same historical situation and reflected a common world economic and power stratification. The slave trade preceded the imperialist partition and economic exploitation of Africa; in fact it may have been a necessary prerequisite for colonial conquest, since it helped deplete and pacify Africa, undermining resistance to direct occupation. Slavery contributed one of the basic raw materials for the textile industry, which provided much of the capital for the West's industrial development and economic expansionism. The essential condition for both American slavery and European colonialism was the political domination and the technological superiority of the Western world in relation to peoples of non-Western and nonwhite origins. This objective supremacy in technology and military power buttressed the West's sense of cultural superiority, laying the basis for racist ideologies that were elaborated to justify control and exploitation of nonwhite people. Because classical colonialism and America's internal colonialism developed out of similar technological, cultural, and power relations, a common *process* of social oppression characterized the racial patterns in the two contexts—despite the variations in political and social structure.

There appear to be four basic components of the colonization complex. The first component is the mode of entry into the dominant society. Colonization begins with a forced, involuntary entry. Second, there is the impact on culture. The effects of colonization on the culture and social organization of the colonized people are more than the results of such "natural" processes as contact and acculturation. The colonizing power carries out a policy that constrains, transforms, or destroys indigenous values, orientations, and ways of life. Third is a special relationship to governmental bureaucracies or the legal order. The lives of the subordinate group are administered by representatives of the dominant power. The colonized have the experience of being managed and manipulated by outsiders who look down on them.

The final component of colonization is racism. Racism is a principle of social domination by which a group seen as inferior or different in alleged biological characteristics is exploited, controlled, and oppressed socially and psychically by a superordinate group. The systems of colonialism that have been most central to the modern era have involved the subjugation of nonwhite Asian, African, and Latin American peoples by the white European powers, although imperial nations have colonized people who were technically considered to be of the same race; examples of such colonization are the British dominion over Ireland, the Hapsburg oppression of Central and Eastern European nationalities, and the Japanese suzerainty in Southeast Asia, which was ended by defeat in World War II. Even in these examples the link between colonialism and racism is indicated by the tendency of the ruling powers to view their subjects as inherently alien, culturally degenerate, and biologically inferior.[4]

The concept of colonization stresses the enormous fatefulness of the manner in which a minority group becomes a part of the dominant society. The crucial difference between the colonized Americans and the ethnic immigrant minorities is that the latter have always been able to operate fairly competitively within the relatively open spaces of the capitalist class order. They came voluntarily in search of a better life. They have worked predominantly as free laborers; therefore their movements in society have been less controlled. Finally, as white Europeans they could achieve a sense of membership in the larger society by making minor modifications in their ethnic institutions.

In present-day America, a major device of black colonization is the powerless ghetto. As the Haryou Report describes the situation:

> Ghettoes are the consequence of the imposition of external power and the institutionalization of powerlessness. In this respect, they are in fact social, political, educational, and above all—economic colonies. Those confined within the ghetto walls are subject peoples. They are victims of the greed, cruelty, insensitivity, guilt and fear of their masters . . . .
>
> The community can best be described in terms of the analogy of a powerless colony. Its political leadership is divided, and all but one or two of its political leaders are shortsighted and dependent upon the larger political power structure. Its social agencies are financially precarious and dependent upon sources of support outside the community. Its churches are isolated or dependent. Its economy is dominated by small businesses which are largely owned by absentee owners, and its tenements and other real property are also owned by absentee landlords. Under a system of centralization, Harlem's schools are controlled by forces outside the community. Programs and policies are supervised and determined by individuals who do not live in the community.[5]

Many ethnic groups in America have lived in ghettos. What makes the black ghettos an expression of colonized status are three special features. First, the ethnic ghettos arose more through voluntary choice: the choice to immigrate to America and the choice to live among fellow ethnics. Second, the immigrant ghettos of the inner city were one- or two-generation phenomena—way stations along the road of acculturation and assimilation. When ethnic communities persist, they tend to reflect voluntary decisions to live among one's fellows and maintain group institutions, as in the case of the so-called "gilded ghettos" of the Jewish suburban middle class. The black ghettos on the other hand have been more permanent, though their boundaries expand and change and some individuals do escape them. But most relevant is the third point, that black communities are, to a great extent, controlled from the outside. For many Europeans—the Poles, Italians, and Jews, for example—there was only a brief period, often less than a generation, during which their residential buildings, commercial stores, and other enterprises were owned by outsiders. Afro-Americans are distinct in the extent to which their segregated communities have remained under outside control: economic, political, and administrative.

> When we speak of Negro social disabilities under capitalism . . . we refer to the fact that he does not own anything—*even what is ownable in his own community*. Thus to fight for black liberation *is to fight for his right to own*. The Negro is politically compromised today because he owns nothing. He has little voice in the affairs of state because he owns nothing. The fundamental reason why the Negro bourgeois-democratic revolution has been aborted is because American capitalism has prevented the development of a black class of capitalist owners of institutions and economic tools. To take one crucial example, Negro radicals today are severely hampered in their tasks of educating the black masses on political issues because Negroes do not own any of the necessary means of propaganda and communication. The Negro owns no printing presses, he has no stake in the networks of the means of communication. Inside his own communities he does not own the houses he lives in, the property he lives on, nor the wholesale and retail stores from which he buys his commodities. He does not own the edifices in which he enjoys culture and entertainment or in which he socializes. In capitalist society, an individual or group that does not own anything is powerless.[6]

And what is true of business is true also for the other social institutions that operate within the ghetto. The educators, policemen, social workers, politicians, and others who administer the affairs of ghetto residents are typically whites who live outside the black community. Thus the ghetto plays a strategic role as the focus for that outside administration which in overseas colonialism is called "direct rule."

The colonial status of the Negro community goes beyond the issue of ownership and decision making within black neighborhoods. Despite the fact that blacks are numerically superior to many other interest groups, the Afro-American population has very little influence on the power structure and institutions of most of the larger cities. A recent analysis of policy making in Chicago estimates that "Negroes really hold less than one percent of the effective power in the Chicago metropolitan area. (Negroes are 20 percent of Cook County's population.) Realistically the power structure of Chicago is hardly less white than that of Mississippi."[7]

Although the Chinese-American experience has not yet been adequately studied, it may be worthwhile to consider briefly how "Chinatowns" relate to the two ideal types, the voluntary ethnic community and the involuntary racial ghetto. Like the blacks, the Chinese have faced intense color prejudice and a racist housing market. However, a major divergence from the Afro-American pattern is suggested by the estimate that the "income of Chinese-Americans from Chinese-owned businesses is in proportion to their numbers 45 times as great as the income of Negroes from Negro-owned businesses."[8] The strength of Chinese business and community institutions appears to be related to the fact that traditional ethnic culture and social organization, in which entrepreneurial values were strong, were not destroyed by slavery; it may also be that the group's relatively small numbers made systematic oppression less central to American capitalism. Yet these facts in and of themselves do not prove the absence of colonization. Chinese middlemen played a major role in the exploitation of the masses of their own group: Chinese contractors supplied and managed the indentured laborers that worked in the mines and on the railroads. The Chinatowns of America may be viewed as neo-colonial enclaves in which a business class has been able to gain wealth and political power within the ethnic community. In the larger society, however, the Chinese are ultimately powerless, controlled by outside political and economic arrangements.

Colonization outside of a traditional colonial structure has its own special conditions. In America the group culture and social structure of the colonized are less developed and less autonomous; the colonized are a numerical minority; and they are ghettoized more totally, yet are more dispersed geographically, than people under classic colonialism. All these realities affect the magnitude and direction of reaction by the colonized. But it is my basic thesis that the most important expressions of protest in the black community during the recent years reflect the colonized status of Afro-America. Riots, programs of separation, politics of community control, black revolutionary movements, and cultural nationalism each represents a different strategy of attack on domestic colonialism in America. Let us now examine some of these movements from this perspective.

RIOT OR REVOLT?

The so-called riots are being increasingly recognized as a preliminary if primitive form of mass rebellion against colonial status. There is still a tendency to absorb their meaning within the conventional scope of assimilation-integration politics; some commentators stress the material motives involved in looting as a sign that the rioters want to join America's middle-class affluence just like everyone else. That motives are mixed and often unconscious; that black people want good furniture and television sets like whites is beside the point. The guiding impulse in most major outbreaks has not been integration with American society, but an attempt to stake out a sphere of control by moving against that society and destroying the symbols of its oppression.

In my critique of the McCone Report (see Chapter 8), I observe that the rioters "were asserting a claim to territoriality, making an unorganized and rather inchoate attempt to gain control over their community turf." In succeeding disorders also the thrust of the action has been toward ridding the community of the alien presence of white officials, rather than killing white people, as in a conventional race riot. The main attacks have been directed at the property of white businessmen and at the police who operate in the black community "like an army of occupation," protecting the interests of outside exploiters and maintaining the domination over the ghetto of the central metropolitan power structure.[9] The Kerner Report misleads when it attempts to explain riots in terms of integration: "What the rioters appear to be seeking was fuller participation in the social order and the material benefits enjoyed by the majority of American citizens. Rather than rejecting the American system, they were anxious to obtain a place for themselves in it."[10] More accurately, the revolts pointed to alienation from the system on the part of many poor, and some not-so-poor, blacks. Again as I argue with respect to Los Angeles: the sacredness of private property, that unconsciously accepted bulwark of our social arrangements, was rejected. People who looted—apparently without guilt—generally remarked that they were taking things that "really belonged" to them anyway.[11] Obviously the society's bases of legitimacy and authority have been attacked. Law and order has long been viewed by Afro-Americans as the white man's law and order; but now this characteristic perspective of a colonized people is out in the open. The Kerner Report's own data question how well ghetto rebels have been buying the system: In Newark only 33 percent of self-reported rioters said they thought this country was worth fighting for in the event of a major war; in the Detroit sample the figure was 55 percent.[12]

One of the most significant consequences of the process of colonization is a weakening of the individual and collective will to resist oppression. It has been easier to contain and control black ghettos because communal bonds and group solidarity have been weakened through divisions among leadership, failures of organization, and a general dispiritment that accompanies social oppression. The riots were a signal that the will to resist had broken the mold of accommodation. In some cities they represented nascent movements toward community identity. The outbursts stimulated new organizations and movements in several riot-torn ghettos. If it is true that the riot phenomenon of 1964–1968 has passed its peak, its historical import may be more for the "internal" organizing momentum that was generated than for any profound "external" response by the larger society in facing underlying causes.

Despite the appeal of Frantz Fanon to young black revolutionaries, America is not Algeria. It is difficult to foresee how rioting in our cities can function in a manner similar to the situation of overseas colonialism where such outbursts were an integral phase in a movement for national liberation. By 1968 some militant groups (for example, the Black Panther Party in Oakland) had concluded that ghetto riots were self-defeating for black people in the present balance of organization and gunpower—endangering their lives and their interests—though they had served to stimulate both black consciousness and white awareness of the depths of racial crisis. Such militants have been influential in "cooling" their communities during periods of high riot potential. Theoretically oriented black radicals see riots as spontaneous mass behavior, which must be replaced by a revolutionary organization and consciousness. Despite the differences in objective conditions, violence seems to have served the same psychic function for young ghetto blacks in the 1960s as it did for the colonized of North Africa described by Fanon and Albert Memmi—the assertion of dignity and manhood.[13]

For a period during the 1960s and early 1970s riotlike political action shifted from the urban ghetto streets to more limited and focused institutional settings. One example was the high schools and colleges, where a white European cultural system carried out the psychic and intellectual colonization of people of color. The second was the prisons, whose inmates are disproportionately black, brown, and lower class. In confining within its walls a significant segment of those who have reacted against racial and colonialism overtly and aggressively, although not always with political consciousness, the prison is a concentrated essence of the colonial relationship. It is therefore not surprising that it became a new breeding ground for nationalist and revolutionary organization.

Cultural Nationalism

Cultural conflict is generic to the colonial relation because colonization involves the domination of Western technological values over the more communal cultures of non-Western peoples. Colonialism played havoc with the national integrity of the peoples it brought under its sway. Of course, all traditional cultures are threatened by industrialism, the city, and modernization in communication, transportation, health, and education. What is special to colonialism is that political and administrative decisions are made by colonizers toward the end of managing and controlling the colonized peoples. The boundaries of African colonies, for example, were drawn to suit the political conveniences of the European nations without regard to the social organization and cultures of African tribes and kingdoms. Nigeria as blocked out by the British included the Yorubas and the Ibos. The recent civil war was at least partially a by-product of the colonialist's disrespect for the integrity of indigenous cultures.

The most total destruction of culture took place not in traditional colonialism but in America. As E. Franklin Frazier stressed, the integral cultures of the diverse African peoples who furnished the slave trade were destroyed because slaves from different tribes, kingdoms, and linguistic groups were purposely separated to maximize domination and control. Language, religion, and national loyalties were lost in North America much more completely than in the Caribbean countries and Brazil, where slavery developed somewhat differently. On this key point America's internal colonization has been more total and extreme than classic colonialism. The British in India and the European powers in Africa were simply not able—as outnumbered minorities—to destroy the national and tribal cultures of the colonized. Recall that American slavery lasted 250 years and its racist aftermath has lasted another 100. Colonial dependency in British Kenya and French Algeria lasted only 77 and 125 years, respectively. In the wake of this more drastic uprooting and destruction of culture and social organization, much more powerful agencies of social, political, and psychological domination developed in America.

> Colonial control of many peoples inhabiting the colonies was more a goal than a fact, and at Independence there were undoubtedly fairly large numbers of Africans who had never seen a colonial administrator. The gradual process of extension of control from the administrative center on the African coast contrasts sharply with the total uprooting involved in the slave trade and the totalitarian aspects of slavery in the United States. Whether or not Elkins is correct in treating slavery as a total institution, it undoubtedly had a far more radical and pervasive impact on American slaves than did colonialism on the vast majority of Africans.[14]

Yet a similar cultural process unfolds in both contexts of colonialism. To the extent that they are involved in the larger society and economy, the colonized are caught up in a conflict between two cultures. Fanon has described how the assimilation-oriented schools of Martinique taught him to reject his own culture and blackness in favor of Westernized, French, and white values.[15] Both the colonized elites under traditional colonialism and perhaps the majority of Afro-Americans today experience a parallel split in identity, cultural loyalty, and political orientation.

The colonizers use their culture to socialize the colonized elites (intellectuals, politicians, and middle class) into an identification with the colonial system. Because Western culture has the prestige, the power, and the key to the limited opportunity available to a minority of the colonized, the first reaction seems to be an acceptance of the dominant values. Call it brainwashing, as the Black Muslims put it; call it identifying with the aggressor, if you prefer Freudian terminology; call it a natural response to the hope and belief that integration and democratization can really take place, if you favor a more commonsense explanation; however the process is defined, this initial acceptance crumbles in time on the realities of racism and colonialism. The colonized, seeing that his success within colonialism is at the expense of his group and his own inner identity, moves radically toward a rejection of the Western culture and develops a nationalist outlook that celebrates his people and their traditions. As Memmi describes it:

> Assimilation being abandoned, the colonized's liberation must be carried out through a recovery of self and of autonomous dignity. Attempts at imitating the colonizer required self-denial; the colonizer's rejection is the indispensable prelude to self-discovery. That accusing and annihilating image must be shaken off; oppression must be attacked boldly since it is impossible to go around it. After having been rejected for so long by the colonizer, the day has come when it is the colonized who must refuse the colonizer.[16]

Memmi's book, *The Colonizer and the Colonized,* is based on his experience as a Tunisian Jew in a marginal position between the French and the colonized Arab majority. The uncanny parallels between the North African situation he describes and the course of black–white relations in our society is the best impressionist argument I know for the thesis that we have a colonized group and a colonizing system in America. His discussion of why the most radical French anticolonialist cannot participate in the struggle of the colonized is directly applicable to the situation of the white liberal and radical vis-à-vis the black movement.[17] His portrait of the colonized is as good an analysis of the psychology behind black power and black nationalism as anything that has been written in the United States.

> Considered *en bloc* as *them, they* or *those,* different from every point of view, homogeneous in a radical heterogeneity, the colonized reacts by rejecting all the colonizers *en bloc*. The distinction between deed and intent has no great significance in the colonial situation. In the eyes of the colonized, all Europeans in the colonies are de facto colonizers, and whether they want to be or not, they are colonizers in some ways. By their privileged economic position, by belonging to the political system of oppression, or by participating in an effectively negative complex toward the colonized, they are colonizers. . . . . They are supporters or at least unconscious accomplices of that great collective aggression of Europe. . . .
> The same passion which made him admire and absorb Europe shall

make him assert his differences; since those differences, after all, are within him and correctly constitute his true self. . . .

The important thing now is to rebuild his people, whatever be their authentic nature; to reforge their unity, communicate with it, and to feel that they belong.[18]

Cultural revitalization movements play a key role in anticolonial movements. They follow an inner necessity and logic of their own that comes from the effects of colonialism on groups and personal identities; they are also essential to provide the solidarity that the political or military phase of the anticolonial revolution requires. In the United States an Afro-American culture has developed out of the ingredients of African world views, the experiences of slavery, migration, and the northern lower-class ghettos—and, most importantly, the political history of the black population in its struggle against racism. That Afro-Americans are moving toward cultural consciousness in a period when ethnic loyalties tend to be weak (and perhaps on the decline) in this country is another confirmation of the unique colonized position of the black group.

THE MOVEMENT FOR GHETTO CONTROL

The call for black power unites a number of varied movements and tendencies. Although agreement on a unified program has not yet emerged, the most important emphasis seems to be on the movement for control of the ghetto. Black leaders and organizations are increasingly concerned with owning and controlling those institutions that exist within or impinge upon their community. The colonial model provides a key to the understanding of this movement; indeed, advocates of ghetto control have increasingly invoked the language of colonialism in pressing for local home rule. The framework of anticolonialism explains why the struggle to put poor people in control of poverty programs has in many cities been more important than the content of these programs and why it has been crucial to exclude whites from leadership positions in black organizations.

The key institutions that anticolonialists want to take over or control are business, social services, schools, and the police. Though many spokesmen have advocated the exclusion of white landlords and small businessmen from the ghetto, the idea has evidently not caught fire among the blacks, and little concrete movement toward economic expropriation has as yet developed. Welfare recipients have organized in many cities to protect their rights and gain a greater voice in the decisions that affect them. Larry Jackson observes that "there is no organizational structure in the black community which can equal (on a national level) the number of troops that the National Welfare Rights Movement can politically engage in literally hundreds of cities across the country."[19] However, because the problems of welfare do not cut across class lines, whole communities have not mounted direct action against this form of colonialism. Thus, schools and the police have been the crucial issues of ghetto control politics.

The Schools

In many cities during the late 1960s educational priorities shifted from integration to community control, New York and Brooklyn being the most publicized examples. Afro-Americans demanded their own school boards, with the power to hire and fire principals and teachers and to construct a curriculum that would be relevant to the special needs and culture of ghetto youth. Black students across the country have been active in high schools and colleges, protesting in behalf of incorporating black power and black culture into the education system. Consider how similar the spirit behind these developments is to the attitude of the colonized North African toward European education:

> He will prefer a long period of educational mistakes to the continuance of the colonizer's school organization. He will choose institutional disorder in order to destroy the institutions built by the colonizer as soon as possible. There we see, indeed a reactive drive of profound protest. He will no longer owe anything to the colonizer and will have definitely broken with him.[20]

Protest and institutional disorder over the issue of school control in New York City came to a head in 1968. The procrastination in the Albany state legislature, the several crippling strikes called by the teachers' union, and the almost frenzied response of Jewish organizations made it clear that decolonization of education faces the resistance of powerful vested interests. Funding for the experimental school districts was ended after one year, and the limited autonomy that had been granted these districts was incorporated into a more general plan of decentralization. The defeat of "community control" in New York may have contributed to its failure to spread rapidly to other major cities.[21]

The movement reflected some of the problems and ambiguities that stem from colonization within the borders of the "mother country." The Afro-American community is not parallel in structure to the communities of colonized nations under traditional colonialism. The significant difference here is the lack of fully developed indigenous institutions other than the church. Outside of some areas of the South there is really no black economy, and most Afro-Americans are inevitably caught up in the larger society's structure of occupations, education, and mass communications. Thus the ethnic nationalist orientation, which reflects the reality of colonization, exists alongside an integrationist orientation, which reflects the reality that the institutions of the larger society are much more developed than those of the incipient nation.[22] As would be expected, the movement for school control reflected both orientations. The militant leaders who spearhead such local movements may be primarily motivated by the desire to gain control over the community's institutions—they are anti-colonialists first and foremost. Many parents who support them may share this goal, but the majority are probably more concerned about creating a new education that will enable their children to "make it" in the society and the economy as a whole; they know that the present school system fails ghetto children and does not prepare them for participation in American life.

In many communities black leaders are now struggling for measures that fall between the poles of integration and community autonomy: for example, control over special programs, ethnically oriented curricula, and "alternative schools" within a racially heterogeneous institution or district. And by 1971 the ways and means of achieving integration had reappeared as a major national controversy as the Nixon administration backtracked on the busing issue. As more cities and school systems move toward black majorities, however, demands for community control are likely to emerge again.

The Police

There has been a growing recognition that law enforcement is particularly crucial in maintaining the colonized status of black Americans. Of all establishment institutions, police departments probably include the highest proportion of individual racists. This is no accident, since central to the workings of racism are attacks on the humanity and dignity of the subject group. The police constrict Afro-Americans to black neighborhoods by harassing and questioning them when they are found outside the ghetto; without provocation they break up groups of youths congregated on corners or in cars; and they continue to use offensive and racist language no matter how many seminars on intergroup understanding have been built into the police academy. They also shoot to kill ghetto residents for alleged crimes such as car thefts and running from officers of the law. According to a recent survey:

> In the predominantly Negro areas of several large cities, many of the police perceive the residents as basically hostile, especially the youth and adolescents. A lack of public support—from citizens, from courts, and from laws—is the policeman's major complaint. But some of the public criticism can be traced to the activities in which he engages day by day, and perhaps to the tone in which he enforces the "law" in the Negro neighborhoods. Most frequently he is "called upon" to intervene in domestic quarrels and

break up loitering groups. He stops and frisks two or three times as many people as are carrying dangerous weapons or are actual criminals, and almost half of these don't wish to cooperate with the policeman's efforts.[23]

Thus the police enforce the culturally repressive aspects of middle-class American values against the distinctive ethnic orientations of Afro-American and other minority subcultures. It has been observed that few whites are arrested for gambling despite its popularity in a variety of forms; blacks, however, are arrested unduly for this offense and similar crimes like making noise in public. The Detroit officer David Senak as described by John Hersey[24] well exemplifies how individual policemen can become moral crusaders against "deviant behavior" and how the black community is particularly vulnerable to such cultural aggression.

Police are key agents in the power equation as well as in the dramas of dehumanization and cultural repression. In the final analysis they do the dirty work for the larger system by restricting the striking back of black rebels to skirmishes inside the ghetto, thus deflecting energies and attacks from the communities and institutions of the larger power structure. In a historical review, Gary Marx notes that since the French revolution, police and other authorities have killed large numbers of demonstrators and rioters; the rebellious "rabble" rarely destroys human life. The same pattern has been repeated in America's recent revolts.[25] Journalistic accounts suggest that police see themselves as defending the interests of white people against a tide of black insurgence; the majority of whites appear to view "blue power" in this same light.[26] There is probably no other opinion on which the races are today so far apart as they are on the question of attitudes toward the police.

Set off in many cases by a confrontation between an officer and a black citizen, the ghetto uprisings have dramatized the role of law enforcement and the issue of police brutality. In their aftermath, movements have arisen to contain police activity. One of the first was the Community Alert Patrol in Los Angeles, a group organized to police the police in order to keep them honest and constrain their violations of personal dignity. This was the first tactic of the Black Panther Party, which originated in Oakland—perhaps the most significant group to challenge the police role in maintaining the ghetto's colonized status. The Panthers' later policy of openly carrying guns (a legally protected right) and their intention of defending themselves against police aggression brought on a series of confrontations with the Oakland police department. In 1968 when I first drafted this chapter I wrote: "All indications are that the authorities intend to destroy the Panthers by shooting, framing up, or legally harassing their leadership—diverting the group's energies away from its primary purpose of self-defense and organization of the black community to that of legal defense and gaining support in the white community." Within three years all these "indications" had materialized into hard fact. The Panthers suffered critical losses to their leadership and organizational unity, and their cofounder Huey Newton publicly criticized his party for isolating itself from the problems and concerns of the black community.

There are three major answers to "police colonialism," which correspond to reformist and more radical approaches to the situation. The most elementary, and most superficial, focuses on the fact that ghettos are overwhelmingly patrolled by white rather than by black officers. Therefore, the first proposal—supported today by many police departments—is to increase the numbers of blacks on local forces to something like their distribution in the city, making it possible to reduce the use of white cops in the ghetto. This reform should be supported for a variety of obvious reasons, but it does not get to the heart of the role of the police as agents of colonization.

The Kerner Report documents the fact that in some cases black policemen can be as brutal as their white counterparts. I have not found data on who polices the ghetto, but statistics showing the proportion of blacks on the overall force are available for many cities. In most places the disparity is so striking that white police must predominate in patrolling black neighborhoods. Among the thirty cities listed by *Ebony* magazine, in the modal case the proportion of blacks in the population was three to four times as great as their proportion on the police force; for many cities this ratio was five, ten and even twenty times. In Oakland 34.5 percent of the population was black; only 4.7 percent of the policemen were black. For Boston the percentages were 16 and 2, for Cleveland 39 and 5, Dallas 25 and 2, Birmingham, 42 and 2! There were only five cities where the ratio was less than two to one, that is, where the proportion of black cops was slightly more than one-half their percentage in the town as a whole: Gary, Washington, D.C., Atlanta, Philadelphia, and Chicago.[27] These figures suggest that both the extent and the pattern of colonization may vary from one city to another. It would be useful to study how black communities differ in degree of control over internal institutions as well as in economic and political power in the metropolitan area.

A second more radical demand is that the police must live in the communities where they work. The idea is that black officers who lived in the ghetto would have to be accountable to the community; if they came on like white cops then "the brothers would take care of business" and make their lives miserable. In many cities large numbers of policemen, like other public employees, reside in adjacent suburbs; they have resisted the demand of political leaders and pressure groups that they live where they work on the grounds that it singles out their occupation for discriminatory treatment.

The third, or maximalist, position is based on the premise that the police play no positive role in the ghettos. It calls for the withdrawal of metropolitan officers from black communities and the substitution of an autonomous indigenous force that would maintain order without oppressing the population. The precise relation between such an independent police, a ghetto governing body that would supervise and finance it, the city and county law enforcement agencies, and the law itself is as yet unclear. It is unlikely that any major city will soon face these problems as directly as New York did in the case of its schools. Of all the programs of decolonization, police autonomy will be most resisted. It gets to the heart of the way the state controls and contains the black community by delegating the legitimate use of violence to police authority.

The various black power programs that are aimed at gaining control of individual ghettos—buying up property and businesses, running the schools through community boards, taking over antipoverty programs and other social agencies, diminishing the arbitrary power of the police—can serve to revitalize the institutions of the ghetto and build up an economic, professional, and political power base. These programs seem limited; we do not know at present whether they are enough in themselves to end colonized status. But they are certainly a necessary first step.

Yet they have dangers and pitfalls. Just as the limitation of a riot "strategy" became apparent, and just as the cultural movement bears a potential tendency toward antipolitical withdrawal that would have little impact on the condition of the poor and dispossessed, so ghetto control politics—indeed "black power" itself—faces the possibility that its programs and political thrust could be co-opted by the larger system of power. A number of radical political analysts already see a new stage of neocolonialism in which Afro-American leaders, under the black power banner, exercise a form of "indirect rule" over their internal communities, whose people are then more efficiently exploited and controlled by an ever-flexible corporate capitalism.[28] While this eventuality is not to be discounted, I do not look for such a pat and facile solution to what Franz Schurmann has called a key contradiction of American capitalism—that between the emerging black cities and the white suburbs.[29]

THE ROLE OF WHITES

What makes the Kerner Report a less-than-radical document is its superficial treatment of racism and its reluctance to confront the colonized relation between black people and the larger society. The report emphasizes the attitudes and feelings that make up white racism, rather than the system of privilege and control, which is the heart of the matter. With all its discussion of the ghetto and its problems, it never faces the question of the stake that white Americans have in racism and ghettoization.

It is not a simple question, but this chapter should not end with the impression that police are the major villains. As I have argued in Chapter 3, all white Americans gain privilege and advantage from the colonization of black communities. The majority of whites also lose something from this oppression and division in society. Serious research should be directed to the ways in which white individuals and institutions are tied into the ghetto. Let me in closing suggest some possible parameters.

1. It is my guess that only a small minority of whites make a direct economic profit from ghetto colonization. This is hopeful, in that the ouster of white businessmen may become politically feasible. Much more significant, however, are the private and corporate interests in the land and residential property of the black community; their holdings and influence on urban decision making must be exposed and combatted.[30]

2. A much larger minority of whites have occupational and professional interests in the present arrangements. The Kerner Commission reports that 1.3 million nonwhite men would have to be upgraded occupationally in order to make the black job distribution roughly similar to that for whites. The commission advocates such upgrading without mentioning that 1.3 million specially privileged white workers would lose in the bargain.[31] In addition, there are those professionals who carry out what Lee Rainwater has called the "dirty work" of administering the lives of the ghetto poor: the social workers, the schoolteachers, the urban development people, and of course the police.[32] The social problems of the black community will ultimately be solved only by people and organizations from that community; the emphasis within these professions must shift toward training such a cadre of minority personnel. Social scientists who study and teach courses on problems of race and poverty likewise have an obligation to replace themselves by bringing into the graduate schools and college faculties men and women of color who will become the future experts in these areas. For cultural and intellectual imperialism is as real as welfare colonialism, although it is currently screened behind such unassailable shibboleths as universalism and the objectivity of scientific inquiry.

3. Without downgrading the vested interests of profit and profession, the real nitty-gritty elements of the white stake are political power and bureaucratic security. Although few whites have much understanding of the realities of race relations and ghetto life, I think most give tacit or at least subconscious support for the containment and control of the black population. And whereas most whites have extremely distorted images of black power, many—if not most—would be frightened by actual black

political power. Racial groups and identities are real in American life; white Americans sense they are on top, and they fear possible reprisals or disruptions were power to be more equalized. There seems to be in the white psyche a paranoid fear of black dominance; the belief that black autonomy would mean unbridled license is so ingrained that such reasonable outcomes as black political majorities and independent black police forces will be bitterly resisted.

On this level the major bulwark of colonization is bureaucratic security, which allows the middle classes to go about life and business in peace and quiet. The black militant movement is a threat to the orderly procedures by which bureaucracies and suburbs manage their existence, and I think today there are more people who feel a stake in conventional procedures than there are who gain directly from racism. In their fight for institutional control, the colonized are not playing by the white rules of the game. These administrative rules have kept them down and out of the system; therefore blacks are not committed to running institutions in the image of the white middle class.

The liberal, humanist value that violence is the worst sin cannot be defended today if one is committed squarely against racism and for self-determination. Some violence is almost inevitable in the decolonization process; unfortunately racism in America has been so effective that the greatest power Afro-Americans wield today is the power to disrupt. Racism has fractionated the black population, making unity of political action difficult. A unified people and movement would have power to implement its goals and force changes on the society that would go far beyond disruption. If we are going to swing with these revolutionary times and at least respond positively to the anticolonial movement, we shall have to learn to live with conflict, confrontation, constant change, and what may be either real or apparent chaos and disorder.

A positive response from the white majority needs to be in two major directions at the same time. First, community liberation movements should be supported in every way by pulling out white instruments of direct control and exploitation and substituting technical assistance to the community when this is asked for. But it is not enough to relate affirmatively to the nationalist movement for ghetto control without at the same time radically opening doors for full participation in the institutions of the mainstream. Otherwise the liberal and radical position is little different from the traditional segregationist position. Freedom in the special conditions of American colonization means that the colonized must have the choice between participating in the larger society and in independent structures of their own.

6   Racism and Culture

While writing *Racial Oppression in America,* I was also reading the literature on colonialism in Asia, Africa, and Latin America. That literature fascinated me, especially the wealth of evidence that European colonialists were unable to appreciate, and often even to recognize, the cultural beliefs and practices of the indigenous peoples whose lands they had conquered and occupied. My research resulted in chapters on black culture and on Chicanos (Chapters 7 and 10) and in the chapter that follows, in which I discuss the insights I had gathered on "the intimate, yet antagonistic relation between racism and culture."

A CENTRAL idea in my work is the antagonistic yet intimate relation between racism and culture. Cultural domination is a major instrument of racial control, and oppression has a negative, weakening effect on the cultures of dominated groups. During the colonial experience the many dimensions of racism in its relation to culture were highlighted. European rule caused acute conflicts between Western societies and non-Western peoples, conflicts that were exacerbated by the white man's deep sense of racial superiority. At the same time, colonialism's attack on nonwhite cultures—and the color line it institutionalized—set into motion new movements of race consciousness, cultural revitalization, and political nationalism, movements that contributed to the emergence of new nations and group identities. Whereas racism tends to undermine culture, its special intensity in certain societies appears to be linked to an existing weakness in the integration of the national heritage. Racism fills a void and ironically helps cement the oppressor's culture. Chapters 7 and 10 deal with the impact of white racism on the cultures of Afro-Americans and Mexican-Americans; the remarks in this chapter suggest a more general approach to the topic.

RACISM AS THE NEGATION OF CULTURE

Racism can be defined as a propensity to categorize people who are culturally different in terms of noncultural traits, for example, skin color, hair, structure of face and eye. Obviously the human failing of imputing social significance to these differences—a failing Western Europeans have had to an extreme—underlies the fatefulness of race in recent history. By its very logic racial thinking emphasizes the variations between groups rather than the things they have in common. Further, it tends either to ignore the existence of culture or social heritage or, more often, to mini-mize its importance in accounting for real differences. Since virtually every nation, tribe, or ethnic group defines its uniqueness in terms of cul-ture—its history, religion, ritual, art, philosophy or world view—rather than in terms of "blood," racism as a view of reality violates the auton-omy and self-determination of peoples. It rejects their own definition of themselves and substitutes one based on the framework of the oppressor.

One tradition of British colonials was to call all indigenous people of color "niggers" despite the incredible diversity in history and culture among the Africans, Indians, Burmese, and Chinese who received this appellation.[1] In England today West Indians, Africans, Pakistani, and East Indians are lumped together as "blacks." In a similar manner Amer-ican GIs in "police actions" in Asia have used the term "gook" to refer, successively, to Koreans, Chinese, and Vietnamese. These racial defini-tions have permitted whites to order a universe of unfamiliar peoples without confronting their diversity and individuality, which are products of rich and distinct cultural traditions. Such a propensity to excessive cat-egorization is fundamental to racism; another example is the tendency to view members of the same minority in global generalized terms when the group may be quite differentiated in a variety of ways.

More important than such mental mechanisms have been the actions of white Europeans as they colonized the world, and the objective conse-quences of their acts. Especially in the early period, the colonial powers set out to weaken the cultures of the colonized. Missionaries, often the advance guard of Western expansion, were fortified by an almost fanati-cal belief in the virtues of European religion, morality, and customs. Such an ingrained sense of moral rectitude was responsible for the inability of many Europeans to comprehend other ways of life and led to barbaric attacks on pagan artifacts and social institutions. In Goa and a number of other Asian cities, for example, Western missionaries destroyed Hindu temples, shrines, and priceless works of art.[2] In Central Africa they attempted to outlaw the *lobala,* an exchange of cattle in the betrothal cer-emony, on the grounds that it was a bride-purchase, a mercenary custom that profaned the marriage sacrament. The *lobala* was the institution around which the entire social organization of these cattle-raising tribes revolved; its elimination would have meant a total breakdown in social order.[3] Every competent survey of Western colonialism reveals countless similar examples.[4]

The depreciation of the cultural integrity of non-Western people appears to be a result of specific values and emphases within the Western ethos, not just a matter of ignorance, arrogance, and ill will. The leading concepts of Western culture, intensified in Protestantism, include control and dominance, property and appropriation, competition and individualism. These values have worked well in support of racial oppression and cultural domination: equalitarian and democratic themes have been weak countertrends at best. Particularly important has been the conflict between the Western technological orientation or engineering mentality and the more organic, harmonious notions of the relation between man and nature that were held by the societies dominated by colonialism. The aggressive implementation of such an exploitative attitude toward the external world often disrupted non-Western ways of life and contributed to the white man's depreciation of people of color.

For the European mentality "the apparent inability of the African to dominate his environment provided perhaps the basic proof of his backwardness. . . . Nothing, as Lord Bryce remarked, was more surprising to the European than the fact that savages left 'few marks of their presence' on their physical environment. . . . The savage, he argued, had 'no more right to claim that the land was made for him than have the wild beasts of the forest who roar after their prey and seek their meat from God.' Bryce's view was standard."[5] Similar arguments belittling the Native Americans' claim to their continent were popular in the United States. Englishmen evaluated other cultures primarily in terms of their mastery of nature—but the mastery had to be achieved in the British manner. African footpaths were winding and therefore objects of ridicule: "the straight line, a man-made construct, was indicative of order and environmental control."[6]

THE TENSION BETWEEN RACE AND ETHNICITY

Systems of racial oppression tend to undermine ethnic groups and ethnicity as a principle of social organization. One of the most profound consequences of colonialism was its creation of races and racism through weakening the relevance of other human distinctions. The extreme case was slavery in the New World.

It is an error to assume that slave traders and plantation owners always saw their captives as an undifferentiated mass of black Africans. In North America, as well as in the Caribbean and Brazil, a crude working knowledge of African tribal diversity and social character existed. Thus some West African peoples were viewed as good workers, whereas others were considered less desirable because it was believed that they were more likely to rebel, escape, fall ill, or even commit suicide in the state of bondage.[7] Yet the logic of slavery had to weaken, if it did not necessarily eliminate, the long run significance of ethnic ties. Cultural groups were broken up, in part because it was the more convenient administrative arrangement, in part because traders and planters were aware that tribal fragmentation would reduce the ability of slaves to communicate and resist. With time it became "natural" to treat the bondsmen as a more or less homogeneous mass of Africans. This took place earlier and more thoroughly in the United States because favorable economic conditions made it possible to reproduce the slave population through natural increase, which ended the need for new imports from Africa. In Brazil and the Caribbean, slaves were more typically worked to death; continuous replenishment through the slave trade maintained the relevance of African ethnicity much longer.[8]

The slave system created the "New World Negro" out of a mélange of distinct cultural groups. In a similar fashion, racial practices common to the European powers in Africa—despite their different colonial policies—created the identities of Negro and African and a corresponding sense of blackness and African-ness among the disparate populations south of the Sahara. Ndabaningi Sithole quotes a saying of the Ndau-speaking people of Rhodesia: "'*Muyungu ndiye ndiye*'—'the white man is the same the world over.' By this they mean to say that the white man the world over likes to rule and humiliate the black man."[9] It is important to stress that race awareness and racial thinking of this type were almost nonexistent in Africa before white rule.[10] A critical consequence of Western colonialism has been to bring racial divisions and racial thinking to parts of the world and to social groups where they previously held little sway. This cannot be dismissed as false consciousness, a purely mental trip, for to the extent that the West introduced systems of labor and social organization in which color rather than kinship or ethnic group determined social position, race became a socioeconomic reality at the expense of cultural definitions.

It was not possible to override ethnic and cultural differences in the classical situation of overseas colonialism. Ethnic groups were rooted in the land and the natural clusterings of people. Western cultural domination had relatively little direct effect on the traditional ways of life of the Asian and African masses. It was the "assimilated" elites, taught in missionary schools or other centers of Western education, for whom ethnic loyalties became less than central. Furthermore, the Western powers often fostered ethnic divisions and exacerbated cultural conflict by importing nonindigenous peoples to serve certain functions. The British policy of indirect rule was based on maintaining the traditional authority of tribal chieftains as long as they remained subservient to colonial power. The French used militia and policemen from one colony, for example Senegal, to put down disturbances in other territories. The English brought East Indians to their colonies in the West Indies, Africa, and Asia to work as laborers and to fulfill administrative and business roles; people from the Middle East often became small traders in African and Asian colonies.[11]

In addition to races, racism, cultural pluralism, and ethnic conflict, nations and nationalism were further unanticipated consequences of Western colonial rule. Movements of reaction against the colonial cultural attack were especially significant for emerging national consciousness. The first and most characteristic cultural resistance was the maintaining of values and ways of life in the face of Westernization. Where disruption of culture did take place, new religious movements and cults often emerged, based on some combination of old and new, but carrying within them an overt or covert attack on white domination and values.[12] Such religious developments were followed by politically oriented and often race-conscious movements such as *négritude,* which sought to restore the validity and dignity of the cultural heritages impugned by Western racism and to challenge its cultural domination. These forms of cultural resistance contributed to the developing abilities of colonized people to organize for national independence.

Race replaced ethnicity most completely in slave and postslavery societies, above all, in the United States. Many of the ambiguities of American race relations stem from the fact that two principles of social division, race and ethnicity, were compressed into one. With their own internal ethnic differences eliminated, people of African descent became a race in objective terms, especially so in the view of the white majority. Afro-Americans became an ethnic group also, one of the many cultural segments of the nation. The ethnicity of Afro-America, however, is either overlooked, denied, or distorted by white Americans, in part because of the historic decision to focus on the racial definition, in part because of the racist tendency to gainsay culture to people of color beyond what they may have assimilated directly from the European tradition. This merging of ethnicity with race, in the eyes of people of color as well as of whites, made it inevitable that racial consciousness among blacks would play a central part in their historic project of culture building, and that their institutions, politics, and social character would be misinterpreted in a restricted racial paradigm.

For those Africans who escaped the slave trade and remained at home, ethnic realities have persisted. Because the colonialists drew their boundaries in disregard for cultural facts, ethnic groups are major social forces in the internal differentiation of African nations today. A paradox of the colonial encounter with culture lies in the fact that the stronger ethnicity in the classical situation has resulted in a weakening of the national unity of many new independent states—though cultural continuity has undoubtedly strengthened social institutions and personal identities—

whereas in the United States the more complete development of the racial basis of collective identity among Afro-Americans, which weakened group and individual integrity, ironically created the conditions for a more unified regrouping and a new sense of peoplehood unimpaired by ethnic division. (The major ethnic group within the black population has been the West Indian.)

Up to now I have focused on racism's impact on the cultures of the oppressed. How racism relates to the oppressor's culture is another crucial, though relatively unexplored, issue. It is plausible to assume that the finding of modern psychology that people who are least secure and integrated in personality structure have the greatest need for racist and other distorted belief systems might apply also to nations and their cultures. The special intensity of racial feeling among settler populations and in the cultures of new societies that develop by fragmentation from older national traditions[13] seems to confirm this insight. The new society is characterized by a weakness in cultural identity, a lack of great tradition, an absence of a sense of distinctiveness. Winthrop Jordan has suggested that racist thought contributed to the resolution of such cultural problems among the white American settlers who used African people as "contrast conceptions" to help define themselves.[14] The fear of chaos, even of reversion to barbarism, that comes from the weakness of civil constraints in frontier situations is dealt with by projecting all the undesirable (but dangerously appealing) possibilities associated with savagery and uncivilized animal existence on a scapegoat race.[15] The colonial society of overseas Europeans was even less integrated culturally than the new society in America; in such a context racism and obsessive denigration of the native population became the single most important unifying thread in the lives of the white group. Racial oppressors, in the process of attacking the cultural realities of the oppressed, are engaged in fortifying their own precarious cultures; this tradeoff is another example of the exploitative thrust of white Europe in its historical encounter with peoples of color. Those who believe that racial oppression is on its way out, or can be readily eliminated in American life through reforms that guarantee greater equality in living standards and political participation, fail to reckon with the "integrating" role that racism performs for the society and the depths to which it has penetrated the national culture.

7   Black Culture and Its Critics

The idea that African Americans have a real and vibrant ethnic culture has become so widely accepted that it may be hard to imagine how radical that position was when I wrote "Black Culture and Its Critics" in 1967. At the time the prevailing orthodoxy in the social sciences was just the opposite. American Negroes had lost all of their African heritage in the course of slavery, and whatever distinctive culture they might seem to have was simply a reflection of their economically disadvantaged, lower-class status. In his 1966 book *Urban Blues* on the performance style of black musicians, the anthropologist Charles Keil dissented from this viewpoint and argued that the Afro-American idea of "soul" was the essence of black culture. In a long review in *Trans-Action,* the sociologist Bennett Berger wrote that Keil had missed the boat: a culture based on poverty could not be a genuine ethnic culture. Berger's review was brilliant, but to my mind, dead wrong. So my rejoinder, also published in *Trans-Action,* was the first version of the chapter that follows.

"Black Culture and Its Critics" caught an early wave of what would become a decade of ferment in Afro-American consciousness. Led by civil rights militant Stokely Carmichael, who had insisted in 1966 that only blacks could define their own political and cultural realities, Afro-Americans began to reject white standards of beauty, to "talk black," and to put down those they saw as "acting white." These developments were followed a few years later by demands for black studies programs in colleges and high schools and the replacement of the word "Negro" by "black."

Racism alone didn't account for the failure—among ordinary Americans and social scientists alike—to see and acknowledge black culture. In large part people went astray because Afro-American ethnicity did not conform to the prevailing model of ethnic culture derived from the experiences of European immigrant groups. The latter brought with them their own languages, religions, and memories of a national homeland, whereas Americans of African descent were originally a legal category in this country and not a nationality or even a sociological group. A long slow process of group formation and culture building began during slavery and was influenced not only by bondage and lower-class status, but also by Africa, life in the South, Emancipation, northern migration, and, above all, the struggle to survive a racist society.

THE VIEW that black people lack any characteristics of a distinctive nationality, that they are only Americans and nothing else, has become almost a dogma of liberal social science. Gunnar Myrdal and his great book *An American Dilemma* set the tone for the present outlook.[1] In this influential and voluminous work there is no chapter on Afro-American culture and only a sketchy treatment of the black community. Furthermore, Myrdal's statement that the Negro is "an exaggerated American" and that his values are "pathological" elaborations on general American values has been widely quoted for a generation.[2] In 1963 another influential study of ethnic groups in New York took a similar position. "It is not possible for Negroes to view themselves as other ethnic groups viewed themselves," wrote Nathan Glazer and Daniel Patrick Moynihan, "because—and this is the key to much in the Negro world—the Negro is only an American and nothing else. He has no values and culture to guard and protect."[3]

It is misleading to give the impression that the standard position has been advanced only by white liberal sociologists. On this point, E. Franklin Frazier was at least as influential as Myrdal. Perhaps the leading black sociologist of his generation, Frazier took issue with the anthropologist Melville Herskovits, who in his *Myth of the Negro Past* had imputed African origins to many, if not most, Afro-American social and cultural patterns.[4] Frazier's view was published in 1957 in the revised edition of his comprehensive work, *The Negro in the United States:*

> As a racial or cultural minority the Negro occupies a unique position. He has been in the United States longer than any other racial or cultural minority with the exception, of course, of the American Indian. Although the Negro is distinguished from other minorities by his physical characteristics, unlike other racial or cultural minorities the Negro is not distinguished by culture from the dominant group. Having completely lost his ancestral culture, he speaks the same language, practices the same religion, and accepts the same values and political ideals as the dominant group. Consequently, when one speaks of Negro culture in the United States, one can only refer to the folk culture of the rural Southern Negro or the traditional forms of behavior and values which have grown out of the Negro's social and mental isolation. Moreover, many of the elements of Negro culture which have grown out of his peculiar experience in America, such as music, have become a part of the general American culture.
>
> Since the institutions, the social stratification, and the culture of the Negro minority are essentially the same as those of the larger community, it is not strange that the Negro minority belongs among the assimilationist rather than the pluralist, secessionist or militant minorities. It is seldom that one finds Negroes who think of themselves as possessing a different culture from whites and that their peculiar culture should be preserved.[5]

Despite this prevailing point of view, the studies of southern towns and northern ghettos undertaken from the 1930s through the 1950s are rich in evidence of distinctive institutions and unique ways of looking upon life and society that read very much like descriptions of ethnic cultures.[6] Yet, until recently, the positive assertion of black culture has been confined to nationalist and political circles; it has not been defended in academic research. During the 1960s, the recognition of Afro-American ethnicity finally crept into the social sciences. One of the first instances was the anthropological study *Urban Blues*. Charles Keil used the blues singer and his audience as the raw materials to outline the distinctive traits and ethos of black American culture, the core of which he located in the ideology of *Soul*. The importance of the Soul idea to Keil is its suggestion that "Negroes have a dearly bought experiential wisdom, a 'perspective by incongruity,'" that provides black Americans a unique outlook on life that cannot be shared by whites.[7]

Urban Blues evoked an incisive critique by the sociologist Bennett Berger. In the context of a generally positive review, Berger attacked Keil's major thesis at three pivotal points. First, he asserted that Soul theorists romanticize Negro life and thereby lose sight of the fact that "black culture" is at bottom only an American Negro version of lower-class culture. Second, because this culture has no future, analytical appreciation of it may be misplaced. Lower-class culture in America is no basis for the development of a national consciousness and ethnic solidarity. Since it has no appeal to the socially mobile, it can only interfere with progress toward integration and equality. Finally, Berger argued that black cultural spokesmen are only confusing the intellectual atmosphere and obstructing the road to Negro progress and racial harmony. As intellectuals and political men they have the obligation to specify clearly what in Afro-American culture is to be affirmed, so that everyone can see whether anything solid or meaningful is involved. But, speaking so generally if not demagogically, black spokesmen have failed in their obligation, Berger noted.[8]

With unusual cogency, Berger has expressed a position that is held by many people today, including scholarly experts in the study of race relations. In the pages that follow I argue that this perspective is based on a number of misconceptions about culture and ethnicity in modern American society. It reflects a restricted usage of the idea of culture and, even more important, a mechanical application of the model of immigrant assimilation to the very different cultural experience of black people in America. I argue further that the inability to perceive the realities of Afro-American ethnicity is related to the complexity of black culture, its diverse and paradoxical elements, as well as to a failure to grasp the fact that racism and its legacy, black political history, are central to this cultural dynamic. In addition, the position is based on a static, deterministic approach to cultural development, one that minimizes its open-ended quality and therefore underplays the role of consciousness and culture building in affecting that development. And finally, the conventional sociological position is yet another reflection—albeit in liberal form—of the ideological imperative of a racist society, which ignores, discredits, or depreciates the cultural realities of people of color. Let us examine each of these issues in turn.

THE UNIQUE CULTURAL PROCESS

The premise that informs Kenneth Stampp's history of slavery—"that the slaves were merely ordinary human beings, that innately Negroes *are,* after all, only white men with black skins, nothing more, nothing less"—is plausible to a degree.[9] As Frazier stressed, the manner in which North American slavery developed—in contrast to Caribbean and South American slavery—eliminated the most central African traits, those elements of ethnicity that European and Asian immigrants brought to this country: language, dress, religion and other traditional institutions, and a conscious identification with an overseas homeland. Scholars of postslavery societies concur that "Africanisms" are least apparent in the United States. The cultural critic Janheinz Jahn concluded that the American Negro novel was the only stream of black literature outside the African or neo-African tradition.[10] But the African heritage approach to black ethnicity can be misleading. Its proponents typically assume that there is only one generic process—the model of European ethnic assimilation—through which nationality cultures and the dominant American ethos have interacted What must be understood is that the Afro-American historical experience and the experiences of other third world peoples have unique features that suggest a cultural development that has reversed the path traveled by the European ethnics.

Howard Brotz has observed that the "no Negro culture" argument rests on the assumption that an ethnic group must possess three attributes—a distinctive language, a unique religion, and a national homeland.[11] This position is derived from the classic anthropological conception, or *holistic view,* of culture, which points to an integrated way of life and system of customs, institutions, beliefs, and values that fit together into some organic whole, perhaps dominated by a central ethos. This idea of culture was developed from the study of primitive peoples and contributed to the overemphasis on social integration that characterizes *functionalist theory* in the social sciences. Yet it does point up the unity of the heritages that the various immigrant groups brought to America. The parallel holistic cultures of the African peoples were destroyed in America because groups of slaves from the diverse tribes, kingdoms, and linguistic groups were consciously broken up so that language, religion, and national loyalties were lost. But ethnic cultures as organic, holistic ways of life did not last very long for the immigrant nationalities either, and in fact the idea of a holistic culture is less and less applicable to any group in a modern urban society. Today when we characterize Jews, Italians, or Greeks as ethnic groups, we are referring to a different notion of culture, one that locates ethnicity in certain distinctive values, orientations to life and experience, and shared memories that coexist within the framework of general American life styles and allegiances. Most sociologists and laymen find little difficulty in calling American Jews an ethnic group despite the fact that in most of their institutional and cultural behavior Jews are eminently American and middle class. Still, there are distinctive cultural orientations—a peculiarly ethnic style of humor, for example—that come from a common historical and social experience.

Let us look more closely at the model of ethnic group assimilation that dominates sociological thinking about nationalities. The holistic way of life was introduced with the immigrant group's first entry or, more accurately, early in the peak period of its immigration. It soon gave way to the demands of the American environment and the competition of domestic ways of life. Typically, after one generation an ethnic culture developed out of old-country elements, American ways, and original adaptations to the immigrant's situation. Such a culture was more fragmented and full of normative and value conflicts than the traditional one; yet it still provided some round of life and center of community for the group. As time went on the number of people involved in the more traditional holistic cultures declined, and the emerging ethnic-American cultures took on more and more characteristics of the larger society. Assimilation meant modifying or giving up certain ethnic institutions and culturally distinct values as the generations followed one another. The process tended to be one-way and nonreversible, from immigrant extra-national status to ethnic group to assimilation, though Will Herberg has noted that ethnic identity is sometimes reasserted by the third generation.[12] The means that move this process forward are occupational mobility and the ethnic group's increasing contact with dominant institutions, especially education.

Very little of this fits the cultural experience of Afro-Americans. How a minority group enters the host society has fateful—if not permanent—consequences. The very manner in which Africans became Americans undermined original culture and social organization. The slave-making operation vitiated the meaning and relevance of the traditional, specific African identities. On the other hand, black people did not enter this country with the group identity of Negro. As Singer has pointed out, blacks at first constituted a sociolegal *category,* rather than a group in sociological terms.[13] Therefore the cultural process could not be one of movement from ethnic group to assimilation, since blacks were not an ethnic group. What took place was not acculturation but an incorporation into a legal status that did not permit the collective autonomy, nor the social and economic progress, that accompanied assimilation for other minorities. It was a forced deculturation, a spurious assimilation. At the same time, beginning with slavery, the group- and culture-building process began among the black population, and the development of an ethnic group identity and distinctive culture has been going on ever since. But this cultural process is infinitely more complex than that for the immigrant groups. One reason is the general reversal in direction. But it is not a simple one-way process in the opposite direction, from "assimilation" to ethnic group; the black cultural experience is more like an alternating than a direct current. The movement toward ethnicity and distinctive consciousness has been paralleled by one toward becoming more "American" in action and identity. Sometimes these conflicting vectors characterize different time periods; sometimes they reflect different segments of the large and diversified black minority; sometimes both contradictory cultural tendencies have been present simultaneously and within the psyche and social orientations of a single individual. Underlying these phenomena are the many and varied historical and social conditions that have produced Afro-American culture. Black culture cannot be understood in terms of the model that is reasonably satisfactory for the European ethnic groups.

THE DIVERSE SOURCES OF AFRO-AMERICAN CULTURE

The idea of black culture meets resistance because the term itself contains a number of ambiguities. To many liberals, the term *black culture* appears unacceptable and even racist because it threatens the distinction between race and culture—a distinction that is a basic principle of the modern scientific outlook, the special contribution of anthropology to that outlook. But if it is understood that in this context black refers to ethnic realities and experiences and not to color per se, the grounds for this objection disappear. A further problem is that black culture has several connotations. The two most common usages are conflicting, to a degree. On the one hand, the term refers to the totality of the culture that is lived and possessed by black Americans. On the other hand, it connotes those traditions, symbols, and meanings that are specially associated with black people and their experience. The culture of black Americans (first meaning) and Afro-American ethnic culture (second meaning) are not identical, though the two overlap. The relation between these two referents must be clarified to avoid confusion.

Those who deny the reality of black culture argue that people of African descent in America live and think much like other Americans. This is true, for the culture of Afro-Americans is in some ways like that of all human beings in the world; in other ways it is specific to the concerns and values of all Americans; in still other ways it is considerably diversified by differences in region, social class, age, and sex. It is also uniquely ethnic in some other ways. But to argue that black people must think and feel alike and that the culture of a group must be in every way different from that of other groups in order to qualify as cultural is to set up a standard for black culture that would disallow the cultural realities of all peoples! Jahn makes this point tellingly with respect to African culture:

> If in places the reader is inclined to object that what we are expounding as an aspect of African culture plays a part also in other cultures, that the meaning of life is also stressed in European culture, that the spoken word has the greatest significance also in other cultures, above all in illiterate ones, that rhythm has its functions among all peoples, that even in the Christian middle ages the picture has also functioned as a symbol, ideogram, and sensory image, and that therefore all these so emphatically African matters are not after all so original—then let him recollect that all human cultures resemble one another up to a point, that different cultures only value their common elements differently, in so far as one puts the accent here, another there, and that it is the ordering, the relation of the elements to one another that determines the difference between the cultures.[14]

Just as the culture of black Americans consists in part of life styles and values that were originally Euro-American, Afro-American ethnic culture is also to a considerable degree part of the larger American cultural panoply. Building from the base of their special oppressed situation, blacks have contributed much (in relation to reward and recognition, overcontributed) to the language, lore, art, and styles that are today available to Americans of every ethnic origin. It is this mutual interaction and interpenetration between the Euro-American and the Afro-American streams that make the question of black culture so paradoxical and therefore impervious to precise analysis.

The poetry of Melvin Tolson, based upon the integration and striking concatenation of thematic materials from the African, European, American, and Afro-American traditions, abounds with these paradoxes. Consider the following passage from *A Harlem Gallery*:

> Frog Legs Lux and his Indigo Combo
>   let go
>   with a wailing pedal point
>   that slid into
>   Basin Street Blues

       like Ty Cobb stealing second base:
Zulu, King of the Africans,
arrives on Mardi Gras morning;
the veld drum of Baby Dodds'
great-grandfather in Congo Square
pancakes the first blue note
in a callithump of the USA.
And now comes the eve of Ash Wednesday.
Comus on parade!
All God's children revel
like post–Valley Forge
charivari in Boston celebrating the nuptials of
a gay-old-dog minuteman with a lusty maid.[15]

And when Tolson introduces an ethnic metaphor suddenly into a "universal" discussion of aesthetics, the effect is powerful:

    An artist makes what he can;
    every work of art asserts,
      "I am that I am."
      So leave the rind to the pedant
    and the bone to The Hamfat Man.[16]

In the present essay I focus primarily on Afro-American ethnicity, though I do move back and forth at times between the two major referents of black culture. I attempt some broad generalizations about the historical and contemporary conditions that have given rise to distinctive cultural orientations. The special target of my wrath is the view that the ways of life of black people in America is primarily a class, namely, a lower-class, phenomenon. Poverty is only one source of black culture, and, as I shall attempt to prove, even the lower-class traits and institutions have been modified by strictly ethnic values. Among the other sources of the culture are Africa, the South, slavery, Emancipation, northern migration, and, above all, racism. That racial oppression provides the basis for a more elaborate and more ethnic cultural response than does class exploitation and lower-class status is central to my thesis.

The African Heritage

In *The Myth of the Negro Past,* Melville Herskovits places emphasis on the continuity between African and American black life styles. His thesis has been too easily dismissed as exaggeration, in part because his own conception of culture as specific institutions and traits undermined the power of his argument and evidence. Only a modicum of such specific practices could be maintained in the slave condition. But if the essence of culture is viewed instead as the more subtle human orientations to the problems of existence, as ways of being in the world, as ethos or philosophy of life, then the entire matter of the African-ness of black Americans must be reviewed once again. Sociology and anthropology may have misread these realities because they are expressed more profoundly in literature and art than in the conventional data of the social scientist. The close fit between African cultural assumptions and the world view that is called Soul in the United States, between African aesthetics and the themes underlying Negro American music and literature, suggests that those black nationalists who have for generations insisted on the relevance of the African heritage may have grasped a significant truth.[17] As Arnold Toynbee noted in his *Study of History,* modern scholars assume that Asian societies have been westernized because so much of "our" material culture—our techniques and products—has been widely diffused. He argues that the souls of these civilizations, where the people really live, have not been seriously penetrated or transformed.[18] Thus, because we have viewed culture primarily in its material and behavioral aspects rather than in the spiritual life of a people, we may have exaggerated the westernization of Afro-Americans in the United States.

Without doubt, the salience of African culture for Afro-American ethnicity was reduced by the fact that these orientations and ways of thought were transmitted for the most part subliminally, rather than through conscious awareness and identification. We can assume that the slaves and later the freedmen who created and sang new musical forms, expressed themselves in *nonstandard (black) English,* moved about in distinct fashions, and worshiped in their own way did not know that they were behaving according to African linguistic, aesthetic, and theological precepts—as contemporary scholars are now discovering.[19] The black community's revived interest in Africa—a product of that continent's anticolonial movements and the emergence of independent nations there, as well as of the domestic struggle—is stimulating serious research by both black and white scholars, which in time should provide a clearer understanding of how African cultural values interacted with, and were modified by, specific American conditions.

From the beginning Africa's role was consistently obscured by the frenzied racist imageries of the continent as a cesspool of savagery and barbarism.[20] The Western nations have until recently assumed that Africa had no history and that consequently blacks were people without a past.[21] The stigmatization of Africa was evidently more pronounced among Protestant nations. Though racist in their own way, such countries as

Brazil and Cuba have officially recognized African contributions to their national cultures. North Americans only on rare occasions acknowledge the Indian influences on our culture and history; at other times the importance of the Negro to our society may be referred to—but *never* the impact of *Africa* and its cultures. This phenomenon must have been important in alienating Afro-Americans from a sense of their own past, including a partly self-imposed tendency to deny and reject the bond with Africa.[22]

The South as Neo-African

Our society's repression of Africa has distorted—in racist fashion—the realities of cultural influence in the nation as a whole. Thus, we say that many Negroes speak with "a southern accent," and the implicit assumption is that, in their imitating ways, blacks picked up this slow, modulated drawl from the whites—when the fact is that southerners in general, whites as well as blacks, speak with *African accents*.

In the future, the pioneering studies of the American South will be based on research into the ways in which the distinctive patterns and ethos of the region were shaped by the culture of Africa and the black presence. Even such classic interpreters of the inner essence of southern culture as Wilbur Cash and James Agee paid very little attention to the Afro-American influence.[23] When the neo-African character of the South has been properly recognized, then this region can be viewed as the black analog to the European immigrant's old country, and in the South we will find also the roots of the two additional criteria of ethnic peoplehood: language and religion, the distinctiveness of which has been overlooked because of the surface similarities to white counterparts. Ralph Ellison and Calvin Hernton have pointed out how much the black man's attitudes and cultural styles reflect the patterns of this region, for the southern heritage has been carried to the northern cities and is constantly refurbished through visiting and new migration.[24] Obviously much of black religion, "soul food," music, and language overlaps with southern poor white culture. Undoubtedly there was mutual interaction; yet it is likely that the African was the more vigorous cultural influence.

The Culture of Slavery

Slavery may be viewed as the third great source of black American culture. Here, under seriously restricting conditions, Afro-Americans began developing their own communities and codes of conduct.[25] Many persisting themes in the black experience emerged from the situation of servitude: the search for freedom and self-determination, ambivalence toward the white master class and white people in general, the centrality of religion, and the special role of the woman in the family. To slavery also more negative adaptations and character types owe their origins—for example, the submission, timidity, fear, and manipulation embedded in the "Uncle Tom" orientation. It is these kinds of cultural adaptations that many nationalist leaders have been trying to stamp out in their attacks on "the slave mentality."

Because racist ideology blotted out the significance of African realities for black life and for the culture of the South, slavery came to be viewed as the be-all-and-end-all of the social heritage of American Negroes. Such a view of the black experience and its corollary that an Afro-American culture is nonexistent, or at best a cruel joke, is well expressed by a leading literary figure:

> I think I know why the Jews once wished to survive (though I am less certain as to why they still do): they not only believed that God had given them no choice, but they were tied to a memory of past glory and a dream of imminent redemption. What does the American Negro have that might correspond to this? His past is a stigma, his color is a stigma, and his vision of the future is the hope of erasing the stigma by making color irrelevant, by making it disappear as a fact of consciousness.[26]

Emancipation and Migration

A further source was Emancipation: the promises, the betrayals, and the frustrations that followed upon release from bondage. Because slavery restricted free movement to the ultimate, a period of great mobility followed in its wake.[27] The promise of the North, the attractions of industry, and the push from a depressed Southland, set the stage for ghetto life in the urban North. This is the source of black culture that is most clearly tied to poverty and lower-class existence. And yet the black ghetto is different from the ethnic ghettos of the Irish, Jews, or Italians because it comes out of a different history, that of slavery, southern jim crow, and a northern migration that only in part parallels a transoceanic search for a better life. Whereas the immigrant ghettos allowed ethnic cultures to flower for a period, in the long term they functioned as way stations on the road to acculturation and assimilation.[28] But the black ghetto has served as a central fixture of American racism's strong resistance to the assimilation of black people. Thus the ghetto's permanence has made it a continuing crucible for ethnic development and culture building.[29]

The Lower-Class Component

The black ghettos are overwhelmingly made up of people with low incomes, and poverty is the first fact of life. This has encouraged the view that the ghetto subculture is lower-class culture, or the "culture of poverty" to use Oscar Lewis's now fashionable phrase. Such an interpretation is based on the liberal assumption that Afro-Americans lack distinctive ethnic or national characteristics and the social science discovery that lower-class groups in America share somewhat deviant orientations and ways of life, or a subculture.[30] Since black Americans are overwhelmingly in the low-income population, then whatever appears to be distinctive in the ghetto must be due to class status rather than ethnicity.

Although Charles Keil did not deal explicitly with the analytical problem of class and ethnic contributions in his *Urban Blues,* his critic Bennett Berger based a rebuttal on the premise that ghetto culture is essentially lower-class in character. I think Berger found Keil's emphasis on Soul very convenient to his position, since this elusive and yet real cultural symbol does contain many of the values, orientations, and virtues that have been historically attributed to the poor and downtrodden. Berger (drawing from Keil) interprets Soul as a stereotype that flatters the oppressed black lower class and thus can serve as a compensation, an ideological palliative for its discontents:

> ... strong emotions and feelings, especially when shared with others; something pure, nonmachined; staying power and wisdom through suffering; telling it like it is, being what you are, and believing in what you do. The concept suggests further a tight intermingling of sex, love, and reciprocal responsiveness which constitute the pattern of Negro Dionysianism, manifest in the swing of the blues-jazz-gospel musical milieu and in the brilliant, moving, linguistic innovations which spring from it. The pattern emphasizes the erotic, the frenetic, and the ecstatic—a pattern which when made ideological constitutes a claim to emotional depth and authenticity.[31]

As this capsule summary suggests, there are many themes in ghetto life that can be identified in other lower-class groups, among the Latin American poor described by Lewis, for example, or in the immigrant ghettos of the Irish and the Poles. Some of these themes are expressive of a present-oriented style of life, characterized by minimal planning and organization. Religion is a dominant value and release; crime, hustling, rackets, and other forms of "deviance" are commonplace. Economic pressures strain the family, and "matriarchal" trends are visible. Aggression and violence are more everyday occurrences than in middle-class neighborhoods—at least in their public expression. Personal releases that some sociologists label "immediate rather than deferred gratifications"—sex, drinking, drugs, music—are emphasized in the life organizations of individuals. A sense of fatalism, or apathy, a quasi-paranoid outlook (the "world is against me") pervade the streets, where the public life of the lower-class subculture is set.

That the black ghetto shares these realities with other lower-class milieus and that these themes flow primarily from the condition of poverty I do not doubt. But that is not the whole story. Even the class-based characteristics gain an ethnic content and emphasis when people with unique problems live under similar conditions and associate primarily with one another for generations. The best accounts of Afro-American life reveal how street society, the behavior of youth gangs, and family relations are richly endowed with a peculiarly black style.[32] The cultivation of a black style is emphasized in speech, movement, dress, and of course music and dance.[33] And as Hortense Powdermaker observed in the 1930s, a Negro church service is a totally different happening from a poor white one, despite the fact that the two share some common religious origins and institutional forms.[34]

Berger correctly observes that lower-class traits do not become institutionalized or legitimated. But when class traits are modified and given ethnic content by a national group, they may become institutionalized, that is, conscious, expected, and infused with value (which can be positive or negative). Afro-Americans have long infused value into their music; today southern food, modes of walking and talking, and even an alleged "supersexuality" have become symbols of group identity and cohesiveness. (The development of ethnic cultural values does not, of course, preclude ambivalence; the fact that many people may feel ambivalent toward these phenomena is no argument against their cultural reality. Just the contrary!)

The controversy about the "matriarchy" best illustrates my thesis. Although in recent years social scientists like Moynihan have exaggerated and distorted the subject, the special and different role that the woman and mother have played in the black family and community is a perennial theme in Afro-American life and literature. The black woman (and the cognate issue of male–female relations) is a continuous topic of discussion in black circles, in informal sessions as well as public debates. The emphasis in some parts of the Afro-American movement on black manhood is a reaction to the role of the woman as much as to a racist society's denial of dignity and opportunity. Unlike the lower-class situation where a matrifocal theme operates amid a patriarchal value system that obscures a consciousness of this trend, blacks have directly confronted the issue. In the past few years the so-called matriarchy has been talked about, joked about, defended against, debated pro and con, and more and more actively acted upon—for example, in selecting leadership in community groups. The assessment of the historic position of the woman and the relative roles of male and female in the family, community, and liberation movement is undergoing a spirited reexamination today. This kind of cultural ferment is not characteristic of lower classes or even working classes in America. It points to a dynamic of self-definition through which an ethnic group is shaping its character.

The class and ethnic factors in Afro-American culture are intimately intermingled and thus difficult to distinguish. The effort must be made, however, because the intellectual and social consequences of this apparently innocent distinction are considerable—as I suggest in my conclusion.

RACISM

The paradox of black culture is its ambiguous debt to racial oppression. Whereas racism attacks culture at its very roots, and white supremacy in American life and thought has worked tooth and nail to negate the past and present cultural realities of Afro-America, the centrality of racial subjugation in the black experience has been the single most important source of the developing ethnic peoplehood. Racism has been such an omnipresent reality that the direct and indirect struggle against it makes up the core of black history in America, just as the way in which each individual confronted it can be seen as the distinguishing mark of her or his personal biography.[35] It is through this continuing struggle to surmount and change a racist social system—a struggle which began at least with Emancipation, and has stepped up to new levels each generation, after periods of decline, to the zenith of the present day—that black Americans have created a *political history*. This political history is the core of the distinctive ethnic culture and the clue to the contemporary revitalization movement which celebrates blackness.

Despite the Kerner Report, it is still difficult for most whites to accept the unpleasant fact that America remains a racist society. Such an awareness is further obscured by the fact that more sophisticated, subtle, and indirect forms, which might better be termed neoracism, tend to replace the traditional, open forms that were most highly elaborated in the old South. The centrality of racism is manifest in two key characteristics of our social structure. First, the division based upon color is the single most important split within the society, the body politic, and the national psyche. Second, various processes and practices of exclusion, rejection, and subjection based on color are built into the major public institutions (labor market, education, politics, and law enforcement), with the effect of maintaining special privileges, power, and values for the benefit of the white majority.

Historians and other analysts of American life are today discovering the prominence of racism and the implicit assumptions of white superiority in the national experience. Specific racist practices and systems of thought have had a profound impact on the career of black ethnicity in

America. The alienation of slaves from their African cultural heritages has already been discussed. A subsequent expression of this destructive and exploitative dynamic was the practice of appropriating the cultural creations of Africans in the New World for the purpose of profit. Jazz and other musical forms are the classic example, but it persists widely in many variations such as the present-day absorption of ghetto language by the mass media and white youth cultures. A third variation of the racist dialectic is the tendency to deny the legitimacy, or even existence, of distinctive ethnic orientations and creations, a common premise in contemporary "liberal" ideology.

Yet it was the same racist society that willy-nilly encouraged the development of Afro-American culture. Blocking the participation of black people in the dominant culture meant that the human need for symbols, meaning, and value had to be met elsewhere. There must have always been many who found these meanings in "separatist" ethnic forms; there were others who sought them in the attempt to enter fully into the larger culture. Whereas many blacks have always known that racism was no aberration but an institution built into the fabric of American life, the dominant tendency may have been a more optimistic attachment to the nation's ideals of equality and democracy, combined always with a sharp awareness of the opposing reality. But even the acceptance of American premises necessitated group struggles against racism that would translate such ideals into practice. Expressed both in collective and in individual efforts to transcend its crippling effects on life, liberty, and the pursuit of opportunity, this century-long battle against racism has created a legacy—the political history of black people within the United States. This political history is the solid core, the hard-rock nonmystical aspect of Afro-American culture.

A unique political history plays an essential role in the development and consolidation of ethnic groups as well as nations. For the Irish-American community in the late nineteenth and early twentieth century, Ireland's struggle against England and the heroes of that national movement were central concerns. As many have noted, the Jews may be the purest example of a people that has institutionalized its political history into culture, ritual, and sacred values. The Old Testament depicts the political vicissitudes of the Jewish nation, and the religious holidays memorialize this millennial struggle for liberation. Perhaps then the attempt of many black nationalist groups to memorialize the date of Malcolm X's birth or assassination as an official holiday—which in some communities has been successful—can be understood as a similar recognition of the relation between political history and national culture.

The content of black political history is beyond the scope of this essay.

It is clear, however, that in the past two decades there has been a significant change in its intensity and nature, a change that lies behind the present-day ferment and interest in black culture. In the past the Negro masses—like the lower orders of all colors and nations in most eras—were primarily passive politically, acted upon more than acting. Since the 1954 Supreme Court *Brown* decision (that last major turning point in American race relations that was initiated by a decision of a "white" institution), blacks have become the most important social force acting to change the nation's social structure. Beginning in the mid-fifties they have been creating the big news in domestic American history.

Despite the fateful reciprocity of black and white in America (a theme that has been stressed in the essays of James Baldwin and the fiction of William Faulkner and W. M. Kelley),[36] Afro-Americans share a consciousness of a common past (and a concomitant national or ethnic identification) to which other Americans are not privy. How could whites perceive, react, and relate to slavery, Emancipation, to the South and its history of jim crow and lynching, to early twentieth-century race riots, and even to Montgomery and Watts in the same way as blacks? No matter how democratic our ideals and how sensitive our human capacities, we were *on the other side* sociologically and existentially.

The point I am belaboring has been made succinctly by a reflective blues singer, Al Hibbler. When Charles Keil asked him what it takes to make a Soul singer, Hibbler listed three ingredients, "having been hurt by a woman," "being brought up in that old-time religion," and "knowing what that slavery shit is all about."[37] In a nutshell, this is the essence of the distinctive political history that lies behind the reality of black ethnicity—since no white American can really know "what that slavery shit is all about." Hibbler, of course, was referring not only to the past.

The black man's unique sociopolitical experience also lies behind other elements of Afro-American culture that have been stressed recently. The Soul orientation can be thought of in Dionysian terms and thus be linked to poverty and lower-class status. But it can also be looked at as a philosophy of life or world view that places tragedy, suffering, and forbearance in a more central position than does the dominant American ethos. The construction of an orientation toward inner experience that clashes with the more external instrumental orientation of our industrial culture reflects as much the racism that has excluded black people from American life as it does lower-class status per se.

Another corollary of racism is the prominence of *survival* as a focal concern in the Afro-American culture. The preoccupation with survival is worth examining because of its remarkable salience and because it may appear to be only a reflection of poverty and lower-class status. It is common for black people to argue that the white race would not have survived had it been subject to the conditions, past and present, that their group has been subject to. Indeed, the biological survival and numerical increase of Afro-Americans, along with the continual renewal of their cultural energy, is a remarkable historical achievement. This sense of tough resilience is one of the central themes in the blues and in the mystique of Soul. In the ghetto there is consensus that the problem of every individual is "making it." "How you makin' it, man," is a common form of greeting. This idea of survival now dominates much of the rhetoric of black American leaders. Because white power is threatened by the numerical increase of the black population, particularly in the cities, such measures as birth control campaigns aimed at welfare clients, the draft policies of the Vietnam war, and the plans to put down ghetto riots with heavy military equipment have been interpreted as potentially genocidal strategies.

Poverty and lower-class existence per se make survival an inevitable and insistent preoccupation. But the Afro-American's self-conscious concern with survival and "making it" only reflects in part alimentary and economic subsistence needs. When black people talk about surviving, they are even more pointedly referring to the problem of maintaining life, sanity, and dignity in a racist society. The backdrop of the "making it" imagery is the presence of the Klan, lynch mobs, ghetto police, and the closed, restricted white power and economic structures. "Making it" appears to be a response to poverty and blocked economic opportunities, but "making it with dignity" is the response of a suppressed national group with distinctive ethnic values to defend. Here I refer to the more subtle pressures of white institutions to remake Afro-Americans in those middle-class ways that acceptance and success seem to require. Constraints against the expression of black ethnicity and style are interpreted as racist, and a major factor behind the increasing ambivalence toward integration is the fear that it will lead to assimilation and thereby threaten cultural survival.

This suggests another reason why Afro-American culture has been relatively "invisible." Blacks have learned to respond to racist depreciation and opportunistic cultural appropriation by concealing many of their deeply held patterns from the white world. White America therefore has not been prepared to respond to any affirmation of black culture beyond the conventional and usually racist stereotypes. Today this old adaptation is dying out as a new mood of pride motivates black people to celebrate rather than to deny ethnic values.

Racist social relations have different cultural consequences from class relations, and therefore black culture cannot be forced into the Procrustean bed of lower-class culture in the way that Marxists at one time and some liberal social scientists today have wanted to reduce race relations to class relations. For several centuries blacks in America have lived together in ways that are markedly different from those of the lower and working classes. The manner in which they have been compelled to relate to individual whites and to the larger society has been markedly divergent from the typical relations of the lower classes to the middle classes or from that of the proletariat to a capitalist social order. Racism excludes a category of people from participation in society in a different way than does class hegemony and exploitation. The thrust of racism is to dehumanize, to violate dignity and degrade personalities in a much more pervasive and all-inclusive way than class exploitation—which in the United States, at any rate, has typically not been generalized beyond the "point of production." Racist oppression attacks selfhood more directly and thoroughly than does class oppression. For these reasons, racial and class oppression—while intimately interacting—have diverse consequences for group formation, for the salience of identities based upon them, and for individual and group modes of adaptation and resistance. Class exploitation does not per se stimulate ethnic and national cultures and liberation movements; colonialism and domestic racism do.

Oscar Lewis has recently noted a complementary and conflicting relation between the culture of poverty and ethnic group cultures. The classical lower-class culture characterized by apathy, social disorganization, aggression, sexuality, and other themes lacks strong ethnic as well as organized political traditions. When an ethnic culture is viable or when political working-class consciousness is cultivated (as Lewis believes has taken place among the Cuban poor), the culture of poverty with all its negative and problematic effects declines.[38] If Lewis is correct—and he makes sense to me—the black culture movement among Afro-Americans may represent the revival of ethnic consciousness—the strengthening of the ethnic cultural component, at the expense of the lower-class component.

CULTURE BUILDING AND ITS PRESENT-DAY ROLE

The existence of an Afro-American culture does not make black people less American, though it conditions their relation to American life in distinctive ways. The society's ways of doing things have been a major if not an overwhelming influence on black community standards. Because blacks were stripped of their original religion, language, and institutions, they were particularly vulnerable to American values. Prevented from equal participation in their pursuit, however, blacks assimilated them from a unique perspective, that of the outsider. Thus a deep skepticism about the big myths of America has been a recurring mood of the black experience, along with a yearning for their realization. Of course black culture accepts the American emphasis on money, the material accoutrements of affluence, and many other goals—probably including even the suburban life style. In its racist dimension America excludes people of color and maintains the ghettoized communities that provide fertile ground for ethnicity, while in its inclusive, mass homogenizing dimension America beckons blacks and all others to identify with its material and ideal symbols and to participate in at least the middle levels of consumption and life styles. Out of these contradictions have emerged a distinctive ethnic consciousness of the social costs of American values and a sensitivity to the hypocrisy in public and private life and to the gap between the ideal and reality. This long-term awareness appears today to be changing into a more outspoken and outright rejection of American middle-class values by a substantial number of young Afro-Americans.

The fact that black Americans are more actively rejecting the society and its values at a time when that social order has begun to open its doors to their participation appears paradoxical. To some degree and in some cases this may be a defense mechanism, a protection against the anxieties of openness, competition, and new possibilities. But from another point of view, the paradox is resolved if we understand the special career of Afro-American ethnicity discussed earlier. In contrast with the European immigrants, the period of integration and potential assimilation for blacks is coinciding with the upsurge of the group's sense of peoplehood and with the institutionalization of its culture, rather than with the decline of these phenomena. Because Afro-American culture is a homegrown product, it continues to develop within the matrix of American society. The result is that blacks are becoming more and more bicultural, able to shift back and forth between two social worlds.

Furthermore, blacks are an extremely large and highly differentiated minority, particularly in comparison to the immigrant groups who inspired the sociologists' model of ethnic group assimilation. Most of the latter were small, their members concentrated physically in a few cities and socially in the lower classes. During the long periods of black cultural development the Afro-American minority has become more and more differentiated. The middle classes grow; new political and religious movements proliferate; the black population spreads out more evenly across the country—though it is now predominantly in the urban centers. The diverse "subcultures" within Afro-America—regional, religious, class, and age-based—complicate the overall ethnic development, which moves at an uneven pace, intensifying the ambiguities and paradoxes in the relation between the racial order and the larger society. It is precisely this ambiguous or paradoxical character of black culture that makes it especially critical for group formation and personal identity. The immigrant ethnics had a clear-cut and holistic "traditional culture"; this gave them implicit strength and bargaining power in the game of assimilation and acculturation. They had something deep inside the group and the individual to fall back upon in the event the American staircase became blocked or its climb too perilous. The black man has faced the American colossus with his original culture shattered. But most important, racism is more profound in its destructive impact on personal identity than the prejudice and discrimination that was leveled against the nonblack outlanders.

The present cultural ferment in the Negro community is not totally new, of course. Well known is the Harlem renaissance of the 1920s, which saw the emergence of a group of self-conscious black intellectuals and artists, along with a somewhat parallel nationalist political development, the Garvey movement. This earlier cultural renaissance came after the post–World War I setbacks to racial democratization, just as today's cultural movement gained its power from the limited successes and possibilities of the civil rights movement—specifically the failure of integration to become a socioeconomic reality. But if culture building feeds on "backlash," this does not mean it is a temporary will-of-the-wisp that will die out when integration finally hits its stride. The totality of the racial experience of the last twenty years is beginning to teach some white people what most blacks have probably always known—that racism is not a dying phenomenon in American life, confined largely to decadent southern elites and their "redneck" allies. Unfortunately it is on the way out only in these more blatant forms. In various and subtle ways, racism and neoracism permeate the social institutions of society, North, South, West, and East. Thus the black culture movement is a reasonable response to the realities of a society that in its present socioeconomic and psychic organization is not going to accept people of African descent without imposing ceilings on their human possibilities. The stronger that Afro-American ethnicity becomes, the greater the possibility for black people to utilize both group power and individual mobility to take what they can from, and give what will be accepted to, this basically racist society—a process that in time will contribute to its transformation. For in American life, ethnic culture is identity, and there is no individual or group progress without a clear sense of who one is, where one came from, and where one is going.

The black consciousness and culture-building movements of today seem much more significant than the earlier Harlem development, though for a nonhistorian this can be only an impressionistic guess. Today's movement is more widespread; it is taking place in every major locale, not just New York. It encompasses large segments of the black bourgeoisie and working-class masses, rather than primarily marginal people and intellectuals. The appeal of black culture seems especially strong today to the occupationally and socially mobile, a group that in the past tended to resist ethnic identification.[39]

The young are of course at the forefront of the black culture and black power movements. Ironically, if Claude Brown is correct, E. Franklin Frazier may have had much to do with this generational change in the outlook of the "black bourgeoisie." Brown mentions that Frazier's lectures and his book *Black Bourgeoisie* had a great impact on his own thinking and, presumably, that of other college students. Of course, there is a sense in which these mobile black youths did not have to be motivated to become different from their parents; in America all young people are predisposed to reject their elders and break away from their parents' life patterns. But in so clearly dissecting the group-denying and self-negating hangups of their parents, Frazier also helped teach the young generation to identify with their own blackness and with the oppressed ghetto masses. Many middle-class college-educated youth have taken on the tasks of attempting to organize politically, as well as to articulate self-consciously, the less conscious cultural values of the lower-class black community.

CONCLUSION

Many liberal intellectuals assume that talk of black culture is mainly rhetorical. They arrogantly demand that its spokesmen clearly define its content and function. Bennett Berger expressed this position well when he asserted that "once the radicals invoke the perspective and rhetoric of Black culture, they place themselves under the intellectual obligation to concern themselves with clarifying precisely *what* patterns of Negro culture they are affirming, *what* sources of institutional support for these patterns they see in Negro social organization, and *how* these patterns may be expected to provide the bases of 'racial pride' and 'ethnic identity' sufficient to motivate the Black masses to claim both their full rights as Americans *and* the nation's respect for their ethnicity."[40] The fallacy here is that the black intelligentsia is expected to provide a clear statement of what its culture is—something that American social scientists have not adequately accomplished for the society as a whole.

The concept of culture—as well-taught undergraduates should know—is very sticky and troubling. Much scholarly controversy and uncertainty surround its essential features. American culture is a most vague and amorphous reality; it simply cannot be pinned down as neatly and conveyed to us as graphically as the ethnographer can capture the culture of a tribal people. This may be partly because we are all caught up in it; more probably it reflects the diversity, the contradictions, and even the weakness of meaning systems and of central patterns in American life. As Harold Cruse has emphasized, it is the lack of ethnic unity, distinctiveness, and indigenous creativity in the white American heritage that has made our society so receptive to and needful of the cultural contributions of black people.[41] It is indeed an irony that the cultural stream within American life whose reality and legitimacy are most systematically denied is its single most vigorous ethnic tradition.

Despite the variety of meanings attached to black power, a common theme is that of self-definition. Self-definition implies that whites no longer can demand that blacks do this or that; Afro-Americans now select the time, place, and manner in which to reveal their plans and strategies outside the group. As a matter of fact, the project of cultural clarification that Berger calls for has been a constant preoccupation in the black experience; what is new today is that many whites are interested in the problem, and consequently a decision has been made to exclude them from the settings in which these complex issues are hammered out. In addition to all-black conferences and informal meetings, the major forums for the discussion of Afro-American ethnicity include black studies departments in universities and colleges and an increasing number of new magazines and journals.

That whites are no longer calling the shots on these matters is the great and historic gain of two decades of black protest. The white intellectual and social science communities are no longer the primary interpreters of black people and their culture. Yet while our academic theorizing is no longer as central as it once was, the black political and cultural movement still operates within those American conditions that we affect. For this reason, white social scientists have a responsibility to probe deeply into the assumptions and consequences of our characterizations of racial realities.

The demand that black spokesmen give us the lowdown once and for all on black culture so that we can define our attitude toward it overlooks a reality that is more profound than new "nationalist" rules for intergroup relations. It reflects a static approach to social and cultural reality. It assumes that Afro-American culture is "all there," or all-determined, needing only to be fully detected so that the chaff can be separated from the wheat. On the contrary, this culture, like all cultures, but today even more so, is *in process*. It is a dynamic, open-ended phenomenon, and that is why it is becoming such a central concern of the protest movement. On the basis of the culture that has already been built out of the experience of the (until recently relatively quiet) masses, a more self-conscious and explicit national culture is in the process of development. This requires the synthesis of the orientations of the predominantly lower-class ghetto dwellers with the articulations of the intellectual and political leaders, the middle classes, and the marginal people, who play a crucial part as cultural enunciators and systematizers.

The opinion that black culture is only a lower-class life style and that Afro-Americans have no ethnic traditions to value and defend falls within a general concept that I call neoracism. Superficially the argument seems to be that blacks are as American as whites and therefore their cultural orientations reflect their social class position. But, as I have maintained in this essay, such an approach ignores the group-forming and culture-producing effects of racism; therefore, as an analytical position, it leads to the minimization of the reality of racial oppression. This position leads further to an overconcern with the pathological features of the black community at the expense of its unique strengths and contributions, since the culture of poverty is generally (and correctly) seen in terms of the predominance of suffering and the destruction of choice and of human possibilities. If Afro-American culture is only lower-class culture, then the questionable assumption that *all* black people want integration, mobility, and assimilation seems justifiable as a basis for institutional policy; it is therefore not necessary to consult, to offer alternative choices, or to respect individual diversity. Furthermore, this position is historically tied to past patterns of negating or appropriating the cultural possessions and productions of black people. The racist pattern was to destroy culture, to steal it for profit, or to view it contemptuously or with amusement. The neoracist equivalents today are to deny that culture exists or to envy and desire the values that blacks create and defend as their own. (Witness the pathetic need on the part of many young and not-so-young liberal and radical admirers of the Negro movement to feel that they, too, have Soul.)

The denial of Afro-American ethnicity is the more serious form that white appropriation takes today. Through abstract and intellectual analysis, the full implications of which are not always clearly perceived, the social scientist has attempted to undermine the claims of black Americans to a distinctive ethos and value system. The very existence of our possibility to so influence the cultural process is based on the original alienation of black people from their African traditions. Because black Americans could use only the English language to carry on their business, their politics, and their intellectual life, their physical and moral communities became vulnerable to the penetration of white Americans, a penetration that other ethnic groups—insulated by exotic languages, religions, and other institutions—could escape. Thus, the original stripping and the subsequent appropriation of indigenous black culture opened up the Negro community to economic and political colonialism, to the contamination of group ideology by alien, pride-destroying perspectives, and to the participation of paternalistic whites in racial movements.

It is time for social scientists to insist that there are no exceptions to the anthropological law that every group has a culture: if black Americans are an ethnic group then they possess an ethnic culture; and just as the Jews explain to the world what Jewish culture is about and Italians define Italian-American culture, we will learn what Afro-American culture is from American blacks—when they are ready to tell us—rather than from our own dogmas and fantasies.

Part Two

Institutionalized Racism

8 Whitewash over Watts

The Politics of the McCone Commission

In retrospect, the August 1965 riots in the Watts neighborhood of South Central Los Angeles can be seen as a fault line dividing the 1960s in two. During the first half of the decade the civil rights movement continued to pursue its goal of racial integration, and though its tactics grew more and more militant, the tenor of racial politics remained relatively moderate. But the Watts riots changed the national climate, setting the stage for the Black Power and black nationalist movements that soon followed.

The five days of violence left thirty-four dead, virtually all of them African Americans shot by the police, and $40 million of damage inflicted on businesses and other property. Like the assassination and funeral of John F. Kennedy less than two years earlier, television images of the Watts riots electrified the populace, and the revolt's "Burn, baby burn" slogan became part of the nation's consciousness.

I was invited to join the research staff of the commission appointed by Governor Pat Brown to investigate the causes of the rioting. Since the McCone Commission seemed to reflect the concerns of Los Angeles's elites rather than those of the low-income citizens of the riot area, I began to prepare a survey of the attitudes of the black population of Los Angeles toward the August events. But I was naive to think that I could steer the commission's report away from its law-and-order approach. Soon, the commission began to sabotage my efforts to carry out that survey, and my only recourse was to pack my bags and return to Berkeley.

In the essay that follows I compare the gulf between Watts and affluent Los Angeles to that between natives and colonial masters, suggesting that the events are better understood as an anticolonial uprising, rather than a racial revolt. Not only did this mark my first use of the "colonial analogy" to interpret black–white relations in America, it also marked my discovery that the essay form was an ideal vehicle to analyze the big news of the day, one in which I could combine my youthful passion for journalism with the analytical tools I had learned as a sociologist.

I like to think that this essay, along with similar critiques by other social scientists, helped people to look at the events in Watts and the even more destructive revolts that followed in Detroit and Newark in a deeper, more complex way. Two and a half years later in March 1968, when another governmental riot commission appointed by Lyndon Johnson published its findings, the Kerner Report was much more serious, detailed, and satisfactory.

On July 27, 1919, a clash of whites and blacks at a Chicago beach resulted in the drowning of a Negro boy and served as the spark to what was to remain the most violent racial outbreak in American history until 1965. For four days black and white mobs were virtually uncontained and it was almost another week before the state militia was able to withdraw, on August 8. The final toll read 38 dead (23 black, 15 white), 537 injured (of whom two-thirds were black), and 1,000 people homeless (primarily whites). Less than two weeks after the end of the rioting Governor Frank Lowden of Illinois appointed a twelve-member Commission on Race Relations "to study and report upon the broad questions of the relations between the two races." The hearings and research, which the commission began three months later, occupied them for an entire year; the greater part of 1921 was spent in writing the 672-page report, which appeared in 1922 as *The Negro in Chicago: A Study of Race Relations and a Race Riot.*[1] The commission was most fortunate in selecting for its major investigator Charles S. Johnson, a young graduate student at the University of Chicago, who decades later was to produce a number of classic studies of the American Negro.[2] Thus the 1919 Chicago riots resulted in a significant analysis of the events themselves, as well as of the sociological structure of race relations and of a northern black community, which served for decades as a model of social science.

On August 24, 1965, just one week after public order had been restored in the south-central area of Los Angeles known as Watts, Governor Pat Brown of California announced the appointment of an eight-man commission of leading citizens. In his charge to the group (which came to be known as the McCone Commission, after its chairman, John A. McCone, former head of the CIA), Brown asked it to "prepare an accurate chronology and description of the riots"; "to probe deeply the immediate and underlying causes of the riots"; and finally to "develop recommendations for action designed to prevent a recurrence of these tragic disorders."

For what appears to have been political considerations connected with possible repercussions of the Watts affair on the 1966 gubernatorial campaign, the commission was given December 1, 1965, as the deadline for the completion of its report. Thus only 100 days were available for a "deep and probing" analysis of one of the most destructive incidents of racial violence in American history.

In an atmosphere of speedup that made work on an automobile assembly line appear leisurely by comparison, the commission held a series of sixty formal hearings before which eighty sworn witnesses, including city and police officials, leaders and citizens of the white and black communities, eventually appeared. It also selected a full-time staff of thirty, primarily lawyers and legal-oriented investigators, to carry out the day-to-day work of assembling data and preparing the report. The staff called upon the services of twenty-six consultants (chiefly university professors in the social sciences) for advice and the subcontracting of research, interviewed ninety persons among the 4,000 arrested, and opened an office in the riot area to take testimony from local citizens. After a total expenditure of $250,000, Commissioner McCone presented the report to Governor Brown with the fanfare of television on December 6.

In view of the conditions under which it was hurried into existence, it should be no surprise that *Violence in the City—An End or a Beginning?* is a slim volume with only eighty-six pages of blown-up type.[3] But the report of the McCone Commission is not only brief, it is sketchy and superficial. Its tone and style are disturbing. There is much glib writing, and the approach as well as the format is slick in the manner of illustrated news weeklies. The depth analysis of this fateful outbreak can be read by an average reader in less than an hour—allowing ample time for contemplating the many photographs, both color and black- and-white.

My comparison with the careful and considered report of the Illinois governor's commission of 1919 that required three years of planning, research, and writing may well be unfair. But with the sizable, budget and all the academic expertise available, more was to be expected than the public relations statement of the California commission.

Not only the size and style of the McCone document are disturbing. Its content is disappointing both in its omissions and in its underlying political and philosophical perspectives. There is almost nothing in the report that is new or that gives consideration to the unique conditions of Los Angeles life and politics. As Los Angeles councilman Billy Mills commented, most of the material in the report documented conditions in the ghetto that have been common knowledge to sociologists and the informed public for a generation. The events of the rioting were covered in greater breadth and depth in the daily reporting in the *Los Angeles Times,* a sense of their larger meaning conveyed more perceptively in any of a number of hour-long television documentaries.

More appalling are the report's deeper failures. With a narrow legalistic perspective that approached the riots in terms of the sanctity of law and order, the commissioners were unable (or unwilling) to read any social or political meaning into the August terror. There was no attempt to look at the outbreak from the point of view of the black poor. The commissioners also played a dangerous game with the problem of responsibility. The Negro community as a whole is absolved from responsibility for the rioting while local and national leaders (civil rights moderates and extremists alike) are taken to task for inflaming mass discontent and undermining commitments to law and authority. (In a two-page dissenting comment appended to the main report the Reverend James E. Jones, a black commissioner, criticized the report for attempting "to put a lid on protest.")[4]

In a crude attempt at "horse trading" in the responsibility market, the positions of the Los Angeles police department and city administrators are consistently protected. By discounting the relevance of police provocation and city policies without presenting any facts or evidence, the commission not only protected powerful interests, it abdicated its mandate to seek out facts and establish as best it could the objective reality. My most general and most serious criticism of the report is this violation of the responsibility to seek truth and the frequent hiding behind opinion and hearsay.

CAUSES OF THE WATTS "REVOLT"

Lurking behind the Watts violence are three basic problems, according to the McCone Commission:

1. the widespread unemployment and "idleness" in the ghetto
2. the cultural and educational backwardness of black children, which prevents the schools from preparing them for the labor market and integrating them into society
3. the troubled state of police-community relations in the Negro neighborhoods

The Crisis in Employment

The chapter on employment is forthright in its emphasis on jobs as a central problem and correct in its understanding that male dignity and family responsibility can hardly be expected when men are unable to find steady work. For example: "The most serious immediate problem that faces the Negro in our community is employment—securing and holding a job that provides him an opportunity for livelihood, a chance to earn the means to support himself, and his family, a dignity, and a reason to feel that he is a member of our community in a true and very real sense."[5] The commission calls upon federal, state, and city government to create jobs for the black and Mexican-American poor. Corporations and labor unions are asked to end discrimination once and for all and to police their progress by keeping careful records on minority employment. Because the commissioners are convinced that the majority of jobless Los Angeles Negroes are presently unemployable, they call for an expanded and better-coordinated program of job training; they wisely recommend that control of this effort be within the black community.

These proposals on employment are worthwhile and necessary, but they encourage a deceptive complacency. The report does not probe sufficiently into the depth and seriousness of the problem. There is no con-

sideration of the impact of population trends and technological developments on the availability of jobs, especially for the unskilled, and no willingness to face the escalating employment needs in the rapid expansion of
the minority population of Los Angeles. The report is irresponsible,
because its style and tone convey the impression that its relatively mild
and moderate recommendations provide real solutions.

Educational Inequality

The treatment of education is the one section of the McCone Report that
is based on a careful and firsthand study. Kenneth A. Martyn, professor
of education at Los Angeles State College, investigated five areas within
the Los Angeles City Unified School District as a commission consultant.
Student achievement was compared for four "disadvantaged areas" (of
which two were primarily black and close to the riot centers) and one
"advantaged" area (predominantly white upper middle class). Average
student reading performances in the fifth, eighth, and eleventh grades
reveal a consistent backwardness in the lower-class black and Mexican
districts. The gap is most dramatic at the eighth grade, since by the
eleventh many of the poorest "achievers" are already dropouts. The average student in the white middle-class area is in the 79th percentile in reading vocabulary based on national norms; the average students in "Negro"
Watts and Avalon are in the 13th and 14th percentiles; the average percentiles in the primarily Mexican areas of Boyle Heights and East Los
Angeles are 16th and 17th.

Martyn investigated the possibility of discrimination in educational
facilities. Some inequalities were found, but hardly enough to explain the
systematic backwardness of minority students. The commission therefore
ascribed the problem of school performance to what today is fashionably
called a *culturally impoverished environment*. Parents have little education and their own background does not foster an orientation toward
achievement and learning; crowded housing conditions are not favorable
for disciplined study; and the precariousness of employment and the lack
of models of achievement may further dull incentive. In order to break
this pattern and "raise the scholastic achievement of the average Negro
child up to or perhaps above the present average achievement level in the
city," the commission calls for an intensive infusion of educational
resources into the black community, focusing on three programs:
preschool learning on the model of Headstart, the reduction of class size,
and the improvement of academic and behavioral counseling.

The McCone Report accepts the conventional position that it is the
"vicious circular" connection between education and employment that is
the crux of the dilemma of the Negro poor. It places its main bet on edu-

cation and the future, rather than on creating jobs to solve the problems of the present. If the achievement levels of present and future generations of black children can be sufficiently raised, they will be motivated to remain in the school system and assimilate the skills and training that will begin reversing this cyclical process. Unfortunately, the middle-class ethos underlying the commission's emphasis on future orientation and achievement is irrelevant to the needs and outlook of the lower-class adult group whose problems of work and training are likely to intensify.

But even with a crash program in education, can the average ghetto youth be motivated toward achievement and excellence when the condition of his people and community place him in a position of alienation and powerlessness vis-à-vis the larger society? What is missing in the report's analysis is a total picture of the Watts community as consistently deprived and disadvantaged in relation to Los Angeles as a whole. Fragmented hints of this picture abound in the report, particularly in the excellent discussion of the woefully inadequate transportation system, but the fragments are never pieced together. If they were, municipal officials would then have to bear some responsibility for permitting this systematic deprivation to persist. By singling out education as the strategic sphere for ameliorative efforts, the commission aims its biggest guns on the target area in which the city's hands are relatively "clean" and in which it is relatively easy to suggest that the cultural backgrounds and individual performances of black people themselves account for a good part of the problem.

The Police Issue

> If we don't get no good out of this, it will happen again. By good I mean an end to police harassment, and we need jobs. I got eight kids, and I've only worked 10 days this year. I ain't ever been a crook, but if they don't do something, I'm gonna have to take something. I don't know how they expect us to live.
>
> —"A young man in a striped shirt," quoted in Louise Meriwether, "What the People of Watts Say," *Frontier* (October 1965)

When an oppressed group breaks out in a violent attack on society and its representatives, the underlying causes are those long-term elements in its situation that have produced its alienation and despair. Immediate causes are the short-run irritants and grievances that have intensified feelings of anger and hatred and focused them on specific targets. The immediate grievances and conditions that spark illegal violence must have the effect of weakening the oppressed's normal disposition to accept, at least overtly, the authority structure and legal norms of the society—otherwise mass violence could not erupt. The young Watts man quoted above seems to be saying that from his standpoint "jobs" are the underlying cause, "police harassment" the immediate issue. The governor's commission disagrees with his analysis and has its own explanation for the ghetto's sudden loss of commitment to the legal order.

It answers its own question "Why Los Angeles?" in a way that almost totally relieves the city and county of implication. The rapid migration of southern blacks to the city's ghetto serves as their starting point, for these migrants are unrealistic in expecting that California living will solve all their problems. In the context of this "crisis of expectations" black frustration and despair were fanned by three "aggravating events in the twelve months prior to the riots":

> Publicity given to the glowing promise of the federal poverty program was paralleled by reports of controversy and bickering over the mechanism to handle the program here in Los Angeles, and when the projects did arrive, they did not live up to expectation.

> Throughout the nation, unpunished violence and disobedience to law were widely reported, and almost daily there were exhortations, here and elsewhere, to take the most extreme and even illegal remedies to right a wide variety of wrongs, real and supposed.

> In addition, many Negroes here felt and were encouraged to feel that they had been affronted by the passage of Proposition 14—an initiative measure passed by two-thirds of the voters in November 1964 which repealed the Rumford Fair Housing Act and unless modified by the voters or invalidated by the courts will bar any attempt by state or local governments to enact similar laws.[6]

To locate the argument it is necessary to pass over the invidious and insidious tone of this passage—the back-of-hand slap at the national civil rights movement, the implication that our country's injustices to people of color are as much "supposed" as "real," and the incredible insinuation that Afro-Americans required political spokesmen to tell them they were being affronted by the passage of an initiative in which 70 percent of their white fellow Californians said, "We don't want you moving into our neighborhoods." But the point is clear. Aside from some blunderings over the antipoverty war, it was Negro leadership that undermined the commitment of law-abiding black citizens to authority and legal methods of redressing their grievances. What is important is the assumption that the black poor's acceptance of political authority was not weakened by its own experience with police and other official representatives of society, but was instead subverted by an extremist and opportunist leadership.

Such an analysis gives the commission a free field to discount the role of the Los Angeles police and their presence in the ghetto as immediate precipitants of the violence. In short, the commission has "bought" the line of Chief of Police William Parker, who has consistently argued that the riot was a revolt of the criminal and lawless element, prodded on by a black leadership that inflamed the Los Angeles black community with the "bugaboo" of "police brutality."

The report devotes a chapter to law enforcement and police–community relations. It takes note of the severe criticism of the police department by many black witnesses and frankly admits "the deep and longstanding schism between a substantial portion of the Negro community and the police department." Considering the virtual unanimity in the black community concerning police practices as the foremost immediate cause of the outbreak, why did not the commission seriously investigate the role of law enforcement in the ghetto? The commission acknowledges that *feelings* of oppressive police action were significant conditions of the rioting. It violates its responsibility to truth and impartiality by refusing to examine the factual basis of black opinion while stating the beliefs and hearsay of white officers in an aura of established truth:

> The police have explained to us the extent to which the conduct of some Negroes when apprehended has required the use of force in making arrests. Example after example has been recited of arrestees, both men and women, becoming violent, struggling to resist arrest, and thus requiring removal by physical force. Other actions, each provocative to the police and each requiring more than normal action by the police in order to make an arrest or to perform other duties, have been described to us. (28)

Precisely the same line is taken with respect to Chief Parker. The commission duly notes that the outspoken chief is a focal point of criticism and is distrusted by most blacks. They feel he hates them. Yet the report conveniently omits all rational and objective bases for such "beliefs," including a whole series of public statements made long before the riots.[7] The inference is that "Negro belief" rests on misinterpretation of fact and paranoid reactions.

However, not only embittered black attitudes, but facts exist about the police presence in the ghetto—if the commission had only looked for them. For example, a study by a Youth Opportunities Board was available to the commission. It was based on intensive interviews with 220 people in the Watts, Willowbrook, and Avalon districts, undertaken only two years before the outbreak in this very area. The sample included 70 delinquent and nondelinquent children, 26 parents, and 124 high administrators and lesser personnel of the major agencies in the community (schools, welfare and probation, recreation and youth groups). Attitudes toward the critical agencies of the community were probed, and it was found that of all the "serving institutions" of the larger society, the object of the greatest hostility was the police department. A majority of adults as well as children felt that the behavior of the police aggravated the problems of growing up in the black community rather than contributing to their solution; this was in direct contrast to their attitudes toward the schools, the parks, the health services, and the probation officers.[8]

The real issue has perhaps been muddied by the outcry against "police brutality," the term that blacks use to sum up their sense of grievance against law-enforcement agents. The police liberalization policy of recent years may well have reduced the number of cases of "classic" brutality, like beatings and cruel methods of questioning. What the black community is presently complaining about when it cries "police brutality" is the more subtle attack on personal dignity that manifests itself in unexplainable questionings and searches, in hostile and insolent attitudes toward groups of young Negroes on the street or in cars, and in the use of disrespectful and sometimes racist language—in short, what the Watts man quoted above called "police harassment." There is no evidence that this assault on individual self-esteem and dignity has ceased.[9]

Another facet of police brutality is the use of excessive force to control criminal and illegal behavior. Characteristically the commission neglected its opportunity (and obligation) to assess the use of force by the various law enforcement agencies that put down the August violence, despite its considerable attention to their logistical and coordination problems and the concern of blacks and liberal groups like the ACLU with what appeared to be unnecessary shootings of looters, including young children.

The police chapter is primarily devoted to the adequacy of procedures presently available for processing complaints against officer misconduct and to recommendations for improving both them and relations in general between law enforcement and the black community. Yet, the demand of Negro leaders and white liberals for an independent civilian review board is described as "clamor"; the proposal is rejected because this device would "endanger the effectiveness of law enforcement." Experience with its use in two cities "has not demonstrated" its "advantages," but characteristically no evidence is given and the cities are not even named. Instead the report advocates strengthening the authority of the present Board of Police Commissioners, the civilian heads of the department, and establishing the new position of inspector general under the authority of the chief of police. The latter "would be responsible for making investigations and recommendations on all citizen complaints." In addition, the police should improve its community relations programs in the ghetto areas and strive to attract more blacks and Mexicans to careers in law enforcement. That there might be a connection between the way in which white police operate in the ghetto and the remarkable lack of interest of black youth in such careers never enters the heads of the commissioners.

The report correctly notes that all seven riots in the North in 1964 (as well as the one in Watts) began with a police incident and in every case "police brutality" was an issue. But in a monument to twisted logic it concludes from these observations:

> The fact that this charge is repeatedly made must not go unnoticed, for there is a real danger that persistent criticism will reduce and perhaps destroy the effectiveness of law enforcement. (29)

Instead of asking why poor blacks come to believe that law and authority are not their law and their authority, the report goes on to preach sanctimoniously:

> Our society is held together by respect for law. A group of officers who represent a tiny fraction of one percent of the population is the thin thread that enforces observance of law by those few who would do otherwise. If police authority is destroyed, if their effectiveness is impaired, and if their determination to use the authority vested in them to preserve a law abiding community is frustrated, all of society will suffer because groups would feel free to disobey the law and inevitably their number would increase. Chaos might easily result. (Ibid.)

CHARACTER OF THE WATTS OUTBREAK

There is very little explicit consideration of the character and meaning of the outburst in the McCone Report, in spite of its great concern with causes. The commission missed an important point of departure by not viewing the Watts violence as a problematic phenomenon, the essence of which needed to be determined through a careful weighing of evidence and through social and political analysis. For this reason the report's assumptions must be inferred because they are introduced in passing and never clearly spelled out.

The perspective of the analysis is overwhelmingly riot control rather than collective or crowd behavior. The attempt of "responsible" leaders to cool off the mobs is discussed, but the major emphasis is on the tactics used by the various law enforcement agencies. After a fairly thorough discussion of the arrest that set off the events, the black people who participated in violence are almost excluded from the story. The very language of the report suggests that it has pre-judged "the meaning of Watts."[10] On its opening page, it calls the outbreak a "spasm" and "an insensate rage of destruction." Later it calls it "an explosion—a formless, quite senseless, all but hopeless violent protest." Only in the discussion of the business targets that were looted and burned does the commission attempt to find a meaning or pattern in what the rioters did, and here they conclude—unlike most informed observers—that there was no "significant correlation between alleged consumer exploitation and the destruction."

The legalistic perspective of the commission and its staff seems to have blocked their sensitivity to the sociological meaning of the riots. When they view them simply as an uprising of the criminal element against law and order (aggravated of course by the social, economic, and political causes of frustration already discussed), the commissioners need not look seriously at the human meaning of the turmoil, nor need they understand what messages may have been communicated by the rocks, gunfire, and Molotov cocktails. Let us not romanticize the Watts violence. I don't claim that everyone involved and everything done had rational motives. But it is a more humble and scientific attitude to leave the question open and to examine the limited evidence that is available. For the assumption of meaninglessness, the emptying out of content and communication from any set of human actions—even nonrational violence—reduces the dignity of the actors involved. In the present context it is a subtle insult to the Los Angeles black community. The report ostensibly avoids such an insulting stance by minimizing participation and exculpating the bulk of the community from responsibility for the antisocial outbreak—but not its leaders, of course, who aggravated the underlying tension.

> In the ugliest interval which lasted from Thursday through Saturday, perhaps as many as 10,000 Negroes took to the streets in marauding bands. . . . The entire Negro population of Los Angeles County, about two thirds of whom live in this area (that of the riots), numbers more than 650,000. Observers estimate that only about two percent were involved in the disorder. Nevertheless, this violent fraction, however minor, has given the face of community relations in Los Angeles a sinister cast. (1)

No evidence is presented for the 2 percent estimate, nor for the total of 10,000 participants on which it is based. We are not told how the commission defines being "involved in the disorder." A number of distortions are apparently obvious, however. Even if 10,000 was the upper limit, this figure would indicate participation by far more than 2 percent of the blacks in Watts. The curfew area, with some 50,000 residents, contains many neighborhoods of comfortable middle-class people who were far from the riot center; they should be eliminated from a calculation of the extent of participation in an outbreak of the poor and dispossessed. Second, the total population figures include women, children, and the aged. A more appropriate (and still difficult) question would concern the extent of participation of young and mature black men in the low-income districts that were the centers of the action.

Unfortunately, I cannot answer this question precisely, but in view of the commission's unscientific methodology and dubious deductions there is no reason to accept their view of the participation issue. Consider on this matter the opinion of Bayard Rustin, who visited Watts with Martin Luther King a few days after the outbreak:

> I could not count heads but reports I have received and my experiences with the people leads me to believe that a large percentage of the people living in the Watts area participated. Most of them did not themselves loot and burn but they were on the streets at one time or other.[11]

As Rustin suggests, the question is not simply how many engaged in lawless acts. Essential to the meaning of the revolt is the attitude of the "nonparticipants" toward those who erupted in hate and violence. In the most popular revolutions it is only a small minority that storms the Bastille or dumps tea in Boston Harbor. Only through considering the attitudes of the "silent mass" is it possible to know whether the Watts riots represented an action by a large segment of the Negro poor of Los Angeles rather than a cutting loose of a small "violent fraction." Had the McCone Commission done its job, it would have conducted a systematic survey of community opinion to determine the distribution of sentiment in black Los Angeles.

My informants reported widespread support within the ghetto for the violent outbreak. Moral approval (as well as active participation) was stronger among youth and among the poor and working class. Old people and middle-class Negroes were more likely to feel ambivalent and to hold back. But there seems to have been at least some participation from all segments of the black community. In the countless interviews and feature stories that appeared in the press and on television, Watts citizens were more likely to explain and justify the riots rather than to condemn them; certainly the mass media would have little interest in censoring accounts of black disapproval. In a statewide public opinion survey conducted in November, 1965, only 16 percent of the blacks interviewed attributed the riots to "lack of respect for law and order" in contrast with 36 percent of the whites; "outside agitators" were seen as a most important cause by a scant 7 percent of the blacks compared with 28 percent of the whites. Seventy-nine percent of the black respondents fixed upon "widespread unemployment" and "bad living conditions" as prime causes, compared with only 37 percent of the whites. And months after the rioting a poll conducted by ABC Television found that the proportion of Watts residents who felt that the summer's events had helped their cause was twice as large as of those who felt it had hurt them.

If the Los Angeles revolt was not simply a "spasm" of lawlessness reflecting the violent inclinations of a minor criminal group; but represented instead the mood and spirit of the low-income black community, then we must look more closely at what the crowds were attempting to communicate.

As the Governor's report correctly notes, the uprising was not organized in advance. Yet it was neither formless nor meaningless. The people on the street were expressing more than the blind rage and the antiwhite hate epitomized in the "Burn, baby, burn" slogan. They seem to have been announcing an unwillingness to accept indignity and frustration without fighting back. In particular, they were communicating their hatred of policemen, firemen, and other representatives of white society who operate in the black community "like an army of occupation." They were asserting a claim to territoriality, making an unorganized and rather inchoate attempt to gain control over their community, their "turf." Most of the actions of the rioters appear to have been informed by the desire to clear out an alien presence, white men, rather than to kill them. (People have remarked how few whites were shot, considering the amount of sniping and the degree of marksmanship evidenced in accurate hits on automobile lights and other targets.) It was primarily an attack on property, particularly white-owned businesses, and not persons. Why not listen to what people in the crowds were saying as Charles Hillinger of the *Los Angeles Times* did on the night of August 13.

"White devils, what are you doing in here?"
"It's too late, white man. You had your chance. Now it's our turn."
"You created this monster and it's going to consume you. White man, you got a tiger by the tail. You can't hold it. You can't let it go."
"White man, you started all this the day you brought the first slave to this country."
"That's the hate that hate produced, white man. This ain't hurting us now. We have nothing to lose. Negroes don't own the buildings. You never did a decent thing in your life for us, white man."[12]

A "NATIVE" UPRISING

Any appraisal of the Watts uprising must be tentative. I suggest, however, that it was not primarily a rising of the lawless, despite the high participation of the lumpenproletariat and the clear-cut attack on law and authority. Nor was it a "conventional race riot," for the Los Angeles terror arose from the initiative of the black community and did not fit the simple pattern of whites and blacks engaging in purely racial aggression. It was certainly not a Los Angeles version of a mass civil rights protest.

Its organization was too loose. More important, the guiding impulse was not integration with American society but an attempt to stake out a sphere of control by moving against that society.

Instead my interpretation turns on two points. On the collective level the revolt seems to represent the crystallization of community identity through a nationalistic outburst against a society felt as dominating and oppressive. The spirit of the Watts rioters appears similar to that of anti-colonial crowds demonstrating against foreign masters, though in America the objective situation and potential power relations are very different. On the individual level, participation would seem to have had a special appeal for those young blacks whose aspirations to be men of dignity are systematically negated by the unavailability of work and the humiliations experienced in contacts with whites. For these young men (and reports indicate that males between the ages of fourteen and thirty predominated in the streets), violence permitted expressing their manhood in the American way of fighting back and "getting even."

The gulf between Watts and affluent Los Angeles is disturbingly similar to that between "natives" and their colonial masters. The Afro-American's alienation from the institutions and values of the larger society was made clear during the revolt. The sacredness of private property, that unconsciously accepted bulwark of our social arrangements, was rejected. Black people who looted, apparently without guilt, generally remarked that they were taking things that "really belonged" to them anyway. The society's bases of legitimacy and its loci of authority were attacked. Law and order were viewed as the white man's law and order. Policemen were the major targets, police activity the main issue, because uniformed law enforcement officers represent the most crystallized symbols and the most visible reality of colonial domination.

Thus Watts was not simply a racial revolt. Negro police and "responsible" moderate leaders also were the objects of the crowd's anger. Black businessmen who were seen as close to the community were spared damage. From the standpoint of the poor, there was thus an implicit division of the black middle class into those two segments that are found in the colonial situation: a "national bourgeoisie" on the side of liberation and a "native middle class" that serves as an agent of the dominant power arrangements.

Frantz Fanon has argued that in violating the integrity of indigenous ways of life and in creating the social status of "natives," colonialism reduced the manhood of the peoples it subjected.[13] The condition of slavery in the United States and the subsequent history of economic exploitation and second-class citizenship have constituted a similar attack on black manhood. A new generation of militants created in the civil rights movement a vehicle for the affirmation of their manhood in the political struggle against its systematic negation. But the nonviolent movement that grew up in the South (with its religiously oriented population, cohesive communities, and clear-cut segregation problems) is not well adapted to the social conditions and psychological temper of northern blacks. Unless new possibilities for the expression of initiative, assertiveness, and control are opened, we can expect violent revolt to become increasingly frequent.

> A young boy, who had been involved in a number of situations of arson, told me that he enjoyed it. "You mean you enjoyed seeing buildings going up in fire?" I asked. "I did," he replied, "because it gave me a feeling of being powerful, of being somebody. And if I can't go downtown and be a man, at least up here I can set something on fire." These youths, blocked from asserting their manhood in constructive ways, turn to violence. And this is a society in which violence has come to be related to manhood.

> In some families Negro men who had participated in the riots were treated with awe and respect by their wives and children. They were no longer the passive victims of the ghetto, to be pited or hated, often both, by their families. Now they were—if even for a moment—men who had asserted themselves through action. A jobless young man of 18 who already had a number of common law marriages and six children by different women, told me that the first time he felt like a man was when he saw the building he set on fire burn to the ground.[14]

The Watts revolt was also a groping toward community identity. South Central Los Angeles has been a vast ghetto with very amorphous neighborhood and district boundaries—and a glaring lack of leadership and organization. Most of the major civil rights groups were nonexistent in the ghetto; the gap between official Negro spokesmen and the poor was even greater than is typical. The word "Watts" itself as a locational reference for the ambiguously defined district around 103rd and Central Avenue had become a stigmatized term among blacks as well as whites and was rarely used by residents. During the August uprising a reversal in all these tendencies became apparent. The mass action strengthened feeble communal loyalties. The term "Watts" appeared painted on walls and windows as an expression of pride and identity. Youth gangs representing the adjacent neighborhoods of Watts, Willowbrook, and Compton ceased their long-standing wars and united to provide a core of organization during the rioting and the subsequent work of rehabilitation. Many middle-class blacks saw that their interests could not be severed from those of the ghetto's poor, particularly when their streets and residences were included within the curfew boundaries drawn by the militia—thus dramatizing the fact of common fate. Since August 1965, a proliferation of community organizing, political action, and civil rights groups have arisen in the Watts area.[15] All these processes—intensified communal bonds, ethnic identity, the hesitant return of the middle class, and a new sense of pride in place—are graphically summed up in the experience of Stan Saunders, a Watts youth who had moved out of the ghetto to All-American football honors at Whittier College followed by two years abroad as a Rhodes scholar. His return two weeks before the revolt may be prototypical.

> At the height of the violence, he found himself joyously speaking the nitty-gritty Negro argot he hadn't used since junior high school, and despite the horrors of the night, this morning he felt a strange pride in Watts. As a riot, he told me, "It was a masterful performance. I sense a change there now, a buzz, and it tickles. For the first time people in Watts feel a pride in being black. I remember, when I first went to Whittier, I worried that if I didn't make it there, if I was rejected, I wouldn't have any place to go back to. Now I can say 'I'm from Watts.'"[16]

The McCone Commission missed the meaning of the Watts revolt because of the limitations inherent in its perspective. The surface radicalism of its language (in calling for "a new and, we believe, revolutionary attitude toward the problems of the city") cannot belie its basic status quo orientation. The report advocates "costly and extreme recommendations," and while many of their excellent proposals are indeed costly, they are by no means extreme.

Truly effective proposals would hurt those established institutions and interests that gain from the deprivation of Watts and similar communities—the commission does not fish in troubled waters. Possibly because they do not want black people to control their ethnic neighborhoods, they do not see the relation between community powerlessness and the generalized frustration and alienation that so alarm them.

In their approach to the problems of Watts, the commission was guided by values and assumptions of a white middle-class ethos, which are of dubious relevance to the majority of lower-class blacks. Their chief hope for the future was the instillation of achievement motivation in the ghetto poor so that they might embark upon the educational and occupational careers that exemplify the American success story. I am not against middle-class values—but in the immediate critical period ahead "middle-classification" will be effective with only a minority of today's poor. Needed were a perspective and set of recommendations that spoke to the collective character of the situation, the overall relation between America's black communities and larger structures of power. The legalistically oriented commission—with primary commitments to control, law and order, a white-dominated status quo, and a middle-class ethic—was not able even to formulate the problem on this level.

POSTSCRIPT 1971

In the six years that have elapsed since "Watts," there have been vast amounts of social research on both the Los Angeles events and other ghetto rebellions that followed. These studies have disproved virtually all of the McCone Commission's sociological generalizations and explanations, and have tended to confirm my dissenting analysis. It may be valuable to summarize the most important of these findings.

First, the thesis that the riots were the work of the "criminal, lawless" elements has been put to rest. In a supplementary volume to the 1968 report of the Kerner Commission, the authors identify this commonly held "riff-raff" theory of ghetto violence, and marshall statistics from a variety of cities to counter it.[17] The UCLA study of the South Central Los Angeles curfew area, undertaken shortly after the 1965 uprising, found that blacks in the lowest income levels were no more likely to riot than others.[18] Indeed riot participation and support tend to be associated with slightly higher-than-average levels of education and political sophistication, as well as with attitudes of racial pride and militancy.[19]

Second, research has found that levels of participation and support were far higher than the McCone estimate. The UCLA investigators calculate that approximately 15 percent of the adult black population were *active* in the events. An additional 35 or 44 percent were active as spectators.[20] All classes of people participated, middle-class as well as poor, employed as well as unemployed, those without arrest records as well as those who had been in conflict with the law. Similar results were found in other cities. The southern immigration thesis did not hold up, either. Sixty percent of the UCLA sample had lived in the city ten years or longer, and support for the revolt was as great among these long-term residents as it was among the more recent arrivals.[21]

Third, the uprising did not look as irrational to the black population as it did to the commissioners. It is true that the majority of the Los Angeles sample decried the burning, sniping, and looting; at the same time they expressed sympathy for those engaged in these acts. They felt that business and other targets were selected because of specific grievances and not at random. Blacks in the curfew zone were twice as likely to feel that the uprising had a purpose or goal than to deny one; incidentally, a white sample was just as convinced that there was no purpose to the violence. Eighty-five percent of these whites referred to the events either as a *riot* or by some other negative expression such as disaster, tragedy, or mess. Only 54 percent of the blacks chose these terms (primarily the riot one); 38 percent preferred to use a more political definition—revolt, revolution, or insurrection.[22]

At the beginning of this chapter a comparison of the McCone Report with the 1922 *Negro in Chicago* study was suggested. In conclusion it might be appropriate to consider briefly the most important riot study which has since appeared, the *Report of the National Advisory Commission on Civil Disorders* of 1968.[23] The connection is a real one, for the staff of the Kerner Commission was quite conscious of the inadequacies of the California study; my critique, which originally appeared in 1966 (as well as others), was studied closely so that similar errors might be avoided.

There is no doubt that the Kerner Report, more than 600 pages long, is a more solid and better balanced work. The amount of time, energy, and social research incorporated is impressive. It is a serious document, filled with countless footnotes, statistical tables, and appendices. It is a good expression of the liberal approach to our racial crisis, whereas the McCone product was a shoddy rendering of the conservative position.

The National Advisory Commission attempted a sociological approach rather than a legalistic, riot-control perspective, though traces of the latter appear in sections. Instead of focusing primarily on law and order, it "introduced" the American public to the idea that white racism was the underlying condition of ghetto violence. The police role in intensifying racial tensions was more frankly dealt with, the opinions of black people were taken more seriously. Thousands of recommendations for change were made. Comprehensive as these were, their goal was limited reform, rather than a basic overhaul of the institutions that make up a racially oppressive society. But even with its own limitations,[24] the report received a cold reception from the administration and, apparently, from the general public.

9   Jury Selection in the Huey Newton Murder Trial

The Black Panther Party was organized in 1966 by two African Americans from working-class backgrounds who met while attending Oakland's Merritt Community College. Although Huey Newton and Bobby Seale put forward a comprehensive ten-point program addressing the needs of the black community, the Panther Party's priority became to curtail the excesses of the police, who routinely harassed the local population. The Panthers were the Oakland police's bêtes noires, literally and figuratively. They carried weapons, challenging law enforcement's monopoly in this area. And in their efforts to keep the police honest and to stop police brutality in its tracks, they patrolled West Oakland in their automobiles day and night. Whenever they saw an officer stop a black person for questioning, they would pull up behind, get out of their car with their weapons visible, and observe the proceedings. Huey Newton, who participated in many of these patrols, also carried a law book, so that if challenged he could recite chapter and verse to defend his group's legal right to do what they were doing.

Newton's trial on the charge of killing a police officer polarized public opinion in the Bay Area. In many whites, Newton and the Panthers awakened archaic fears of slaves in revolt. But they were admired by most black people, even those who would never act so recklessly themselves.

The Panthers also had white allies, including a legal defense team led by Charles Garry and Faye Stender. I volunteered to write a brief for Newton's defense team on how the pervasive racism in the white population would make a fair trial next to impossible. When the judge refused to accept written testimony, I found myself on the witness stand giving a lecture on white racism and suggesting the best ways to find a panel of the least prejudiced jurors. That was when Garry asked me if I would come back the following week and help him select the jury.

As it turned out, I stayed for the entire trial, an experience that radicalized me even further. And after witnessing two months of high drama in a murder case in which the main actors epitomized the most important social and political forces dividing the nation, I was convinced that I had all the ingredients for a nonfiction novel that might rival the kind of books that Norman Mailer and Truman Capote were writing at the time. Unable to carry off such an ambitious project, I settled for the more limited example of sociological journalism that follows.

DURING THE past few years an increasing number of black militants have been arrested and tried in cases arising out of racial and political struggles. Some arrests, such as that of Ahmed Evans of Cleveland, have taken place in the course of ghetto rebellions; others have occurred during more organized demonstrations, particularly on the campuses; many have resulted from individual confrontations with the police. Police incidents precipitated the trials of Black Panthers in Oakland, Los Angeles, Chicago, and New Orleans; other Panther cases in New York and New Haven followed arrests on conspiracy charges. Most recently, the militancy among black convicts, exploding into actions against prison guards, officials, and the judicial process, forms the general background for such celebrated cases as the two groups of "Soledad Brothers," Angela Davis, and Ruchell Magee. Of all these many trials, perhaps none was more pointed in its social, political, and legal implications than that of *The People of California v. Huey P. Newton,* which unfolded in the Oakland (Alameda County) Superior Court before Judge Monroe Friedman during the summer of 1968. The Newton case was strategic because the defendant was the founder and Minister of Defense of the Black Panther Party, the group that had most aggressively advanced the policy of armed self-defense in the northern ghettos; because the Panther leader was indicted on a first-degree murder charge for the alleged shooting of a white policeman; and because this trial dramatized the issues in a way that set precedents for the legal and political climate of many that followed in its wake.

On the morning of October 28, 1967, John Frey, a white Oakland police officer, was shot and killed in a deteriorating section of the West Oakland ghetto. Another white policeman, Herbert Heanes, was shot and wounded. Frey had stopped a car driven by Huey Newton, who received bullet wounds in the stomach and was arrested later that morning at the hospital where he had sought medical attention. Although the prosecutor argued that Newton had pulled a gun and deliberately murdered Frey, the weapon the Panther leader allegedly used was never located. The State's main witness was Henry Grier, a Negro bus driver. Grier stated that he saw Newton fire at Frey, but the credibility of his identification of the defendant was weakened by many contradictions between his grand jury and trial testimonies. Another principal was Del Ross, a black youth, who was expected to testify—in support of the third charge, kidnapping—that Newton had commandeered his car to get to the hospital. Ross's memory went totally blank on the witness stand. Finally, Gene McKinney emerged as the defense's "mystery witness." He had been Newton's companion that morning, and he took the Fifth Amendment when asked about his role in the events. The lack of hard evidence and the confusion that still surrounded the case after all the "facts" had been presented led to what most courtroom observers considered a compromise jury verdict. Newton was cleared of the assault charge against Heanes and convicted of voluntary manslaughter of Frey rather than murder. The third kidnapping charge had already been dropped after Ross would not testify.

The full story of the Newton case is beyond the scope of this study.[1] I concentrate instead on that phase of the trial in which I participated as a consultant to the staff of defense attorneys: the selection of the jury and particularly the attempt to detect the existence of, and evaluate the degree of, racism among white jurors through the voir dire (questioning of prospective jurors). From the standpoint of legal precedent and social interest, one of the many innovative aspects of this trial was the introduction of racism and racial prejudice as a legitimate area for extensive probing of the state of mind of the members of the jury panel. In this chapter I shall discuss how the voir dire worked, how we attempted to uncover racial attitudes, and how the defense staff made its decisions related to jury selection. Limiting our interest to the pretrial phase of the case, we omit the significant legal and sociological issues involved in the trial proper.

The opening segment of *The People of California v. Huey P. Newton* was unusually lengthy, significant in legal issues, and well organized, even for a murder case. Three days were devoted by the defense to the testimony of expert witnesses and to the introduction of motions challenging the system of jury selection in Alameda County. Charles Garry and his associates argued that the method by which jury lists were drawn from the rolls of registered voters resulted in a nonrepresentative panel, systematically underrepresenting members of the black and low-income populations. Furthermore, the defense challenged the very competence of a jury, conventionally drawn and constituted along prevailing concepts of "representative of the community," to provide a fair trial in the case of a black militant leader accused of murdering and assaulting white police officers. It was argued that "a jury of one's peers" in this context must mean a jury drawn from the ghetto, composed primarily—if not entirely—of Afro-Americans with life conditions and experiences similar to the defendant's. The Kerner Report, which had appeared four months earlier, was cited to document the prevailing white racism in America, which makes problematic the unbiased deliberations of the conventionally drawn "representative" jury: Seven expert witnesses, including six social scientists—among them Hans Zeisel, professor of law at the University of Chicago; Nevitt Sanford, a coauthor of *The Authoritarian Personality;* and Floyd Hunter, who had studied the community and power relations in Oakland after his pioneering work *Community Power Structure*—provided research data and expert opinion in support of various aspects of these motions.

The several motions challenging the jury selection system were denied, as was probably expected, but they enhanced the interest and seriousness of the jury selection over the course of the following two and one-half weeks. It took two weeks and the questioning of ninety-nine prospective jurors to constitute the regular jury (defense attorney Garry used all twenty of his peremptory challenges; prosecuting attorney D. Lowell Jensen, now chief district attorney, then an assistant district attorney, of Alameda County, used only fifteen). Approximately two-and-a-half days and fifty-three panelists were required to choose the four alternate jurors, none of whom had the chance to substitute for the regulars during the trial proper.

The voir dire, and in fact the entire trial, provided a natural experiment, a test of the validity of the significant charges contained in the defense motions and in the expert testimony. The methods Garry used to question jurors on social and political attitudes were copied or adapted in other racially and politically relevant trials by attorneys defending both black and white militants.[2] The voir dire was fascinating for the glimpse it provided of the racial attitudes and concerns of a natural sample of American citizens a few short months after the murder of Martin Luther King. Though my analysis is based only on this single case study, I find the experience of jury selection in the Newton case profoundly disturbing with respect to certain fundamental tenets of American justice.

The data that follow should be read in terms of their implications for some basic principles of our legal system. Is it possible to take seriously the norm of the "fair and impartial" juror, especially in racially charged cases, or must we view impartiality as an outdated legal fiction? What does it mean to speak of a jury representative of "the community," when the community itself is split into diverse and often conflicting segments based on race, class, style of life, and political attitudes? Does the present system of challenges, by which counsel are free to eliminate a fixed number of jurors, aid or obstruct the goals of impartiality and representativeness? And, finally, if white racism cannot be adequately uncovered by the innovative methods used by an exceptionally able Newton defense, how can racial prejudice be minimized as a factor in trial by jury?

THE VOIR DIRE IN THEORY AND PRACTICE

The reader unfamiliar with trial procedures must first grasp the basic elements of the voir dire. After a master panel of prospective jurors has been selected and sworn in, portions of that panel are selected at random and assigned in blocs of fifteen to fifty to the various courtrooms where juries are being chosen. The court clerk spins a wheel, the name of a juror from the list is chosen by lot, and he or she is called to the stand. After the judge has read the charges in the case and furnished other instructions, the two opposing counsel are free to question the prospective juror in order to determine her or his state of mind with respect to the legally salient issues of the case.

Theoretically, the purpose of the voir dire is to guarantee a neutral, objective, and relatively unbiased jury. Thus, if the questioning is thorough it elicits information that will permit the elimination of jurors who have close personal ties with one of the parties of the case. Because this was a capital offense, the views of the prospective juror on capital punishment also were relevant. In the context of California law in 1968 as interpreted by Judge Friedman, it was permissible to oppose the death penalty on principle, but not to be so fixed about it that the juror would not consider death at all should the trial result in a verdict of first degree murder and thus require a second trial to deal with the penalty phase.

The theoretical purpose of the voir dire may be realized in the majority of civil and criminal cases in which political and social issues are at most peripheral. But the norm of impartiality is strained to the limit in cases involving black militants. The Newton case was the most highly charged criminal trial in the Bay Area in a decade, probably the most publicized "political" case since the 1930s. On the one side, the mass media had covered the "facts" of Frey's killing and Newton's arrest in such a way that many—if not most—white citizens automatically assumed that the defendant was guilty. Leading citizens, including the Mayor of Oakland, had made inflammatory statements against Newton and the Panthers just before the trial opened. On the other side, black militants aided by white radicals had organized a "Free Huey" movement, asserting that his arrest represented a frameup for the purpose of crushing the Black Panthers. The Newton case thus served to further polarize the extremes of opinion in what may already have been the most polarized metropolitan area in the United States.

The two major symbols in this case were the black militant and the white policeman. (In the trial proper, the majority of defense witnesses were to be blacks, generally but not exclusively "militant" in tone and style; the majority of the prosecution witnesses were to be white officers.) In the late 1960s it was virtually impossible for Americans of any color not to have had some sort of preconceptions toward aggressive black nationalists; in fact most white Americans are considerably threatened on one level or another by militant Afro-Americans. Several prospective jurors in fact expressed the fear that sitting on the jury would invite physical retaliation from the militants.

Attitude toward police is an issue upon which whites and blacks are markedly divided. The problem of impartiality is further compounded by the fact that a significant proportion of the white citizenry have friendly social ties with individuals in law enforcement, whereas almost none from the majority group have similarly close relations with black people, let alone militants. In the Newton jury selection, thirteen of the first twenty persons questioned on this point affirmed that they counted a policeman as a friend or relative. A few of these people admitted that this would bias them as potential jurors; the majority, however, insisted that they could be perfectly neutral. One man, while protesting his impartiality, expressed the opinion that no police officer would ever attack a citizen; others indicated that they would tend to believe the sworn testimony of a law enforcement officer, yet expressed various reservations about crediting a Black Panther witness. In a case whose major actors so epitomized the polar conflicts of our society, the reader can imagine the incredulity of the court audience when one somewhat confused Berkeleyan stated, "I am pro-police but I am also pro–Black Panther so I don't know where I stand."

Despite its theoretical function, the voir dire is actually a contest between the two adversaries with the goal of selecting a jury most favorable to their case. The contestants win a round when they succeed in having the judge accept a challenge "for cause," thus eliminating a prospective juror who appears to be unfavorable to them. In the Newton case, only forty-eight of the ninety-nine prospective jurors who were examined during the selection of the regular jury actually sat in the box for a period of time. The others were either challenged for cause (sending them to be assigned to another courtroom) or removed by stipulation (agreement of the two attorneys in cases of ill health, financial hardship, impending vacations, and the like).

The two main criteria for a challenge for cause were prejudice and a rigid anti-death-penalty stance. Twenty-three from the regular panel were successfully challenged for a state of mind containing bias; in all cases except two or three these were people prejudiced against Newton; they thought that he was guilty, or revealed some other tendency to favor the state's case. Fourteen persons were eliminated because of a fixed opposition to capital punishment. The principle behind a challenge on account of bias toward the defendant seems perfectly clear. It is less apparent why the present law permits a challenge for cause toward persons strictly opposed to the death penalty, since, as attorney Garry repeatedly pointed out, this position need not interfere with neutrality in judging guilt or innocence. A murder trial jury is less representative when people who feel strongly against capital punishment have no chance to become jurors. Some of the social scientists also presented data to show that people opposed to the death penalty tend to be more liberal, humane, and less prejudiced than those in favor of it.[3]

The role of the judge is crucial here since both prejudice and the precise line where opposition to the death penalty results in an inflexible position are extremely vague. But on this score, the court gave something to both sides; Judge Friedman questioned jurors and made his rulings with the intent of trying to keep the juror seated whenever possible. Thus Friedman made it very difficult for Garry to establish prejudice; but he was no easier on Jensen in the latter's attempt to establish a rigid anti-capital-punishment position.

When a possible challenge for cause is at stake, the voir dire resembles a see-saw or tug-of-war in which the prospective juror is pulled back and forth between the two adversary counsel. Jensen interrogated the panel member first; sensing a "friendly" individual with a bias toward the prosecution's views, he presented his questions in such a way as to "coach" the person toward the appropriate responses that make up the front of neutrality. Garry, getting his turn, tried to trip the man up, getting him to reveal apparent bias. Jensen objected or intervened, and getting the man back for questioning, tried to reestablish an impartial position so that the judge would deny the defense's challenge. Or, finding someone opposed to the death penalty, the prosecutor tried to box this potential juror into a rigid position and, if successful, challenged for cause. Then the judge or Garry would intervene, giving the person every opportunity for a more flexible position that might "save" him.

The other element in the contest is the peremptory challenge. Each attorney strove to get an apparently unfavorable juror dismissed "for cause" in order to save his peremptory challenges. Because the Newton trial was a capital case, each party was permitted twenty challenges to be used against people who for some reason did not suit them. No reason is given for challenging peremptorily; it is sufficient that the attorney just doesn't like his face. But, in fact, the adversary counsel tended to base their challenges on information or cues brought up during the voir dire. Thus, another standard function of the questioning is to get a sense of the prospective juror in order to make an intelligent decision whether or not to use a challenge on her or him. But a delicate element is involved here also. If one side questions the juror thoroughly enough to be absolutely sure that this is a man he likes, this will give the opposing counsel information to use his peremptory challenges more intelligently.

It is instructive to examine what kinds of people were thrown out by each side. In keeping with his methodical style, Jensen's challenges could be divided neatly into three main categories: blacks, Berkeley residents, and anti-death-penalty people. He used twenty-one challenges in all, fifteen in selecting the regular jury and six for the alternates.

Eight of the prosecutor's twenty-one challenges were used against Negroes (three of the four who were seated in the regular jury voir dire; five of the five seated during the alternate voir dire). He left one black man,

David Harper, a loan officer for the Bank of America, on the regular jury. Although Jensen might have preferred an all-white jury, he knew that Judge Phillips of the same superior court had recently granted a mistrial when the prosecutor had thrown out every black. (The regular Newton jury contained also one Japanese-American man and two Mexican-American women.) But it is clear that Jensen was doing all that was possible to limit the number of Afro-Americans on the final jury. Of the fifty white people who were "passed for cause," that is, seated, if only temporarily, in the jury box and thus vulnerable to his peremptory challenges, he dismissed thirteen—or 26 percent. Of the nine blacks passed for cause, he threw out eight—or 89 percent.

In addition, the number of Negroes who might have become jurors was already limited by their underrepresentation in the panel and by the tendency of black people to be against capital punishment (a consistent research finding that was brought out in the pretrial testimony of Dr. Zeisel and Dr. Sanford). In the Newton voir dire, ten of the twenty-one blacks called up were challenged for cause because of fixed attitudes against the death penalty; this compares with only sixteen of the 122 whites called up. Of course, these data are not a perfectly accurate indication of racial differences on this issue, even for our limited sample. Persons in the voir dire situation do not always present themselves with complete honesty. It is quite possible that some blacks (as well as some whites) who wanted to avoid judging this highly charged political case exaggerated their negative position in order to avoid service. In the same way, a number of whites whose main interest might have been keeping off the jury claimed prejudice and fixed judgments of guilt. Garry took notice of the racial bias in Jensen's use of his challenges and demanded a mistrial because blacks were being kept off the jury systematically. Judge Friedman, whose brand of liberalism combined an ideology of color-blindness with an intense personal interest in everybody's ethnicity, replied that Mr. Jensen had allocated his peremptory challenges in a most lawyerlike fashion and implied that the charge of racial bias was ridiculous.

The second group of persons dismissed by Jensen were whites who might be suspected of relations or ties with anti-establishment subcultures. During the regular jury voir dire the prosecutor threw out all but one of the seven citizens who lived in Berkeley. (Six were white, one was black. During the alternate jury selection, Jensen dismissed one black Berkeleyan but permitted two whites to remain.) In only one case did the person appear to belong to the "hippie subculture"; he was a long-haired potter who made ceremonial tea bowls and whose main news source was *The Berkeley Barb*. The others appeared only to have soaked up, in various degrees, some of the liberal-to-radical sentiments that are important in this city. In addition to Berkeleyans, women with college-age children, who expressed some sympathy with the "dissenting generation," also were dismissed.

Once again, the use of peremptory challenges in this manner raises questions about the representativeness of a jury in Alameda County, where the city of Berkeley and various youth-radical-hippie subcultures in and out of Berkeley compose a significant minority of the East Bay populace. In residential terms, Jensen seemed to prefer jurors who lived in such middle-class, virtually all-white suburbs as Fremont, Castro Valley, San Leandro, San Lorenzo, Hayward, Livermore, Alameda, and Albany. He challenged only three persons of the twenty-seven passed from these towns; in contrast he dismissed eighteen of thirty-five from Oakland and Berkeley!

Six of Jensen's challenges were used on persons opposed to the death penalty—very often older white women. In fact, every juror who indicated serious reservations about capital punishment and who was not immediately eliminated "for cause" was subsequently removed by the prosecuting attorney. This does not necessarily mean that the final jury contained only people strongly supportive of the death sanction; certainly, many prospective jurors had learned to give the "right answers," glossing over some of their actual feelings. But it does raise the substantive problem of whether a jury in a capital case can be truly representative if it can be composed only of persons favorable to "death," considering that a sizable minority of the population—indeed, almost half—is opposed or ambivalent to this extreme verdict.

Garry, of course, tended to favor those whom Jensen disliked. He never challenged any potential juror who appeared to be against the death penalty. And he never peremptorily challenged a person from a racial minority group. Some Afro-Americans who were temporarily seated were not even questioned by the defense; it was sufficient that they were black people from the ghetto for him to assume that they would be better, more appropriate jurors than the whites. The two Mexican-American women seated, both of whom became final jurors, were asked very few questions, particularly about racial and social matters. The Japanese-American man, also to become a regular juror, was given a similar mild treatment. Garry also tended to distrust people from the white suburban areas; in fact, twenty of his twenty-five challenges were of people from the primarily white communities mentioned above. In addition to Berkeley residents, there was less suspicion of those whites who lived in some of the "mixed" areas of Oakland—such persons were expected to be more appreciative of the social issues in the case.

Age was another category that the defense found relevant: young people in America are more likely to be sympathetic to the black movement than their elders. Despite the fact that the final jury included five people under thirty-five, the panel as a whole appeared to be stacked against the young. My estimates of age distribution (in some cases age was asked, in others I had to rely on guesswork) show that more than half of the regular panelists (fifty-three of ninety-nine) were more than fifty years old. Another thirty-one appeared to be between thirty-five and fifty, leaving only fifteen out of ninety-nine under thirty-five years old. (During the alternate selection, approximately half were over fifty but there was a higher frequency in the twenty-one to thirty-five group, perhaps one-third).

The principles behind the defense attorney's challenges were not so clear-cut as the prosecutor's. Garry is a less methodical personality, and he often made his decision on the basis of an intuitive hunch about the prospective juror. Garry's quick intuition was aided by the force of his personality. Unlike Jensen, whose neutral, bland style evoked a response in kind, Garry related to prospective jurors quite personally. He expressed his feelings freely and, with his strong presence, made it difficult for the other to maintain a neutral stance. Thus while many were "won over," the hostility of some became explicit, and this aided the counsel in sizing them up.

But there is another reason, perhaps the most basic, why the Garry team could never be as sure of their decisions as the prosecutor appeared to be. Garry was committed to the position that a fair trial was only possible with a jury from North and West Oakland, the primarily black ghetto where the defendant lived and the death of the policeman occurred. On this count, virtually all the jurors who were seated in the box failed the test. Whereas Jensen usually challenged a particular juror because he was the one person seated at the time whom he wanted off, Garry was often in the situation of really not wanting at least half of the prospective jurors. Another way of saying this is that the jury panel seemed to contain more "good" prosecution people—that is, ones who were propolice, for "law and order," and at least mildly antiblack—than "good" defense people—ones critical of the police, sympathetic to the need for social change, and problack. Such a distribution undoubtedly reflected the realities of political attitudes among whites in northern California, though the balance may have been further tipped toward the prosecution by the biases introduced along the slow path to jury selection, and feelings were probably intensified by the negative publicity given the Black Panthers and their indicted leader.

Despite all this, there were some patterns in Garry's challenges. A number of young whites with a generally conservative posture, an orientation toward the military and the police, and racial attitudes and general hostility that were only thinly hidden were quickly dismissed. Others who admitted an initial negative attitude toward Newton and the Black Panthers, but somehow survived a challenge for cause, also were thrown out. People who revealed racist attitudes were always challenged, including several whites with more subtle racist tendencies, who expressed rather self-righteous attitudes about their "liberalism." For the most part, however, Garry seemed to rely on his hunches as to whether a particular juror was hostile to him and his client—though he readily sought the advice of other attorneys and consultants like myself before coming to a decision.

How is all this relevant to the larger legal issues raised at the beginning of this chapter? Theoretically, the contest between adversaries during the voir dire should strike a balance, furthering the goal of a jury that is both representative and reasonably impartial. It seems, however, that the dynamics of the peremptory system results in a jury that is more middle-of-the-road than representative of the diversity of a heterogeneous populace. Thus, the prosecutor in this case was able to minimize or virtually eliminate from the final jury Afro-Americans, lower-class people, principled anti-death citizens, Berkeley residents, and persons from dissenting subcultures. Garry may have been successful in eliminating extreme racial bigots, right-wingers, and militaristic police supporters. Granted that the impartiality of all such persons may have been questionable and that the attorneys were practicing good law in these decisions, the analysis at least suggests an impossible contradiction between the goals of impartiality and representativeness in racial and political cases.

GARRY'S USE OF THE VOIR DIRE: MULTIPLE FUNCTIONS

The situation was further complicated for the defense because Garry was employing the voir dire for a variety of purposes, which sometimes appeared to conflict. His first goal was to select the best possible jury for his client. Specifically, this meant getting a majority opposed to the death penalty and selecting a group with as little racism as possible, given the situation. But a second purpose, political education, was almost as important. Garry welcomed the long voir dire period, because his questions and what Jensen called his "speeches" gave him the chance to deepen the sensitivity of the final jury on racial matters, to insist upon the constitutional rights of the Black Panthers, and to dispel automatic assumptions of guilt and the natural tendency to assume that law enforcement always acts within the law.

The problem of combining the best possible legal defense and using the trial as an act of radical political education at times resulted in ambiguity and conflict; in some cases the political goal seemed to supersede the strictly legal one. Although this may be unusual in the profession, it was not unlawyerlike. As Charles Garry saw it, the social and economic circumstances of black people in America and the political actions of his client went to the heart of the legal issues in the case. In his aggressive social critique of racism, Garry was also carrying out the desire of his defendant who preferred the most militant political offensive in the courtroom, even though it might adversely affect his own personal fate.

Then, too, there was a third function for the voir dire from the point of view of the defense. This was to expose the multiple dimensions of racism existing on the panel: outright bias and prejudice; pure ignorance and unconcern about people of color; insensitivity and lack of involvement. This purpose was relevant to the first, that of selecting the most favorable jury, because information gained was useful in making challenges. But it was also necessary in order to establish the inability of a predominantly white and middle-class jury to deal with the case. Establishing that inability would strengthen both the legal appeal that might be necessary and the political attack against racism. It would link the findings of the voir dire to the motion to quash the jury venire, as well as to the testimony of the social science experts. Yet, at the same time, Garry wanted to see his client acquitted; therefore, he would have welcomed a jury composed of lower-class blacks and antiracist whites. Thus, we detect a contradiction in the purposes of the defense: a need to see its attack on the jury system and white racism confirmed, along with a desire for the kind of jury that would undermine its own social and legal critique. The paradox was expressed in a shift in the public statements of the defendant. Before the pretrial proceedings began he stated that he could receive a fair trial only from a jury drawn from the Oakland ghetto. After the final twelve were selected and at the time they began deliberations, he expressed his confidence to the press that they would come to a fair decision and acquit him. (This change was not simply a public relations tactic. The defense team as a whole had expected a much tougher jury and was cautiously optimistic as the deliberations began.)

Finally, the voir dire served a fourth function for defense attorney Garry. Since some two weeks could elapse between the sitting of persons who might become regular jurors and the opening of the trial proper, he had an opportunity to gain their allegiance through the force of his striking personality—expressed most importantly in a winning charm, a spontaneous wit, and the sincerity of his energetic espousal of his client's case. The courtroom style of Garry and the contrasting manner of the prosecuting attorney are worth examining, since they may have been important to the jurors' ultimate outlook.

In the first place, Garry was more personal and also more aggressive than his counterpart. He exuded warmth and a spontaneous interest in the potential juror, whereas Jensen appeared impersonal, mechanical, even cold. The defense counsel would ask old people about their aches and pains; he always seemed to find a personal inroad to a juror. His style was dramatic because his manner and emotions changed so rapidly, from homey chitchat to hostile frontal attack and back again. It was clear that jurors tended to enjoy their exchanges with Garry (though many were also apprehensive and intimidated); it could be a battle of wits, a testing of mettle, a chance to outsmart a clever antagonist or to gain the approval of an important man. In contrast the bloodless quality in Jensen's questioning (toward a hostile juror he came on like a crafty spider rather than like the lion Garry resembled) did not seem to engage the individual deeply.

With middle-aged women Garry was especially effective. A handsome, impeccably dressed man (the journalistic cliché was "dapper"), approaching sixty but looking years younger, only he himself seemed innocent of the seductive, even overtly sexual, nature of his approach. Thus, a standard Garry opener for females was, "Has anything I have asked the other jurors today triggered off something in the crevices of your conscious or unconscious mind that you would like to tell me about?" Finally, we take note of the spontaneity and flexibility of his wit. When it appeared that Garry was making friends through his ready humor, Jensen attempted some jokes of his own, but they always had a forced quality to them. And when the two of them exchanged barbs and jocular comments, it always seemed to be the humor of Garry that won the juror. I shall refrain from documenting these points, since wit depends so much on the situation. The courtroom jokes would probably not impress the reader as funny.

THE SEARCH FOR WHITE RACISM

The Newton voir dire was precedent-shattering, because Garry questioned the prospective jurors at some length about their general racial attitudes. The questions were not directly related to the issue of prejudice in the sense of preconceived opinions about the guilt or innocence of the defendant. Through the weight of pretrial motions and testimony, Garry convinced the Court that a juror's state of mind about black people and current-day racial issues was relevant to his or her ability to be fair and impartial in judging the case at hand. Thus, the defense counsel asked the panel members whether they had heard of white racism, whether they believed it existed in America, what they understood it to mean, and whether they had within them white racist feelings. In the same vein, he probed for knowledge of, definition of, and feelings toward, black power. Prospective jurors were asked their position on Proposition 14, the referendum that overturned the (Rumford) open housing law in California; whether Negroes lived in their neighborhoods; and whether they had ever moved to a new area because "too many black people were moving in." They were asked about unpleasant experiences with "members of the black community" and about their general feelings toward people of color.

The first time a "racial" question was asked, Lowell Jensen usually objected on the grounds of irrelevance and immateriality. Throughout the entire trial the prosecuting attorney attempted to restrict the case to the more narrow framework of facts and strictly legal issues; he constantly asserted that this was not a political case, a racial trial, or a sociological investigation. The three charges against the defendant and the facts related to the charges were the matter of the case from the State's perspective. The presiding judge sustained many of Jensen's objections, but the court record is more impressive for the number of social and racial questions that remained in the voir dire. Perhaps Friedman's most significant restrictive decision was his ruling out matters of race in the nation as a whole—one could ask, for example, only whether black people were deprived or discriminated against in Alameda County. He ruled out of order the question about how a person had voted on Proposition 14; acts in the electoral booth were protected by privacy. He was impatient with "vague" questions related to the juror's perception of social and racial issues; he consistently limited a question to how the particular person felt, thought, or had acted. The judge seemed to favor a colorblind approach to racial matters—after a storekeeper had attested to some difficulties with black customers, he asked gratuitously whether the businessman had ever had any similar trouble with whites.

Since the county's jury panel is supposed to be representative of the larger community, the aggregate of its responses might reflect how East Bay residents were thinking about race and the racial crisis in July 1968. Limiting our discussion to the whites questioned, the results are certainly not very encouraging. Taking all answers at face value for the moment, the predominant way in which these citizens were relating to the racial crisis of the time was *indifference*: lack of knowledge, lack of interest, and certainly lack of personal involvement. There was also a consistent tendency for prospective jurors to say the "right things" in response to certain questions, but these appropriate, even liberal, statements were almost always on the level of clichés rather than opinions suggesting complexity, sophistication, or the experience of feelings seriously dealt with or positions thought through.

Thus, no one questioned on the point had read the Kerner Report, which had made the headlines five months before and was readily available in paperback; only two persons had seen some excerpts from it in the press; almost no one else had even heard of the report. The majority of the panelists had not heard the term "white racism" before Garry used it in court. Many were familiar with the related idea of white supremacy however, and a scattered few attempted a definition of white racism. When asked whether they had racist or racially prejudiced feelings, some denied it completely, some others admitted the likelihood—but it did not seem that many in either group were sure what they were talking about. Black power had been in the news for almost two years; certainly the term had saturated the media as "white racism" had not even begun to do. Most people did recognize the term. They had heard of it; but the great majority claimed they had no idea what it meant. And the minority who had never even heard of black power was larger than the infinitesimal proportion who expressed some understanding of its meaning.

The prospective jurors were on the whole favorable, though ambivalent, toward fair housing. Most were in favor of a man's right to live where he could afford to buy a home. But many were not sure that a law to enforce such a right was a good idea, and a sizable number questioned were equally or more solicitous of a person's "right" to sell to whomever he wished.

The answers—with some important exceptions—suggested that the majority of whites had had little meaningful experience with black people during their lives. A few persons had Negro neighbors, coworkers, or tenants—or had had them in the past—but most appeared to be living a substantially segregated existence. As a result, the answers to questions about general feelings toward black people tended to lack a concreteness based on generalization from any richness of contact. Thus, there was the unconvincing character of such clichés as "all people are the same" or "they're human beings too."

The following excerpts from the court record illustrate the prevailing themes of indifference, ignorance, and detachment:

1. *July 23, Prospective Juror No. 10, a Southern-born skilled worker living in Fremont:*
Mr. Garry: Have you heard of Black Power?
Answer: Yes.
Question: You have any disagreement with the black people's desire for Black Power?
Mr. Jensen: Object to this as being ambiguous.
The Court: Do you know what Black Power is?
Juror: I don't know what their aims are, to be honest with you, sir, no.
The Court: All right.

Mr. Garry: Do you know anything about Black Power at all?

Answer: I have heard of it, that is all. I don't know what it is about.

Question: How does it strike you when you hear about it? What reaction do you get from it when you hear about it?

Answer: Well, I haven't any reaction because I haven't given any thought to it.

Question: Never thought about it at all?

Answer: I didn't give it a thought.

2. *July 23, Prospective Juror No. 8, an elderly woman, husband retired, living in Oakland:*

Mr. Garry: Have you ever heard of Black Power?

Answer: Yes, I have heard of it.

Question: What do you understand Black Power to mean?

Mr. Jensen: Object to that as incompetent, immaterial, improper voir dire.

Juror: I don't know what it means.

Court: She has answered. She doesn't know what it means. Proceed.

Mr. Garry: Do you have any objection to the use of the words, Black Power?

Answer: No, no, I haven't.

Question: Have you ever heard of white racism?

Answer: Yes.

Question: What does white racism mean to you, the term?

Answer: I don't know what that means either, really.

Question: You don't understand what that is either.

Answer: No, that is the first time I heard of it is today.

Question: Not until today, you have never heard of white racism?

Answer: I never heard of it.

Question: You have heard of white supremacy, have you not?

Answer: Yes, I have heard of that.

Question: What does that mean to you?

Answer: Well, I don't know.

3. *July 30, Prospective Alternate Juror No. 2, a middle-aged skilled worker living in Hayward.*

Mr. Garry: Do you know anything—have you ever heard the term called Black Power?

Answer: Yes, I have heard of it. I don't know anything—

Question: (Interrupting) And what is your—do you think that's good or bad?

Answer: Well, I don't think it's too good.

Question: What's wrong with it?

Answer: I don't think—the other term you called, white power, is too good either.

Question: Do you believe that there has been nothing but white power for three or four hundred years in this country?

Answer: Well, I couldn't say.

Question: You don't know whether there has been white racism in America for some three or four hundred years?

Answer: No, I couldn't say.

Question: Well, do you believe there is white racism in Alameda County?

Answer: I don't know.

Question: Do you believe there is white racism right where you are living in Hayward?

Answer: Not that I know of.

Question: Do you think there is such a thing called white power?

Answer: I have never heard of it until the last couple of days here at Court.

Question: Do you believe that the white people are the ones that control the destiny of the Black people in Alameda County?

Answer: I wouldn't know.

Question: Is this because you have never given the matter any thought or you just have never observed it?

Answer: Well, I haven't given it thought and I haven't observed it either.

The important thing about these examples is that they were typical of the responses of a substantial proportion of the whites interviewed. Furthermore, *each of these three prospective jurors was passed for cause.* This means that under our present system, such total ignorance and indifference to racial matters is perfectly acceptable as a qualification to judge the case of a black militant leader. Ignorance and indifference, in fact, increased a potential juror's chance of sitting in the box—if only temporarily. In the Newton case, the type of person that is held up as ideal for a democratic polity—the concerned, knowledgeable, and politically active citizen—had the worst chance of all to become a juror!

Another inference can be made from the voir dire excerpts. People may have been hiding some of their real feelings under the cloak of ignorance. There is no way to ascertain how often this took place; though in individual cases the defense team could sense racist attitudes in persons who were careful to make no biased responses. After several days of questioning, the principals and observers in the courtroom anticipated that overt racists would mask their opinions in one way or another. Thus, when one woman freely admitted that she had moved from a neighborhood because it was becoming a black area (and this woman struck me as being more equalitarian than most on racial matters), the question had to be asked and answered three times, because everyone—judge, counsel, audience— was convinced a mistake had been made. All previous jurors had vehemently denied such a possibility.

Of the 150-odd prospective jurors, perhaps fifty were questioned fairly thoroughly on their racial attitudes. Of these, only *one* man openly expressed general anti-Negro feelings. He said he was quite happy that there were no blacks living near him, that he imagined most people felt like that—at least out his way—and, finally, he never really "had anything to do with them people." He, like the more liberal woman whose family was perhaps the last of the whites to leave a black neighborhood, was dismissed because of antiblack attitudes. Yet a great deal of social research agrees on the conclusion that approximately one-third of white Americans are overt and extreme in their racial feelings. (Most of the remaining two-thirds are prejudiced in more subtle ways, though they would not fit the category of "bigot.") It is logical to assume that a considerable number of the prospective jurors actually lied in denying a general antiblack set. These facts suggest the possibility that from the point of view of defense counsel a juror who is open and honest about his or her prejudices may be a better bet than the apparently nonracist juror.

I am suggesting, then, that even Garry's innovative and imaginative questioning failed to plumb the depths of racial attitudes. Why this was so is to a large extent built into the situation. The question-and-answer format makes it easy for the juror to hide his opinions and protect himself with acceptable answers or feigned ignorance. The adversary situation in the courtroom permits the prosecution counsel to put a stop to sustained questioning in depth. Jensen, for example, objected every time a new question was asked, made interruptions, and otherwise protected the juror against intrusion into his "private" thoughts. And the judge, although he permitted many social issues to be introduced, also took a protective, even paternalistic, stance. When Garry seemed to be pushing someone rather aggressively, Friedman often stopped a line of questioning. Playing the role of benevolent father, he could not permit a person doing his civic duty to experience too much discomfort—unless he himself had become irritated with that person. Part of the problem is the public character of the voir dire. It does not seem sporting to badger and embarrass a prospective juror, to penetrate into his deep prejudices, in front of a large audience.

As an observer and participant of sorts, I felt that the defense's relative failure in uncovering racism was at times due also to weaknesses in Garry's manner of questioning. To my nonprofessional eyes, Garry conducted a masterful trial, and he was especially brilliant in cross-examining witnesses *and* in interrogating jurors. Yet during the voir dire, it was on racial matters that he most often seemed unproductive. I have already mentioned the inherent difficulties in the task; this was also something new in his thirty years of trial experience. Yet from the point of view of the techniques of interviewing that have been developed in the social sciences and clinical fields, Garry made mistakes and wasted valuable time. He had a prepared list of questions that he intended to ask, and he kept asking those questions even when experience showed they produced no useful information. Thus fifteen or twenty persons were asked whether they had read the Kerner Report; one day's work with this question was enough to ascertain that the answer would universally be no. More significantly, the defense counsel often appeared to be asking questions too directly, putting answers in the juror's mouth, rather than querying in the more indirect open-ended manner that elicits fuller and more honest replies. For example, a middle-aged white woman was asked a characteristic Garry question: "Do you have any feelings of white racism?" She answered no. She might have denied prejudice no matter how the question was put, but Garry's wording made it easier to give a negative, essentially uninformative reply. Another question to the same woman was, "Black power, does that create a revulsion in your mind?" Who would answer yes to such a question? The expert interviewer would recommend the open-ended: "Tell me what feelings black power brings to your mind." To a middle-aged woman from Oklahoma, Garry made reference to a previous witness who had said that the Black Panthers made a mockery of the law, and asked, "You don't feel that the Black Panthers do that, do you?" Of course she said no, but we will never know what she would have said to the simple question, "What do you think about this opinion?"

I made some of these criticisms and suggestions to Garry at the time. Perhaps one reason he did not alter his style—considering how open to advice the man is in general—is that the answers to voir dire items were to a great extent irrelevant in the light of his method of work. With intuitive brilliance, he usually sized up the hostility or friendliness of the prospective juror on the basis of more subtle cues, side comments, and general demeanor. If he disliked a juror, he was only interested in a line of questioning if it would prove the basis of a challenge for cause, and such challenges were almost impossible to win on the grounds of general racial attitudes. Therefore he seemed to ask his questions as much to educate and intimidate other panelists and prospective jurors as to gain information. If he had decided a juror was "good" (always in a relative sense) for his defendant, his questions were asked as much to influence the person to see the case as he saw it as to find out more about that person's state of mind.

This might explain what would otherwise be inexplicable omissions in the voir dire. An elderly woman who was to become one of the regular jurors admitted that she had some subjective feelings of racism. Instead of following this up with the obvious query, "Tell me what some of those feelings are," he continued, "And because of these subjective—some subjective feelings you have, do you make allowances for your own shortcomings in that regard?" She answered yes, and although a graduate student would flunk a test in social research for such an obvious error, Garry's method may have been the successful one for his purposes. The woman turned out to be one of the best jurors from the defense's standpoint. Perhaps the persuasive effect of Garry's "too-direct" question was more valuable in educating this woman than the information a better wording might have gleaned.

The strain of the trial was enormous. Garry had his good days and his bad days, and this might explain some of these lapses. Yet it is important for our analysis to note that his difficulties and failures tended to occur while questioning racial attitudes. In searching for the more concrete bias of a fixed opinion in the Newton case, the defense attorney was consistently creative. His flexibility and quickness of intuition here contrasted with the often stumbling mechanical character of the voir dire on race. Unfortunately, there is not space to document this adequately, and the brilliance of the performance comes across only in the courtroom—even the complete rendering of the transcript dulls the shine, since like other dramatic situations, timing and intonation are more central than words. Two examples will show something of his skill.

An elderly retired printer appeared to have great difficulty accepting the premise that a defendant must be considered innocent until proven guilty. Garry submitted a challenge when the gentleman continually refused to accept Newton's innocence: for example, "That's a question (his innocence) I can't answer before I hear the evidence." Jensen argued that it was a matter of semantics, the potential juror being foreign born. The judge concurred, and Jensen was able to drill the man into the "proper" responses. Then Garry resumed the voir dire and the following denouement settled the matter:

Mr. Garry: Mr.——, again I ask you that same question which you have answered three times to me now—

The Court: No. Please ask the question without preface.

Mr. Garry: As Huey Newton sits here next to me now, in your opinion is he absolutely innocent?

Answer: Yes.

Mr. Garry: (Raising his voice dramatically) But you don't believe it, do you?

Answer: No.

The Court: Challenge is allowed.

Garry made another point in the case of a police reserve deputy who insisted he would be impartial. He asked the man whether he was carrying his police badge, and the man had to produce it to the defense attorney. Garry's description of the badge to the courtroom cinched the challenge.

The data I have compiled from courtroom observation and the case transcript reveal that forty-one persons were successfully challenged for the cause of prejudice. In all but two or three cases these people admitted or revealed, under intense cross-examination, a tendency to believe in Newton's guilt, an animosity toward the Black Panthers, or a strong inclination to see policemen as several cuts above other mortals. In bringing such attitudes to the surface, Garry eliminated a substantial proportion of the most negative panel members, whereas in probing on racial prejudice, he was able to eliminate only two—including the one woman previously mentioned whose honesty and openness might have made her a more fair and impartial juror than the average.

Although the above point is important, prejudice in the case may often have been based on a deeper racial bias. A preconceived hostility toward Huey Newton and the Black Panthers in many instances reflected a more general hostility and a fear of black people. The inability to award Newton the presumption of innocence may have been based on unconscious assumptions (and often conscious also) that Negroes are violent and are lawbreakers. Still, it is interesting that people were more honest about case bias than about race bias; the former is still socially acceptable; the latter no longer is.

So far in this essay I have presented a rather dim view of the possibility of deriving a fair and impartial jury for a case such as *The People v. Huey P. Newton,* considering the background and social attitudes of those representative citizens who made up the jury panel. I will attempt to support this position even more vigorously in the concluding section. There remains one positive phenomenon, however, that should not be overlooked. Although struck with the dishonesty and simulation of many prospective jurors, I was impressed and pleasantly surprised by the old-fashioned American "fair play" of quite a few others. Many persons, admitting their bias in the case, stated that they did not think their presence on the jury would be fair to the defendant, and they seemed sincere in saying this. Even when attorney Jensen worked hard to "save" them, coaching them in the proper attitudes, a number maintained their self-doubts: they would be less inclined to credit the testimony of a Black Panther than other persons; they could not set aside the assumption of Newton's guilt, which they had gotten from press accounts; their allegiances were with the police and they would not pretend impartiality. In some cases this frankness may have been prompted by a calculated desire to stay off the jury, but there was still a significant group of prejudiced panelists who did not play the game of giving only the right answers.

The prejudiced and honest individuals may be contrasted with another group, those who denied their biases and tried to hide their preconceptions against Newton and the Black Panthers, but were unable to do so. These were generally conservative men who were aggressive and self-righteous about their political ideas, and who had a great need to make their views known. Thus one man attested to his primary allegiance to "law and order," said he held black militants and the Panthers responsible for riots, but argued vehemently that he would be a fair and impartial juror. Garry was usually able to trip up such persons in their own contradictions and win a challenge for cause. There were parallel examples on the other side of the case. Two or three prospective black jurors openly stated that they had doubts about their impartiality because they had long-standing friendships with members of the Newton family. And there were two or three white liberals or radicals who did not choose to play it cool in order to help the defense use up the peremptory challenges of the prosecution. They proclaimed that their commitment to the black movement and their sympathies with the defendant made them inevitably partial.

How the Defense Made Its Decisions

Despite the fact that the sociopolitical milieu and the panel seemed stacked against the possibility of a truly representative and impartial jury, the defense team nevertheless had twenty peremptory challenges to use, and therefore some degree of control over the jury's final makeup. How, then, did Garry and his associates decide which persons should be dismissed from their seats, and which should be left in the jury box?

In addition to relying on the direct statements, Garry seized upon subtle gestures, cues, and especially side comments to form an intuitive assessment of a person. "Freudian slips" were closely attended to. A very self-righteous liberal, who had been proclaiming his fairness, vision, and social compassion, said, "I don't think I would be *impartial*," when he had intended to say "partial." A prospective alternate protested her lack of bias, despite friendships with police officers, including an Oakland cop who had visited the wounded officer Heanes in the hospital. After claiming to accept the presumption of innocence, which puts the burden of proof on the prosecution, she went on to say that the defendant would have to be "proven innocent."

Apparent lapses or slips were made by "friendly" jurors also, including the pivotal David Harper, the one black man among the final twelve. When Garry asked the bank officer whether he believed Huey Newton killed Officer Frey, Harper answered, with perhaps more emphasis than he intended, "I have *never* been of that opinion." Note how he toned down his very next response: "It is a question of—the opinion that's in my mind is I don't know, and I can subscribe to it." A gratuitous side comment by the same juror was also crucial in contributing to the defense's judgment. When Jensen asked him whether he had ever discussed the case with people at work, Harper replied with a slight trace of bitterness that his colleagues never discuss such matters in his presence—even when Dr. King was shot nobody said anything. It was important for the defense to find evidence of political and racial consciousness in this particular black man since other clues suggested that Jensen wanted him on the jury; in fact, because of such suspicions, Garry questioned Harper at greater length than other blacks.

The defense observed other unintended behavior. The southern-born skilled worker, whose denial of any thought or opinion on black power has already been quoted, was perspiring freely during this section of the voir dire. Other panelists fidgeted uncomfortably under Garry's probing, while disclaiming any attitudes of racial prejudice. On the other side of the fence, a Mexican-American woman gave a little spontaneous laugh when she said no—that she had no feelings of white racism. We interpreted this gesture to mean that she saw herself as a victim of prejudice, rather than a possible victimizer.

Equally or more important were the words a juror chose, his or her side comments and reactions to Garry's questions. Such cues appeared to be the best basis for judgment in those marginal cases where the person was difficult to size up. It was simple to form a judgment when the individual could not mask his attitude. One ex-marine was overeager to be seated, a tendency the defense deeply distrusted because it seemed to imply a wish to send the defendant to the gas chamber. This man gave himself away with smart-aleck grins in reaction to Garry's statements. There is a sense, then, in which the political heat and polarized sentiment about the case were helpful to the defense, since they made it easier to recognize many of the hostile people.

Realizing that the prosecution would dismiss any juror who was overtly friendly to Newton's case, the defense was trying to maximize the number of open-minded members of the jury. We were looking for people who were basically honest, who appeared to have a capacity to learn and grow in the course of the trial, who had some degree of personal empathy—in short, we were looking for good human beings, if I may use such a nebulous concept. How did we intuit such elusive qualities? In one case an elderly Italian-American woman replied, "We can all make mistakes," in response to whether she would be biased by Newton's previous felony conviction; we took this as a sign of personal compassion. A retired small businessman first referred to black people as "colored," an old-fashioned expression, which often indicates a prejudiced orientation. But because he was old and foreign-born, we attributed the usage to the norms of his generation. Later he spoke of an unfortunate experience with a "colored boy" who turned out to be twenty-five years old. When Garry pointed out that Negro adults don't particularly appreciate being called boys, the man seemed genuinely surprised. Rather than reacting defensively, he appeared to understand and to have learned something from the exchange. This incident dove-tailed with a general impression that the man was a warm, empathic person. A similar openness and honesty was conveyed by a middle-aged saleslady who, unlike the previous gentleman, was to remain as a juror for the trial phase. Though by no means politically left or even "liberal," she appeared to be a woman who had thought about racial matters, someone who habitually wrestled with her conscience. She admitted being very upset when a Black Panther spokesman appeared before her church discussion group and accused all white Christians of being racists. His speech and her anger had made her think quite a bit.

In some cases, however, significant cues and side comments were misinterpreted with the result that some unfriendly jurors who could have been peremptorily challenged became a part of the final twelve. There is no way to know whether particular individuals consciously put on a false front, but in one instance the circumstantial evidence was strong. A middle-aged worker in a meat factory, married to an Oakland fireman, was conspicuous for her mod dress (Nehru blouse, medallion, miniskirt) during the first days of the voir dire. When questioned, she appeared sophisticated, liberal, and "hang-loose." She knew that the Panthers were a "militant" group—an admittedly minimal level of political knowledge, but still more than the typical panelist showed. She implied that she and her husband were on friendly terms with the two Negro firemen in his station. When asked whether she had any objection to the Panther terminology of "pig" for policeman, she replied that it wouldn't prejudice her at all. "People used to call them fuzz and that didn't bother me either." I think this comment won Garry over, and he stopped his questioning without going further into the topic of racism, probably expecting that Jensen would eventually dismiss this woman. During the course of the trial her demeanor changed considerably, and the sketchy accounts available suggest that she was one of the more pro-prosecution jurors.

To an observer in the courtroom, some of the defense's challenges may have seemed surprising. Garry was not trying to get the most "liberal" jury in strictly political terms. In fact, three men were seen as potentially dangerous jurors because they took a common present-day position that might be termed "pseudoliberal." A school principal in an all-white suburb would not discuss white racism without making the point that there were also black racists, a category into which he placed the Panthers. He was dismissed by Garry, as was a bank officer from the same suburb, who was certainly one of the most knowledgeable panelists interviewed. The latter gave a good definition of racism, and was the only person who could report the main conclusion of the Kerner Report: "It states there our civil rights problems are primarily due; I believe, to the fact that we have a racist society." But this man implied also that some of our civil rights problems must be due to characteristics of the Negro group. He opposed racial discrimination but was adamant for hiring people on the basis of their qualifications, and it did not bother him that there were no black people in his particular branch bank. He favored open housing, but supported the right of a man to sell property to whomever he wished. It was not just the attitudes of such men that put Garry off. After all, some of the jurors probably had "worse" attitudes. It was a quality of smugness, a cocksureness about the purity of their racial views, that made the pseudoliberal type seem worse than a more open-minded conservative or an apolitical person.

The bases for the decisions discussed may make more sense when placed in the context of how the jury appeared to be shaping up as the two weeks of the voir dire passed. In the first stage, a major concern of the defense was to eliminate or minimize the likelihood of a first degree verdict and the possibility of a death sentence. During this time Garry was as concerned about filling the jury spaces with persons opposed to the death penalty as he was in finding nonracists. If someone looked good on this issue, yet had managed to survive Jensen's challenges, Garry often didn't even question him on racial matters. About half-way through, it began to look to me as if the jury would be at least against capital punishment, and anxieties on this score declined. The jury was shaping up better than had been anticipated; the defense became more optimistic and began to set the higher goal of aspiring toward a jury that would acquit or at least "hang" (in the sense of a *hung*, not a hanging, jury). In this second stage the main quality looked for was the openness, honesty, and capacity for growth that I have referred to. Then about two-thirds through, it became evident that Jensen was going to dismiss all the blacks except the banker, David Harper. This introduced a new element into the calculation because Harper was a strong personality, and the defense was beginning to infer that he might be, or become, sympathetic to their case. In the informal camaraderie among prospective jurors the black banker was developing into a social leader. Garry and Ed Keating hoped that he might become the strong man of the jury, the leading influence, and, indeed, he was later elected foreman. Thus the desire to enhance Harper's position was another reason why the two pseudoliberals discussed above were dismissed. If these highly educated, high-status, and articulate men were empaneled, they might compete with Harper for the role of opinion leader. A final point is that Garry had used up his challenges at a time when Jensen still had five of his, saved by passing his turn. Therefore, toward the end of the selection period, Garry was in a box, and he had to accept the last two or three people seated whether or not they were to his liking.

Though it inevitably involves speculation, one might wonder why the assistant district attorney decided to leave David Harper on the jury, considering that the defense built such considerable hopes around this man. As already mentioned, Jensen threw out every other black person. It is reasonable to infer that he could not challenge every Afro-American without preparing the ground for an appeal that would have met almost certain success. Opting for tokenism, the question is, why Harper? It is my judgment that Jensen liked Harper because he seemed to be a highly assimilated "white" Negro. He was solidly middle class, he lived in a primarily white section of Oakland, and he worked for a conservative institution, the Bank of America. Jensen must have assumed that such an Afro-American would see things from the point of view of established society and would not readily identify with Huey Newton and the ghetto blacks who were to be the defense's witnesses. In conducting his voir dire, Jensen seemed much less comfortable with, and certainly more hostile to, Negroes who were lower- and working-class, from the ghetto, and less acculturated. It was my opinion, even during the voir dire—after all, hindsight is easy—that Jensen was making a serious mistake in choosing Harper for his putative "house nigger" over some other possible candidates for this role. He was evidently unaware that racial nationalism and political militancy are perhaps more likely to be the product of the ambiguous status and identity conflicts of today's middle-class blacks than of the more oppressed condition of lower-class ghetto dwellers.

Aside from the question of Harper, I felt that the district attorney could have worked harder for a jury that would have been tougher and more likely to convict. Had he used all his challenges, some of the people who were mildly congenial to the defense could have been removed and Garry would have been forced to accept two or three quite biased jurors. The constellation would no longer have had that "middle of the road" character, which six weeks later was to result in a compromise verdict. Jensen may have been overconfident about the strength of his case. Perhaps, also, he felt more rapport with the conservative but moderate juror than with the extreme bigot. In addition, he may have had enough of the voir dire and have wanted to get on with the trial.

RACISM AND FAIR TRIALS: SOME CONCLUDING ISSUES

The process by which a trial jury is selected in Alameda County—the voir dire and the challenge system—may be reasonably effective in eliminating those members of the panel who are strongly biased toward a particular side of the case. But the experience of the Newton trial, pioneering as it was in the introduction of racial questions, suggests that this process is ineffective in finding a jury that is the most free of racial bias. In fact, the very procedures by which the twelve final members are selected from the original panel appear to impose obstacles to the seating of a nonracist or antiracist jury.

The remarks I made as an expert witness on racism during the pretrial testimony are relevant here. I began my testimony with the generalization that racism—in the objective sense of control of the society's institutions by white people and systematic subordination of people of color and their relegation to the less powerful, prestigious, and rewarding positions—is a basic reality in America. The subjective aspect of this objective or structural pattern is the white group's sense of its own superiority and the inferiority of blacks and other nonwhites. This sense of superiority is almost inevitable, and it is shared by all white people—on conscious, subconscious, or unconscious levels.

Positive Selection as a Counterbalancing Mechanism

The most effective way to eliminate white racism from the judgment of a racially relevant case would be to form a jury of citizens from the racial minority groups. Although people of color have themselves been influenced by the racist assumptions of American culture, still their experience as victims of discrimination makes them more aware of the totality of circumstances motivating black and other nonwhite defendants.[4] But assuming that the courts are not yet prepared to move this far, we need to devise new tests or criteria for selecting the least racist whites. As yet, such tests do not exist. In response to Judge Friedman's request to propose an improved method, I put forward four tentative criteria along which jury panelists might be evaluated. Granted that my criteria make an extremely tough test and that they are the invention of one sociologist rather than of a commission of social scientists and legal experts, it may nevertheless be informative to use them to evaluate the Newton jury experience.

First, I suggested that the least racist person would not deny racial prejudice, but would be aware that he reflected elements of the society's pervasive racism. He would be sensitive to his racist tendencies, would keep them in his consciousness rather than suppress them, and would, of course, strive to reduce their influence. During the Newton voir dire, most people denied that they had any elements of racism or prejudice within them. Often this closed the discussion, and this denial or "affirmation of purity" made it easier for them to be "passed for cause," that is, seated as prospective jurors. A significant minority of citizens admitted some peripheral prejudices; in some cases the defense appraised this cue as a sign of insight, honesty, and good will—though we may have been misled in one or two instances by putting too much stock in this criterion.

The second criterion dealt with knowledge. In order to combat racism effectively, a white person should not see blacks as "invisible" but should be attuned to the social circumstances of the present and the forces in the past that have produced our racial crisis. Therefore, I suggested that the least racist whites would have some substantial knowledge of the history of race relations and a familiarity with the content and character of Afro-American culture. No questions that really tested this criterion were asked during the voir dire. It was clear that almost no one among the 140 white panelists—like American whites in general—knew anything about black history and culture. Ignorance about racial discrimination and the black movement was the typical pattern. Such ignorance or indifference actually made it easier for the panelists to be seated, since there was no possible line of questioning that might lead to a challenge for cause. And because of the system of peremptory challenges, any prospective juror who could have met this knowledge criterion would have been suspect of problack bias and thus dismissed by the prosecuting attorney!

The third point involved contact and experience with members of the minority group. The social and cultural barrier between whites and blacks is a keystone of the racist system; leading a life that is primarily segregated in terms of work, residence, and friendship in itself reflects and maintains white racism. The vast majority of white panelists in the Newton trial led just such segregated lives, though there were exceptions. Again, attorney Jensen was free to dismiss those few persons who were committed to racial integration in action.

Finally, I suggested that a nonracist must be involved in efforts to combat discrimination and prejudice. Personal, subjective racism can be eliminated or diminished only in the process of undermining the objective racism in the society and its institutions. Thus, another criterion would be some personal project directed toward the goal of racial justice: in local communities, in occupations or professions, or in leisure pursuits, as well as in work with organized political groups. Garry employed this standard when he asked persons who said they disapproved of the exclusion of blacks from their fraternal and leisure associations whether they had ever acted to end this state of affairs. From the voir dire testimony, it is apparent that the overwhelming majority of the potential jurors had never been involved in combating racism. If anyone had testified positively, he would certainly have been challenged by Jensen.

Thus, as I have shown, the logic of the voir dire makes it difficult to minimize white racism in the selection of a jury. This is ultimately a product of the overwhelming presence of racism in our society. People who are somewhere along the line of movement to a nonracist position: the aware, the knowledgeable, the integrated, and those oriented toward change make up only a minuscule proportion of the white population. Such a frequency distribution makes it possible for all such people to be dismissed when they appear. The prosecutor need not worry about using up his peremptory challenges against antiracists, whereas the defense attorney will not have enough to reject all the racists.

There is another factor in the logic of the voir dire and challenge system. The assumption is that every citizen has the makings of a fair and impartial juror; therefore, the sole object of the questioning is to discover any negative factors, bias, prejudice, unusual opinions or personal ties, that might vitiate a juror's impartiality. But racial bias cannot be dealt with as if it were some negative property that can be detected through the voir dire. It is so omnipresent in American society that the only reasonable means of minimizing it in a predominantly white jury entails a process of positive selection: setting up a series of qualifications or tests to identify that *least-racist* minority who then, along with nonwhites, would constitute the panel from which the final jury could be drawn.

The Myth of Impartiality and the Dilemmas of Representativeness

The foregoing analysis raises some serious and possibly insoluble questions concerning the several philosophical and legal tenets that underlie the juridical ideal of the "fair trial." The data from the Newton case suggest that the kingpins of the trial-by-jury system—the impartial juror, the representative panel, and the challenge method—are filled with ambiguities and at war with one another. It is possible that the legal fiction of the "impartial" juror should be disposed of as a "cultural lag" hopelessly out of tune with reality—at least for politically significant and highly publicized cases. A juror without any significant biases relevant to a case like *The People v. Newton* is almost a nonexistent animal.

Further, such a state of mind might not even be desirable. A man or woman without any preconceptions related to a trial growing out of a confrontation between a black militant and a white policeman would have to be a person of apathy, ignorance, even stupidity, or at least someone who is not living in today's social world. The issue of partiality has to be redirected and new questions have to be asked by legal theorists and social scientists. As a start, there may be a need for a separation between the question of being able to act with detachment, an ability that probably requires appreciation of the complexities of race and politics; and the problem of preconceptions with respect to guilt and innocence. We need to know what kinds of biases make a person unfit for fair and deliberate decision making in various kinds of cases; what kinds of conceptions and social attitudes are positive or at least neutral?

Our analysis also reveals a contradiction between the goal of impartiality and that of representativeness. A selection procedure that aims toward maximizing the number of least-partial people (as the present idea of impartiality is conceived) is not likely to achieve the goal of representing well the many cleavages and interest groups that make up a socially heterogeneous population.[5] It will bias the composition toward the middle of the road. As we have seen, the challenge system serves to keep the extremes of political position, cultural style, and racial commitment off the jury. This poses some difficult questions for legal norms. If we see the relevant jurisdiction as the county or the metropolitan area in which a "crime" takes place, then, by this logic, should a representative jury faithfully encompass the depth and pervasiveness of white racism in this "community"? Attorney Jensen, who himself did not play on racial bigotry during the trial, nevertheless seemed to think so. It followed from his concept that the case had "two sides," that the constituency and values of the dead policeman should be taken into account as much as the interests of the defendant. But the case of a criminal defendant is different from that of two adversaries in a case of civil litigation. From the philosophical tenets of our legal system—as I understand them—only the individual Huey P. Newton was entitled to a fair trial. The "justice" accorded the deceased and his family, the wounded officer, the Oakland Police Department, and the white racist community should have been totally irrelevant to the trial that took place. For this reason I cannot subscribe to the argument that a jury representative of the county's actual racial attitudes would serve our ideals of justice and the elusive but still to be pursued goal of a fair trial. This throws the issue back to the perplexing problem that was debated in the defense motions and in the propaganda of the "Free Huey" movement: what is the community that would guarantee a trial by a jury of the defendant's peers?

Internal Colonialism and the Court System

The Kerner Report noted that America was moving toward a society made up of two separate nations: one white and one black. It documents the depth of the racial cleavage and suggests that the experience of life in the dominant white American culture is fundamentally different from that of the subordinated black ghettos of the land. The Kerner analysis thus suggests that an overall multiracial community, of values, interests, and life experience, does not at present exist in the United States and, in fact, has never existed. Sociologically, the white and black populations must be viewed as distinct communities, though there is much overlap and interaction between them, as well as division and heterogeneity within each racial group. If we take this official federal report (and other sociological studies) seriously, we must conclude that a black militant from the ghetto is not being tried by a jury from his community when the panels are selected as they are in Alameda County, California, and in the nation's other metropolitan areas.

As I have argued elsewhere, the black population is not simply a distinct and largely segregated community; Afro-Americans are a nationality that has been colonized within the borders of the United States. The model of "internal colonialism" is gaining acceptance because it alone points to the systematic way in which black ghettos are controlled from outside in a striking parallel to the domination of nonwhite peoples by European overseas powers during the colonialist era.

Our legal forms reflect this situation of internal colonialism even more clearly than other institutions do. In fact, in America the administration of justice for people of color is more directly racial than it was in many contexts of classic colonialism—where native courts and "indirect rule" were common. Thus, a black man like Huey Newton is tried under a system of law developed by white Western European jurists. He is confronted in the black ghetto by white police officers, then indicted by an all-white, or predominantly white, grand jury, prosecuted by a team of all-white district attorneys, tried by a white judge, convicted by a predominantly white jury, and denied bail on appeal by white state appellate courts and a white federal judge. It is not simply the color of the principals that is at issue, but the more profound point that the various officials and processes in the system represent institutions that reflect and are responsive to values and interests of the white majority—a power structure and a community that benefit from keeping black people in "their place," namely, in the ghetto and without power.

The ambiguities, dilemmas, and even contradictions within the law that my case study has uncovered reflect only in part the uneven development of judicial decisions. For the most part they derive from the conflicts and tensions within our society, those same oppressive social conditions that produced the trial of Huey Newton. I believe that the issues at the heart of the case and its jury selection can only be resolved through the dynamics of decolonization, which would establish some form of "home rule" in the black communities.

The problems—political, technical, and legal—in developing radically altered systems of law enforcement and administration of justice are indeed enormous. Members of the legal profession as well as social scientists might begin to devise concrete models of such institutional arrangements—working as closely as is possible with organizations in the ghetto. Let us opt for changing the conditions that result in the need for self-defense and police surveillance in the black community, so that groups like the Panthers can devote their energies to the serious work of organizing the ghetto and so that the great talents and possibilities of the future Huey Newtons will not lie wasting in penitentiaries, but will contribute directly to the well-being of their people.

10   More Than Just a Footnote
Chicanos and Their Movement

At a time when the black movement was getting the headlines and the attention of pol-icy-makers, another ethnic group in California and the Southwest was often over-looked. Along with Indians, Mexicans were the region's indigenous people, and in each of the southwestern states they were the largest minority group. Despite this, most whites, including social scientists, remained fixed on black–white issues. By 1970, however, the fact that Americans of Mexican descent were key players in the political arena could no longer be ignored.

For years Cesar Chavez and a devoted band of associates had been quietly organi-zing the field hands, many of whom were Mexican or Mexican-American, of the farm factories of California's Central Valley. By the mid-1960s their work had begun to pay off. Lettuce workers and grape pickers joined the United Farm Workers and struck for union recognition. In New Mexico, Reies Tijerina was mobilizing *hispanos* in a land-grant movement, demanding the return of the territory that white settlers had illegally appropriated. And in Colorado, Rodolfo "Corky" Gonzáles organized the "Crusade for Justice," harnessing Chicano power to confront the disrespect and the discrimination Mexican-Americans faced in every area of their lives.

Another important figure was Octavio Romano, a Mexican-born anthropologist who taught in Berkeley's School of Public Health. Romano had founded *El Grito,* a literary and intellectual journal, and in 1970 he edited *El Espejo,* an anthology of Mex-ican-American writing. Taken with the power and the beauty of *El Espejo's* poems and stories, I decided to review it. I wanted social scientists to take Mexican-Americans and their work more seriously. I also jumped at the chance to write literary criticism, hav-ing long valued literature over sociology. *Trans-Action* magazine accepted my review and published it in their February 1971 issue as "The Chicano Sensibility."

In editing the original essay I have retained the more general and sociological ideas at the expense of the specifically literary criticism that might not interest readers today.

WHITE AMERICA seems to have discovered the Mexican-Ameri-can people in the last few years. On the rebound after a bad experience with the black movement, rejected liberals have needed new causes to espouse, other oppressed peoples to relate to. The great strike of Califor-nia farm workers provided one such opportunity, and along with Tije-rina's land-grant campaign in New Mexico, the Chavez-led struggle has inspired a raft of journalistic interpretations. Publishers are also bringing out more general books on Mexican themes: sociological analyses, docu-mentary histories, readers and anthologies. In California and the South-west higher education has acknowledged the Chicano presence in ethnic studies programs and admissions policies. Even the Nixon administration is moving in this direction. In a transparent maneuver to further divide the nation's racial minorities, it has announced a decision to deemphasize black problems and to focus on Mexican-Americans, along with Indians and Puerto Ricans. Does this mean we are about to see a new ethnic literature emerge as the brown power and Chicano movements gain prominence in America?

THE PSYCHIC ECONOMY OF SUPPLY AND DEMAND

There is a common belief—to a great extent misleading—that Chicanos have been following in the footsteps of the black movement, though perhaps ten years behind. By this logic we would expect an outpouring of Mexican-American essayists, novelists, memoirists, and political commentators to hit the bookstores and interpret for us their group experience much as Baldwin, Ellison, Brown, Bennett, Malcolm, and a host of others have done for the Afro-Americans. A brief consideration of the market for brown writers as compared to blacks, from the point of view of both supply and demand, raises some doubts about this analogy.

Diversified as is the Mexican-American population, the generalization may be advanced that Chicanos tend to relate differently from blacks to the larger white society and to Anglo culture. A prevailing attitude toward Anglo society and its cultural domination has been indifference. This may be why few Chicano intellectuals and writers have been interested in interpreting their ethnic experience to us white Americans. For several centuries there have been blacks who were inspired to plead their case before the forum of public opinion, somehow maintaining a kernel of optimism and residual belief in the fundamental good will of at least a minority of whites. This optimism and hope for racial justice may be on its way out among the Afro-American cultural elite and the younger generation. Yet it still retains a strong hold on many people. It appears that Mexicans in the United States have rarely held such illusions about our vaunted democratic system.[1] Of course, many individual Mexican-Americans have struggled to make it economically, even disappearing socially and culturally into the Anglo middle-class mainstream. Yet Chicano intellectuals and working people had been living their version of cultural nationalism long before black militants brought the term to public attention a few years ago. Therefore we must be skeptical about the idea that the brown political dynamic is re-creating the black's—the similarity of Brown Beret dress and rhetoric to the Black Panthers' notwithstanding. For the historical and sociocultural context of Mexican-American life has been unique—it cannot be fitted into the pattern of

black–white relations, nor to the model of European ethnic group immi-   4
gration, for that matter.

The shortage of Chicano spokesmen and interpreters is not a matter of paucity of talent or absence of literary and political consciousness. Certainly discrimination and racism, particularly in the schools, have reduced the size of La Raza's cultural and intellectual elites. But Mexican-American writers (and ordinary folk) express themselves either in Spanish or a distinctive ethnic amalgam of English and Spanish. For good reasons that will be discussed later, they do not embrace English as willingly and totally as European ethnics—and Asian-Americans—appear to have done. With a strong aversion to the cultural values of Anglo-American society, Mexican-American writers have looked in the direction of Mexico for their audiences and their careers. Would they have done so anyway even if there had been a domestic market for brown writers? There may be no way to know.

Certain mundane facts explain in part the demand side of the equation, that is, the greater potential readership for black writers that I infer. The Afro-American population may be between two and three times as large   as the combined Mexican- and Latin-American groups. Thus there is a larger audience within the minority sector itself. Geographical distribution may be another factor. Chicanos are concentrated in the West and Southwest; blacks are in all parts of the country. So one might argue that blacks and black power are issues of national concern and national significance, while browns and brown power are only regional matters. Plausible enough, especially when one adds an additional point, the difference in style of protest. Blacks have been dramatic, confronting the power structure head on, calling names, serving ultimata, seizing buildings, burning ghettos. Chicanos appear to have mounted their protests more quietly; the Delano strike persisted for years. Chavez can maintain his commitment to nonviolence and still remain a hero for brown youth. Yet there is Tijerina and the many Chicano student groups who have had confrontations as militant as any—styles of protest are created as much by the media, who have chosen to focus their lenses on the black presence, proportionately deemphasizing the brown, the red, the yellow, and the poor white.

There is something here for the still little-understood psychology of racism. We buy black writers, not only because they can write and have something to say, but because the white racial mind is obsessed with blackness. Ellison's phrase "invisible men" can be somewhat misleading. In the American racist dynamic the black man has been unseen as a person, his individuality lost in the distorted, fantasied conceptions we hold of the group as a whole. But blacks as a collective presence have never been invisible nor inconsequential to American institutions and white psyches. Mexican-Americans, on the other hand, have been unseen as individuals and as a group. How else would you explain the fact that in California and other western states where Mexican-Americans have long outnumbered Afro-Americans, the racially conscious white has been much more attuned to black than to brown people? This is as true for those committed to ending racial injustice as it is for those who strive to keep people of color "in their place," probably even more true.[2]

James Baldwin has pointed to the deep mutual involvement of black and white in America. The profound ambivalence, the love–hate relationship, which Baldwin's own work expresses and dissects, does not exist in the racism that comes down on La Raza, nor in the Chicano stance toward the Anglo and his society. Even the racial stereotypes that plague Mexican-Americans tend to lack those positive attributes that mark antiblack fantasies—supersexuality, inborn athletic and musical power, natural rhythm. Mexicans are dirty, lazy, treacherous, thieving bandits— and revolutionaries. Perhaps only the relaxed mañana–siesta image veils a protest against the harried pace of North American life.

It has been less than a century and a quarter since the United States conquered Mexico, incorporating half its territory, and colonizing the Spanish-speaking, brown-skinned inhabitants who were accorded a nominal citizenship status. In this time, so relatively short compared with our historical encounters with Native Americans and blacks, Anglo and Chicano have lived apart—physically, linguistically, socially, and morally. The two peoples inhabit social and cultural worlds that in some ways are further apart than the distance between ghetto and suburb. Even informed Anglos know almost nothing about La Raza, its historical experience, its present situation, its collective moods. And the average citizen doesn't have the foggiest notion that Chicanos have been lynched in the Southwest and continue to be abused by the police, that an entire population has been exploited economically, dominated politically, and raped culturally. In spite of the racism that attempts to wipe out or, failing that, distort and trivialize the history and culture of the colonized, both expert and man in the street are far more aware of the past and present oppression suffered by blacks.

Mexican-Americans have responded to racist depreciation by calling on the reserve and privacy that appear to be central to the ethos of La Raza. Thus sociologists doing research, like myself, have found that it is much more difficult to get "good interviews" in the barrios than in the black communities—even with Chicano interviewers.[3] Chicano writers— and would-be writers—have apparently responded in the same way, so that it has been extremely difficult for Anglos to get a sense of the brown experience as lived, felt, and interpreted by Mexican-Americans. All this suggests why we need Chicano writing desperately and why we are unlikely to get as much as we could profitably learn from.

CULTURAL IMPERIALISM IN SOCIAL RESEARCH

The quarterly journal *El Grito,* which began publishing in 1967, emerged from the work of a circle of Chicano intellectuals based in Berkeley. The first products of the group were a number of position pieces called the *Quinto Sol Liberation Papers.* The general situation that impelled Quinto Sol to act was the virtual Anglo monopoly of social science studies and characterizations of Mexican-Americans, and the consequent distortion—sometimes subtle, sometimes not so subtle—that accompanies this academic colonialism. *El Grito*'s maiden issue contained editor Octavio Romano's initial exposure of the traditional stereotypes lurking behind the social scientists' conceptions of the Mexican-American personality: "fatalistic, resigned, apathetic, tradition-oriented, tradition bound, emotional, impetuous, volatile, affective, non-goal oriented, uncivilized, unacculturated, non-rational, primitive, irrational, unorganized, uncompetitive, retarded, slow learners, underachieving, underdeveloped, or just plain lazy. In using words as these to describe other people, they thereby place the reasons or causes of 'inferior' status *somewhere in their minds, within the personalities, or within the culture* of those who are economically, politically, or educationally out of power."[4] A year later Romano continued his attack, subjecting most influential monographs in this field to detailed criticism."[5]

To a considerable extent, the black power and black culture movements also are directed against this kind of cultural imperialism. The legitimacy of white "experts" to interpret the historical experience and current realities of Afro-American life is in question, a tendency most dramatically expressed in reactions to the Moynihan Report and William Styron's novel."[6] In the social sciences, Chicanos have been subject even more systematically to interpretation in terms of white middle-class standards and ideologies; furthermore, they have lacked ethnic novelists and essayists who might counter the sociological wisdom. The tendency to exclude Mexican-Americans from the analysis of their own group problems boggles the imagination. Thus the Society for the Study of Social Problems had two panels on rural manpower at their 1969 meetings in San Francisco at which the Delano farm labor strike was a major focus. There was not one Mexican among the eight people who presented and discussed the papers.

Aside from that of Indians, the study of the Mexican-American appears to be our most extreme expression of academic colonialism. The proportion of works written by Spanish-surnamed authors (who were not Mexican "nationals") was 18, 14, and 14 percent in three of the most recent and comprehensive bibliographies in this field. The three lists encompassed 235, 1,541, and 1,408 items by noninstitutional authors, and included published books and articles as well as government reports, hearings, and university dissertations.[7] Thus only *one publication in seven* about Mexican-American issues is written by a member of the group.[8]

Academic and research colonization of Afro-Americans has not been as total, perhaps due in part to the Negro colleges, which have trained a black intellectual elite, and in part to such movements as the Harlem renaissance, which have produced scores of ethnic writers. Thus Afro-Americans have authored many of the major studies of their own communities as well as studies of race relations in general. Approximately 35 percent of the books on racial themes listed in Gunnar Myrdal's bibliography (1944) were authored by blacks. The white advantage was greatest for books published before 1930, when the black proportion was only 27 percent; for those published after 1930 the percentages were essentially equal.[9] A count of E. Franklin Frazier's (1957) bibliography reveals that blacks authored almost as many books as whites (46 percent).[10] In a more recent and especially comprehensive bibliography (1966) black writers produced 33 percent of the studies where racial identification was possible. Interestingly enough, black-authored works outnumbered or equalled white-authored ones from 1930 to 1949 (confirming the findings from Myrdal); after 1950 white researchers overwhelmed blacks in the published literature.[11]

The Chicano experience is full of paradoxes. Facing an awesome array of colonial service anthropologists masked as objective scholars, La Raza itself has not been colonized culturally to the extent that blacks and Native Americans have. Among the racial minorities represented on west coast campuses, Chicanos appear to have retained more of their original culture and community integrity than the others.[12] In the Third World Strike at Berkeley in 1969 it was frequently noted that Chicanos exhibited more solidarity than blacks and Asians (Indian students were too few to permit any comparison); in the classrooms also Chicano students seem especially "together." Perhaps it is obvious why Mexican-Americans have experienced less forced transformation of their social organization and group life than African-Americans and Native Americans have. In the first place, Mexican-Americans were conquered and colonized in their own territory, and they have remained physically and culturally attached to the Southwest despite new migration from Mexico and internal movement in the search for work and better living conditions. They were not uprooted from their homeland and transported across the seas like the blacks, nor pushed across the continent in a 400-year drama of war and removal as were the Indians. And in the second place, because Chicanos are not really immigrants to this country, they do not cheerfully give up their native tongue as did the European ethnic groups and as Anglo schoolmasters expect them to do. Spanish preceded English as the language of the West and Southwest. To Mexican-Americans forced anglicization in language is the final stage in the U.S. conquest of Mexico and its culture. Spanish is thus not only a medium of communication and expression: it is a central aspect of selfhood and group integrity. The lyricism and grace of the language in contrast with the more harsh and blunt qualities of English come to epitomize the overall cultural conflict between colonizer and colonized.

The encounter between Mexican-Americans and the United States is sui generis, it cannot be forced into the ethnic model of immigration-assimilation nor into the category of black–white relations. That is why Chicanos, painfully aware of their unique history, resent and resist being classified, interpreted, or "understood" through analogs with the Afro-American. It is extremely difficult not to do this, because we do not know enough about Mexican-American society to discuss it on its own terms; in this essay I have several times approached the Chicano experience in the context of my own and the Anglo reader's greater familiarity with black realities. Of course, institutional racism, including the license to kill without sanction, has been the lot of all peoples of color in America. Our understanding and conception of racism, even expanding as it has been in recent years, has been built up almost exclusively from the materials of black oppression. The distinctive features of racism directed against yellow, red, brown, and Spanish-speaking have not been explored in a society many of whose unconscious cultural assumptions and patterns of thought polarize around the white–black axis.

Thus liberals and radicals alike in America tune in on the black thing; the intermediary colors strike a weak chord. University departments and administrations make considerably greater efforts to hire blacks than browns. Certainly the latter are in shorter supply, but more important may be the psychic energy available for projects of black inclusion, and the greater emotional payoff. A five-year campaign to increase the numbers of "low income minority" students at the University of California's Berkeley campus has resulted in a black–brown ratio of more than three to one (approximately one thousand to three hundred).[13] The concentration on black problems is a constant tendency of white-initiated conferences on minority groups; in many cases it has led to boycotts, protests, or separate caucuses among Chicano participants. The poverty program tells a related story. In many cities Afro-Americans gained control early in the game, at least on the community level. Spanish-speaking groups, excluded in the action, were put in the position of fighting blacks in order to make a dent in the dynamic of neglect and unconcern that is central to antibrown racism. Even the white left and the student movement in the Bay Area have failed to embrace the campaigns of La Raza militants as wholeheartedly as they took up the Black Panther cause.

"Divide and rule" is, of course, an old trick, a technique made to order for colonialism, which has not only exploited ethnic antagonisms but has actually "created" many of the races and peoples that make up the plural society. There are many obstacles to an authentic cultural pluralism, as well as to third world unity, within the United States. But the furthering of group consciousness on the basis of historical and cultural uniqueness can only serve to clarify the terms on which such developments in the future may emerge.

11 Toward the Decolonization of Social Research

with David Wellman

This chapter was one of the first works to "demystify" the research relationship, presaging similar critiques by feminist scholars that appeared later in the 1970s. My coauthor, David Wellman, was directing the field research for our study, then called *Racism, Manhood, and Culture*, and we drew upon this interviewing project to generalize about the exploitative nature of social research and the need to "decolonize" it. We isolate a number of ways in which behavioral science research reflects control, exploitation, and privilege, the generic components of social oppression, despite the masking of these facts by professional ideologies.

It was inevitable that I would have to face the exploitation inherent in my own research, writing as I was about internal colonialism and conducting a large-scale interviewing project in which African Americans were the most important informants and in which both the principal investigator and his main assistant were white. The paper was first presented at a March 1970 antipoverty conference in New Orleans. A decade later, in 1982, we published an expanded version. The two versions differed on the politically sensitive issue of whether white social scientists should be actively discouraged from studying certain aspects of the black and other minority experiences. The first version, perhaps reflecting the ultra-radical spirit of the late 1960s, called for such a division of labor. A decade later, we had changed our position. I have rewritten the ending of the chapter to reflect our present thinking on this matter, rather than advocating a point of view we have long given up.

DURING THE 1960s many assumptions of the academic world were challenged by events both external and internal to the campuses. There was a growing tendency for powerless and excluded social groups to view academics and their activities politically, to criticize their relation to, and responsibility for, existing economic, social and ideological arrangements. In Latin America as well as Europe and North America, debates raged on the political commitments of social science. Calls arose for a radical sociology and new political sciences, histories and anthropologies that would identify with the interests of oppressed classes and groups.

Robert Blauner and David Wellman, "Toward the Decolonization of Social Research," originally appeared in *The Death of White Sociology*, edited by Joyce Ladner (New York: Random House, 1973). Reprinted by permission of Random House, Inc.

The relationship of social research to ethnic and racial minorities came under particular attack. The idea of internal colonialism was advanced in Latin America as a framework for interpreting the subjugation of Indian populations, and in the United States it became an important paradigm with respect to the oppression of blacks, Chicanos, and other third world people.[1] Though no one seriously questioned the positive contributions that past social science had made to the liberalized climate in which sub-jugated groups were presently intensifying their struggles, the new per-spective indicated that social science research was itself caught up in the colonial relationship between white institutional power and the commu-nities of people of color. As ethnic and racial consciousness exploded in the Black Power movement, the social scientist began to look like another agent of the white power structure. Like the policeman, storekeeper, teacher, and welfare worker, social scientists were usually white outsiders who entered ghettos and barrios to advance personal and institutional goals that were determined outside of the community of study. Their authority to diagnose group problems and interpret culture and life styles conflicted with the demands for group self-definition and self-determina-tion that were central to the new consciousness of the racially oppressed. From such a perspective, the fact that the major studies and analyses of third world people in the United States have been carried out by whites took on new significance.[2]

Movements toward decolonization, which have shaken other areas of culture and politics, thus confronted social research. Social scientists studying race and poverty in the 1960s found that the norms of pure dis-interested scientific investigation were no longer adequate. The "subjects" had changed from "passive objects" to active critics of the research process. The experiences of our own study, the subject of this paper, were profoundly influenced by this new dialogue between social scientists and the racially oppressed.

In 1965 when the senior author began work in the area of black–white relations, he was impressed by an apparent centrality of what might be termed "manhood issues" for understanding both racism and the com-parative position of Negroes in American society. His initial theoretical approach to the low status and problems of black people was in terms of cultural and social determinants within the group, paralleling the sociol-ogists' attempts to understand the relative mobility of various European and Asian ethnic groups in terms of distinctive group characteristics. He was struck by indications of strong tension between men and women in the black community and by a variety of data which suggested that women tended to be relatively more resourceful, assertive and perhaps "less damaged" by the legacies of slavery and discrimination. An early hypothesis was that black lower-class society had innovated a concept of manhood—a street or hustling ideal—that, while viable as a survival technique, actually functioned to impede the integration and success of individuals—and by aggregation, the group as a whole.

About this time Moynihan's report became public. His perspective overlapped with our own in many ways, though there were significant differences. For our work, the key point about *The Negro Family* was not any new facts or theories, but the dialogue opened up by this controversial document. The critical responses, both reasoned and emotional, from the black community and its scholars as well as from white social scientists, were important "inputs" for the clarification of our theoretical position. The emergence of the Black Power perspective the following year, as well as our continuous involvement with groups and individuals in the ghetto, also sharpened our awareness of the complex theoretical and political issues of contemporary racism.

In addition, our own staff members who knew racial oppression from firsthand experience forced us to look more closely at the realities of race. We saw that such questions as manhood and male–female relations could not be isolated from the larger structural pattern of racial domination. To place the problem in its original fashion, no matter how sophisticated and sensitive our research, would have clear theoretical and political consequences. As Moynihan must know by now, *emphasis* is not just a matter of style. Emphasis has substantive implications. Our original one implied a denial of the historical and contemporary power of racism, of power and privilege, as first causes of our racial arrangements. We therefore transformed our project's focus, giving primary interest to racism and institutional conflict, and reshaping within this larger context our concerns with manhood and culture.

Important as theory is, it cannot by itself resolve the contradictions inherent in studies of race relations and third world groups that are conceived and directed by white social scientists. As our project progressed, we became more and more aware of these built-in conflicts between the colonial aspects of racial research and our identification with decolonization movements, between the institutional and professional context of social science and our critical posture toward established theory and practice in sociology. In this chapter we attempt an understanding of these contradictions and at the same time discuss the attempts we made—only partly successful—to move in the direction of decolonization. We have organized our ideas around three sources of the problem that seem the most critical: first, the essentially inegalitarian character of the research relationship; second, its specially oppressive relation to people of color and their communities; and third, the intensification of these dynamics which stems from the structure of the university as setting and sponsor of social research.

SOCIAL RESEARCH AS A REFLECTION OF SOCIAL INEQUALITY

Sources of the Problem

Scientific research does not exist in a vacuum. Its theory and practice reflect the structure and values of society. In capitalist America, where massive inequalities in wealth and power exist between classes and racial groups, the processes of social research express both race and class oppression. The control, exploitation and privilege that are generic components of social oppression exist in the relation of researchers to researched, even though their manifestations may be subtle and masked by professional ideologies.[3]

The behavioral scientist's control over the research enterprise, including all the intergroup interaction which he sets in motion, is supported by the norms of professional autonomy and expertise. According to this view, only the social scientist can define a suitable problem for research because he or she alone knows enough about the theories of the field and the methods by which theories are tested. In this model of science there is no place for the community-of-those-studied to share in the determination of research objectives. The theories, the interests, and the very concepts with which we work respond to the dynamics of increasing knowledge within our individual disciplines and professions, as well as to fashions and status concerns. The life problems and needs of the communities-under-study affect the scholar only indirectly; they are rarely the starting point for theory and research. A similar imbalance in control exists at the point of research production: the administration of a test or questionnaire, the conducting of an interview, even the moment when a participant observer sees something in the field and makes a mental note for his diary. At every stage there is a gulf between the researcher's purposes and the subject's awareness of what the investigator and his research instrument is all about.

Consider the norm of the in-depth interview—the respondent is expected to spill his guts about various aspects of his personal life and his social or political beliefs; the interviewer is supposed to be a neutral recorder, revealing nothing in return about his own life, feelings, or opinions—this might "bias" the data. The monopoly of control continues through the stages of analyzing and publishing the results of a study. The individual research subject's unique outlook and specific responses are typically lost in the aggregate of data which are subjected to standardized statistical summaries, ideal type classifications, or some other operation. Because behavioral scientists write for other scholars and "experts," those who are studied usually can't make head or tail of the research report toward which their own responses contributed. The communication gap between researcher and researched, which probably exceeds that between doctor and patient, serves to maintain the inequality of power between the two mutually interdependent parties and underlies the privileged status and elite outlook that social scientists enjoy in a class society.

Exploitation exists whenever there is a markedly unequal exchange between two parties, and when this inequality is *supported* by a discrepancy in social power. In social research, subjects give up some time, some energy and some trust, but in the typical case get almost nothing from the transaction. As social scientists, we get grants which pay our salaries; the research thesis legitimates our professional status, then publications advance us along in income and rank, further widening the material and status gaps between the subjects and ourselves. Thus many of us know ghetto residents who have said, partly boasting, partly complaining, that they have put a dozen people through graduate school, so studied have some black communities been. Of course, once a study is completed, the chances are that no one in the community ever sees the researcher again. There may be less unhappiness at being used in this way by a budding scholar from one's own ethnic group—but this doesn't change the essentially exploitative character of the relationship, since minority social scientists are still groping toward the forms that would relate their careers to their communities of origin in a meaningful way. Thus there is a growing hostility to universities in many black ghettos (such hostility and indifference has probably always existed among Chicanos).[4]

What keeps the behavioral scientist from perceiving the fact that his project uses people as objects, as things, as means only to his ends? Not ethical insensitivity primarily, though it is true that professional socialization is notoriously indifferent to such philosophical issues. It is the ideology of science that provides rationale and rationalization. For we have been taught that the development of a science is a slow and cumulative process—therefore no quick results should be expected. Only when our science gets it together will we have the theoretical knowledge to provide the basis for solutions to the social and human problems that poor and oppressed people face. Built into the deepest roots of the scientific attitude is the assumption that the accumulation and systematization of knowledge must be in the interest of the common good; in America social science gained justification through its concern for the common man. Some scholars, perhaps many, in our divided society retain this belief; perhaps it is defensible if one's view of science and society is sufficiently long-term.

For the short run, the span of time in which people live their lives, it is seriously open to question.

The poor and the racially oppressed have been promised much from social science. Occasionally a study, a book, or a series of investigations do make a difference to a particular community, or even to national policy as a whole. The Supreme Court's 1954 *Brown* decision responded to briefs that depended heavily on sociological and psychological research. But in the overwhelming number of instances, there is no tangible change in the lives of the subjects—either short run or long run. The poor and the oppressed, with their pragmatic sense and sensitivity to phoniness, knew this long before many of us. The lack of payoff comes from at least two sources—first, the distance between our theoretical and empirical concerns and the life-problems and situations of those we study; second, and ultimately the more crucial, our lack of power to implement and influence change. In many, though not all, problem areas, there is already enough known to tell us what should be done—why, for example, undertake research into the causes of black joblessness when it is clear that most unemployment and underemployment is due to the old-fashioned racial discrimination of employers and unions.

Our Attempts at Reform

We began our research with the idea of building into our project a number of specific strategies that might permit us to transcend the one-sided and exploitative dynamics of the research process. A first principle was paying respondents for the time they spent talking with us. The funding agency budgeted $2,500 to enable us to allot five dollars per interview. We stressed that this money was a wage for labor-time, rather than a bribe for information. In some cases the five dollars made a difference and was appreciated; yet a surprising number of interviews took place freely without any request for compensation. There is growing agreement that funded research on low-income communities should include sizable grants to indigenous people or organizations. It is not clear however that ours was the best way to do this.

A second tactic was an attempt to be honest about the purposes of the research and the difference it would make. The approach was no bullshit. We did not promise to save the world; we did make it clear that we were dissatisfied with the way social scientists have approached race relations and described the experience of black people in America. We hoped to do better, and if we were able to, it would be because we intended to elicit depictions of the realities as perceived by the principal actors, ordinary people, black and white. Therefore we aimed for interviews as unstructured and spontaneous as possible, permitting our workers to converse and exchange ideas with respondents. The interview was conducted as a life history, organized around experiences with major institutions: family, school, work, police, politics, welfare, etc. We wanted to find out where the respondent was at, to get as full a picture of him or her as possible. The point was to be flexible: to get inside the person and evoke a sociological portrait in the respondent's own language. Since our goal in data collection was the lived experience of ordinary people, we had to deviate from conventional notions of the appropriate research staff.

"Science" is usually restricted to "experts" who are traditionally selected by "objective" criteria: formal education, degrees, and research experience. Of course, these criteria effectively exclude people of color from actively participating in studies of their own communities. We decided to consider as "experts" those who had lived the lives we wanted to understand. Thus in selecting the original staff in 1967, degrees and research experience were hardly considered. Of the five black research assistants in a group of seven, only one had a university degree. Three had no association with any college or university. More pertinent to us were their ties to diverse segments of the black community. The five field workers and interviewers included a working longshoreman, a community worker in the schools, a Bohemian-oriented part-time musician, a southern-born civil rights veteran, and a graduate student from a middle-class Berkeley background, the one woman in the group. Their informal education included such schools as street hustling, New Careers and other poverty programs, and civil rights and nationalist movements.[5]

What impressed us about this original staff was an ability to talk about sensitive issues, to draw people out, and to understand the feelings of a variety of sectors of the black community. Training a conventional research team is not easy. The problems are magnified when you begin with a group with minimal exposure to sociological thinking. The problem was compounded by a commitment to use the assistants in conceptualizing problems as well as for data collection. Weekly seminars, attended also by other social scientists interested in race relations, were the format for both training and generating intellectual contributions from the staff.

The seminars began with discussions of the aims and ideas of the project. These seminars accomplished a number of purposes. They allowed the staff to participate actively in the ongoing development of the study. They were also concerned with specific issues of data collection, staff members sharing with each other the various problems faced in their work. We also related current issues to our emerging framework. Although time-consuming, and often frustrating, the weekly seminars were successful. Besides developing a certain collective spirit, they served to formulate and reformulate the basic assumptions and concepts underlying our research. They gave all of us a better grasp of the complexities surrounding race in America.

As our study progressed, we exhausted our original contacts, and it became more difficult to get interviews. Potential respondents would systematically stand us up. People raised questions about our motives. Some refused to have anything to do with us. Others demanded that we offer something besides money in exchange for their time. We became painfully aware that social researchers were not welcome in black and brown communities.

All of us, black as well as white, had to come to grips with this situation. If we were going to make any headway, we had to understand the bases of these anatagonisms. Discussions with reluctant respondents usually evoked two initial questions. One was "What's in it for us?" The other was "What's it going to be used for?" The dialogue didn't end when we answered the first by saying "little" and the second with examples of Ph.D. theses and books, for the two questions were merely the tip of an iceberg. Beneath was a hostility toward the university, toward research in general, and toward sociologists in particular. Probing in these areas revealed a sophisticated consciousness of social processes that negates stereotypes of oppressed people as uninformed, apathetic and apolitical.

Many people resented the fact that the University of California had only recently begun active recruitment of third world students. They complained that they, like everyone else, were paying taxes for the university, yet were virtually denied access to its facilities. Like many institutions, the University of California does not pay city taxes. It owns land which would provide a great deal of revenue if taxed. In short, many considered the university a parasitic institution and wanted little to do with it.

Hostility toward research in general was double-edged. A sentiment frequently expressed was "What good's another book gonna do us? We've been studied to death." Another respondent said, "Nothing is happening. I mean they got research after research and nothing is happening. They darn right exploiting people." Yet this concern took on another, more sophisticated form. Many people seemed to know the difference between theory testing and problem solving. The former was associated with university people, the latter, with people attached to poverty agencies: "You guys are just gonna say something we already know," or "Sociologists just get on my darn nerves. They really do. They take the little research they do and just chew it up and come up with the biggest lies and generalizations that you ever want to hear." Since we were affiliated with a university, we were immediately suspected of either documenting the obvious or of distorting the complex—and thus were a waste of time.

In the ghetto, there is hostility toward research for another reason which may appear to contradict the above. People knew that sociologists have been used by government agencies (for example, police and welfare departments) to develop more sophisticated techniques for the control of poor people. Many blacks saw themselves in a life-and-death struggle with white America. They believed sociologists had taken sides with the enemy and were therefore to be avoided at all costs.

There was also strong resentment toward the labels which social scientists have attached to racial minorities. People resented being tagged "culturally deprived," "disadvantaged," with "matrifocal families." And our respondents knew that this has been primarily the work of sociologists. One thing "Black Power" seemed to mean was freedom to define oneself without interference by sociologists or any other outside group.

We began to realize that this widespread hostility, resentment and fear could not be eased by payments or other devices. The issues were too complicated and deep-seated. It was the entire *relationship* between researcher and researched that was resented. In this relationship the objects of study saw themselves as *exploited*—because books are written but oppressive conditions remain; as *distorted* or *humiliated*—because they get put into invidious categorical bags such as "the culturally deprived"; and as *repressed*—because sociologists intentionally or unintentionally produce studies which are used to keep people in their place. The question that faced us was whether we could change this relationship.

Staff members began to commit themselves in various ways to the people they wanted to interview. Community groups called upon them to work and give technical assistance, and to prepare research for these groups. They had to help out in other mundane ways: making phone calls, writing letters, driving people around to appointments. In short, they had to alter the exploitative relationship which research imposes. In order to gain cooperation from the community, the gap between research and action had to be bridged in the immediate present.

Working closely with community groups posed a challenge to our notions of "objectivity" and other scientific principles. It was not enough to say that information was confidential and informants anonymous. We also had to take positions and become partisan. Concerned about the uses to which sociology can be put, we decided that some data would have to be "classified."[6] We could not consider ourselves dispassionate scientists without responsibility for possible misuses of our knowledge. Our respondents saw to that.

Problems in the University Milieu

The structure of the university is another impediment to the decolonization of research. The barriers which the norms of science throw up are often duplicated by the bureaucratic rules and regulations which govern university operation. Administrative reactions to our staff included defensiveness, skepticism and outright hostility. Everyone hired for research administered by the university must meet university requirements. These criteria had little to do with the realities of our project. On the contrary, the possibility of recruiting ghetto people is limited by the practice of linking job titles and pay scales to formal educational criteria. Often hassled by petty bureaucrats who would not waive such requirements, we had to go to higher levels to hire many of our staff.

The predominantly white, middle-class character of the university presents further problems for the involvement of third world and community people in research. The institute which housed us had long been a leading liberal influence on the campus. But its race relations policies and hiring practices reflected the civil rights emphasis on integration and middle-class Negroes. Its personnel apparently had little experience with lower- and working-class blacks. Our staff felt put off by the vibrations of the place. Secretaries did not always relate cordially to our black field workers; academic associates did not appear to regard them as colleagues in research. Characteristic was a combination of insensitivity and bureaucratic thinking, which, in relation to people of color, adds up to a kind of bureaucratic racism. The worst example of this was expressed by an institute staff functionary who informed one of our most capable assistants that he could not work on the project because his grade-point average was too low. This administrator did not consult with either the principal investigator, the project coordinator, or the Department of Sociology, which had just admitted the researcher to graduate school with a five-year fellowship. Instead she took it upon herself to begin terminating him because he did not meet university requirements. The matter was settled only at a higher level. But it contributed to a developing feeling that in the institute's eyes we were the wrong kind of people.

When the building was robbed—a frequent occurrence, due to its proximity to the high-crime area south of campus—the problem was compounded by the fact that our black researchers tended to be invisible and anonymous people to other institute personnel. Since it was always a black person who was "seen" leaving the building late at night, people were always "just asking" if one of "our people" had been in the night before. We couldn't tell whether the administrators were just checking out leads or actually suspecting us. Since these tensions in part reflected a clash of styles, the paranoia at times was a two-way stream.

Our staff posed other problems that had nothing to do with the milieu of the university, however. Some members viewed their job as a pretty good hustle. There was no clock to punch. People were independent, allowed to gather interviews as they pleased. The only demand was a certain number of interviews a week. Sometimes this autonomy—which we considered crucial to good research—was misused. Objective difficulties in arranging interviews became excuses to goof off. We would give someone a couple of weeks to produce, but if it became evident that he wasn't trying, we had to call him on it. In some instances we had to supervise people more closely than we desired. This produced a degree of antagonism within the staff.

This antagonism may have been fueled by resentment on the part of blacks toward the project's white administration. The white coordinator's job of evaluating interviews made by black staff appeared to epitomize larger patterns of racial domination and colonialism. Those who were graduate students felt a somewhat greater stake in the research; to some degree they could mediate this racial antagonism. They could also carve out a subproject within the whole, to pursue as they pleased. In this way feelings of exploitation were lessened—though not alleviated.

But for those who had no intention of becoming part of the university, the project was just a job. And often they handled it as such. Undoubtedly the expectation that staff members will have a commitment similar to that of the principal investigators reflects the paternalism endemic in both master–apprentice and white–black relations. But beyond these factors there was a residue of resentment traceable to the reality that blacks were being studied by whites. Ultimately this problem can be resolved only when research on the black community is conducted by black scholars rather than white ones.

Concluding Issues and Implications

It is not easy to give a balanced assessment of our project experience. Clearly there was some progress in the direction of decolonization. There was a dialogue with the subjects of our research. When the staff had time to develop real relationships, giving something in return, rapport as well as interviews followed. However, we were not totally successful in even these limited aims. In some instances we failed to overcome the barriers between those with and those without experience in social research. When some staff members did not work out and were let go, we felt uncomfortable; we were never sure we had tried hard enough to incorporate them. Assessing where our responsibility began and their inexperience left off was difficult. Moreover, we never completely eliminated the feeling of exploitation among the staff who remained. If you spoke with some of our staff, they would tell you they felt used. We don't always see it their way and don't fully understand to what degree specific actions on our part or the general context of the research resulted in these attitudes. Perhaps exploitation is inevitable if third world people are not involved from beginning to end in planning, administration and intellectual leadership. For this to happen, however, more must change than individual projects such as our own. The priorities of universities and funding agencies must be reordered.

Our attempt at decolonization was only partly successful for essentially three reasons. First, our understanding of the ramifications of the researcher–researched relationship came too late in the game; we could not fully reshape our strategies and priorities—a total overhaul was necessary, yet some major transformations in theoretical focus and research techniques were the most we could accomplish. This was partly due to the second problem, the limitations of our resources in money, time, and people. If research with communities of the poor and the racially oppressed is to approach reciprocity in exchange values, the cost will be great. This in turn relates to the third shortcoming: because of our limited resources our priority had to be data collection rather than social action and service to the community. In decolonized research these priorities have to be equalized, if not reversed.

What is needed is new organizational formats: centers or institutes that integrate social action, change, and community assistance with the theoretical and empirical goals of the researchers: Such a center would begin with a commitment to the philosophy of serving the interests of oppressed communities, as seen by their citizens and local organizations. Academic research projects would have to be related to these interests and be understood, discussed, and approved within the community. Collection of data and theory-testing would go hand in hand with the work of the center's staff in dealing directly with the needs of a community: problem-solving technical assistance, organizing, education, and, of course, allocating money. Every research inquiry would be part of a team effort in which the action and service components would play an integral part—of course some people would be research specialists, others action men. But the research effort and its personnel would then be identified with a larger unit that was clearly committed to community development and already functioning on behalf of the people rather than against them. Such a concept would require vast financial resources. It is possible that in many states, universities may no longer be the most feasible homes for such centers; other alternatives such as independent foundation-supported entities might be considered.

In the late 1960s many of our problems seemed to stem from the fact that two white sociologists had initiated a study of blacks, were in effect the bosses and the only staff members with long-term responsibility and commitment to the research. Even our project which focused on racism, reflected in its structure and function the prevailing patterns of racial domination. In response to this we advocated a racial division of research labor in the fields of race and poverty. Though we did not say that whites cannot study people of color, we pointed out that certain aspects of racial phenomena are difficult—if not impossible—for members of the oppressing group to grasp. These include the nuances of culture and group ethos; the meaning of oppression, especially psychic reactions; and what is called the black, the Mexican-American, the Asian, and the Indian *experience*. Social scientists realize the need for solid ethnographies of black and other third-world communities and analyses of the cultural dynamics, political movements, and other contemporary realities of the oppressed racial groups. White scholars can best further this goal by facilitating such studies by minority scholars. In this spirit we advocate opening graduate schools to minority scholars and recommend that white sociologists, instead of focusing on people of color, should investigate how racism is embedded in American institutions, culture, and personality.

The number of minority social scientists has increased—both in the professions and in the graduate schools—and a certain amount of ethnography and social history is written by these "insiders." In the society as a whole, unfortunately, the Great Retreat from Race has been reflected during the 1970s in a diminishing research interest in racism. Too many white sociologists, just like their counterparts in the public at large, believe that the reforms of the 1960s effectively eliminated the systematic racism affecting the lives of people of color in this country. In such a context, far from discouraging anyone from studying any aspect of race and racism, today we would welcome the interest of anyone, of whatever color, in examining the realities of our racial arrangements and in striving to make the research relationship a more equal and more humane one.

Part Three

Rethinking Critical Race Theory in a New Era

12   Some Self-Critical Reflections on
Colonized and Immigrant Minorities

It is a mixed blessing for a scholar to become associated with one particular theory, or in science with one momentous discovery. There is a tendency to be labeled forever by that association—as I have been with the idea of internal colonialism—even as your work branches out in different directions, or as you modify or discard earlier positions.

During the mid-1970s I stopped using the colonial analogy. At the time I was still enough of a Marxist to believe that a good theory must point the way to a political practice that resolves the contradictions the theory helps us understand. There was a practical solution for overseas colonialism: the colonizers could be sent back to Europe. And for the most part, they were. But I could find no parallel solution for America's domestic colonialism. Such a disconnect between theory and practice suggested to me an inherent flaw in the conceptual scheme itself.

I was also disturbed by internal colonialism's faddishness among social scientists, too many of whom applied the idea in a manner that seemed mechanical and forced. It was also a time when I felt disenchanted with all theory, sensing that sociologists all too often employ theory to impress their peers, and that our preconceived "theoretical ideas" often get in the way of fresh, creative examinations of social reality.

Without the crutch of an overarching theoretical framework, my new formulations came from immersion in firsthand research. Most important was a twenty-year interview study of blacks and whites that culminated in *Black Lives, White Lives: Three Decades of Race Relations in America*. From my informants I learned many useful lessons about the dynamics of America's racial politics, as well as the interplay of racism's subjective and objective dimensions. The other powerful learning experience has been thirty years of classroom discussions on racial issues—not what you might think of as research, but to me a valid form of what we sociologists call participant-observation.

The chapter that follows is excerpted from a long autobiographical essay in which I attempt to explain the origins of my life-long concern with racial justice and describe how later involvements in questions of race have marked my work, my political commitments, and my personal life.

TODAY WHEN I consider race relations sociology, I am more concerned than I was in the past with the social and political consequences of analytical frameworks and less with their abstract "theoretical correctness." It is in this spirit that I have been reassessing some of my earlier work.

"Colonized and Immigrant Minorities" (see Chapter 4) is a 1971 essay that is still widely read, thanks in part to its inclusion in Ronald Takaki's

1987 anthology, *From Different Shores*.[1] The argument turns on the contrast between the historical experiences of those white European ethnic groups who entered America voluntarily as immigrants, were able to move freely within the society, and worked as free laborers in industrial urban centers, and those of the colonized minorities who became Americans against their will, lacked freedom of movement and access to the labor market, and were subjected to systematic racism rather than just ethnic prejudice.

Today I see that contrast as too sharply drawn. Because the essay was written at the peak of "third world" unity movements, I searched for reasons to include Asians and Latinos within the colonial rubric, forcing them into a kind of theoretical Procrustean Bed. Today I would no longer consider Asians and Hispanics colonized. Even though their historical entry into the United States shared some colonial aspects (especially for the conquered Mexicans), they are essentially immigrant groups. This is important because the American mentality remains that of a nation of immigrants.

It is no accident that the two minority groups that remain the most downtrodden, with significant numbers of their population cut off from structures of opportunity and even mainstream values are those who did not emigrate to the United States voluntarily: African Americans and Native Americans. The "immigrant advantage" is not news to the African-Americans in South Central Los Angeles. I suspect that when they targeted Korean stores in the early 1990s they were protesting something larger than even the murder of a fifteen-year-old black girl. Koreans, along with other immigrants, enter the country and in a relatively short period surpass the economic and social position of the black poor, continuing a dynamic that has been taking place for 125 years.

Yet Koreans and other Asian immigrants—as well as Mexicans and Central Americans—are people of color who meet barriers of race and racism that did not exist for European newcomers. They may be advantaged as immigrants, but they are disadvantaged by their color and by the languages they speak. In the American racial hierarchy, the brown and yellow people occupy a middle ground between black and white. So I would now suggest a three-way, rather than a two-way, classification.

I also would not draw such a total contrast between white ethnic groups and people of color. By highlighting so insistently their differences, my writing contributed to widening the gap between whites and non-whites. The grandchildren of European immigrants who read "Colonized and Immigrant Minorities" in their college classes often feel that the struggles of their forebears have been discounted, and that they, as the descendants of these immigrants, are not given moral standing. When one compares the histories of the Irish, the Italians, and the Jews in America with those of the Africans, the Mexicans, and the Native Americans, one can emphasize either the striking differences due to racism and colonialism or the common experiences of being outsiders, undergoing poverty, and facing prejudice and discrimination. Since the choice one makes is consequential, it is important to strike a careful balance between these two positions.

Though class has by no means replaced race in significance, I find myself searching more often for a class perspective on American society these days.[2] Class analysis and class politics retain more potential for building coalitions than does strictly racial thinking. With all his flaws, Jesse Jackson remains a hero to me because his search for common ground has made him effective in mobilizing midwestern farmers and embattled union members, as well as minorities and the urban poor. I was quite moved when he called the community of Howard Beach "victims of economic violence" after some working-class Italian youths there murdered a black New Yorker, rather than simply dismissing them as "racist."

We need to find some balance between today's emphasis on difference—racial and otherwise—that is our legacy from the 1960s and 1970s and the need to build coalitions across lines of color, ethnicity, and other dividing points. I support multiculturalism, diversity, curriculum reform, and other similar programs that are attacked as "politically correct"—but only in an inclusive context that does not disparage or negate the claims of white people, including white males, to be equal partners in our muddled strivings toward a better society. In my classes I find many sincere whites confused, feeling left out, without authority to speak on matters of race and social justice. White males often feel that they are automatically seen as oppressors, rather than as individuals. I am not just talking about their resentment of affirmative action, but of the yearnings many liberal whites (and conservative ones, too) have to know and relate to blacks, Asians, and Latinos as individuals rather than as members of a group.[3]

The sharp contrast between colonized and immigrant minorities underlies the strong approach to affirmative action along racial lines. My own support of affirmative action is more measured, and my position is more complex than two decades ago. I take seriously the concern of critics about affirmative action's political divisiveness, and I see nothing wrong with pragmatically assessing its utility in specific situations. But I do not agree with Dinesh D'Souza and others who argue that affirmative action has reduced the quality of education at universities like Berkeley. In my classes, more than a few of the brightest students—those with the freshest, most original approach to the subject matter—are black or Latino or Asian, groups that were virtually absent on campus when I began teaching. The situation may be different in other fields. I may attract students whose political commitment and life experience give them a special edge. But when I visit other major universities today, the whiteness of their student bodies comes as a shock and makes me appreciate how Berkeley's ethnic mixture is a very special aspect of the education it offers.

Still, I would not dismiss the ideal of "colorblindness" as archly as I did in my earlier writings. I respect more today this basis of opposition to affirmative action. But I think critics like William Julius Wilson and Paul Starr are wrong when they say its impact has been inconsequential, helping only the already qualified, the prepared, the middle class. I don't consider the blacks and Latinos who work in the building trades and in such municipal jobs as police and firefighting to be middle class; they are working class and their numbers are significant. But I have long felt that the emphasis on affirmative action as the single solution to racial equality has had negative political consequences and needs to be reassessed. I would like to see more emphasis on exploring and overturning traditional modes of discrimination, which because of all the fanfare about affirmative action, most whites no longer think significantly affect racial minorities in America.

I have also been reassessing the concept of racism. I now feel that it was premature to imply, as I did in my earlier writings, that its old-fashioned expressions—bigotry and discrimination—were on their way out, no longer necessary to maintain a racially stratified society that could rely better on a more impersonal institutionalized racism. During the 1960s and 1970s there was this strong tendency to highlight structural explanations of all types and to downplay—almost with scorn—the relevance of cultural values or the importance of racial prejudice. From the people in my interview project I've learned a new respect for the power of beliefs, which in the area of race are deep-seated, but also capable of change. In the recent resurgence of racism, the old-fashioned forms of bigotry and hate crimes—even lynchings, in their northern (baseball bats replacing rope) version—have been most prominent.

13   Talking Past One Another

Black and White Languages of Race

As with many of the essays in Part I, in this chapter I use a dramatic event in American race relations as a take-off point—in this case, the 1991 police beating of a black motorist named Rodney King and the subsequent acquittal of the accused police officers by an all-white California jury in 1992.

During the 1960s, no issue was as likely to inflame race relations as that of police behavior. Most of the urban riots of that decade were set off by acts of actual or alleged police brutality. Over the past three decades law enforcement, like other institutions, has taken steps toward eliminating racist attitudes and behavior. But despite such efforts, officers of the law continue to be involved in the most brutal expressions of racism.

The fact that blacks and whites often see major political events from very different, even opposing, perspectives, has long fascinated me. In exploring these issues, I have sometimes used the college classroom as a sociological laboratory. During the 1960s and 1970s, my courses on race relations often had as many as five hundred students, with a considerable diversity of race, ethnicity, and political opinion. During our quite heated classroom discussions, I came to realize that white students and students of color were working from very different definitions of key terms in the language of race. Above all, they imputed different meanings to the concept of racism.

My focus on the way people understand words in this essay reflects my own growing interest in language, as well as the new importance of socio-linguistic thinking in the larger society. Some of my friends have criticized it for not emphasizing the structures of oppression, as I had in my earlier writing. I understand such criticism, but I don't believe that it is necessary to provide a well-rounded analysis in every published work.

FOR MANY African Americans who came of age in the 1960s, the assassination of Martin Luther King, Jr., in 1968 was a defining moment in the development of their personal racial consciousness. For a slightly older group, the 1955 lynching of the fourteen-year-old Chicagoan Emmett Till in Mississippi had been a similar awakening. The protest and violence in Los Angeles and other cities in late April and early May of 1992, spurred by the jury acquittal of four policemen who beat motorist Rodney King, is another such event.

The aftermath of the Rodney King verdict is seared into the memories of Americans of *all* colors, changing the way they see each other and their society. Spring 1992 marked the first time since the 1960s that incidents of racial injustice against an African American—and by extension the black community—seized the entire nation's imagination. Even highly publicized racial murders, such as those of African American men in two New York City neighborhoods—Howard Beach (1986) and Bensonhurst (1989)—stirred the consciences of only a minority of whites. The response to the Rodney King verdict is thus a long-overdue reminder that whites still have the capacity to feel deeply about white racism—when they can see it in unambiguous terms.

The videotaped beating by four Los Angeles police officers provided this concreteness. To be sure, many whites focused their response on the subsequent black rioting, while the anger of blacks tended to remain fixed on the verdict itself. However, whites initially were almost as upset as blacks: An early poll reported that 86 percent of European Americans disagreed with the jury's decision. The absence of any black from the jury and the trial's venue, Simi Valley, a lily-white suburban community, enabled mainstream whites to see the parallels with the jim crow justice of the old South. When we add to this mixture the widespread disaffection, especially of young people, with the nation's political and economic conditions, it is easier to explain the scale of white emotional involvement, unprecedented in a matter of racial protest since the 1960s.

In thirty years of teaching, I have never seen my students so overwrought, needing to talk, eager to do something. This response at the University of California at Berkeley cut across the usual fault lines of intergroup tension, as it did at high schools in northern California. Assemblies, marches, and class discussions took place all over the nation in predominantly white as well as nonwhite and integrated high schools. Considering that there were also incidents where blacks assaulted white people, the scale of white involvement is even more impressive.

While many whites saw the precipitating events as expressions of racist conduct, they were much less likely than blacks to see them as part of some larger pattern of racism. Thus two separate polls found that only half as many whites as blacks believe that the legal system treats whites better than blacks. (In each poll, 43 percent of whites saw such a generalized double standard, in contrast to 84 percent of blacks in one survey, 89 percent in the other.)

This gap is not surprising. For twenty years European Americans have tended to feel that systematic racial inequities marked an earlier era, not our own. Psychological denial and a kind of post-1960s exhaustion may both be factors in producing the sense among mainstream whites that civil rights laws and other changes resolved blacks' racial grievances, if not the economic basis of urban problems. But the gap in perceptions of racism also reflects a deeper difference. Whites and blacks see racial issues through different lenses and use different scales to weigh and assess injustice.

I am not saying that blacks and whites have totally disparate value systems and worldviews. I think we were more polarized in the late 1960s. It was then that I began a twenty-year interview study of racial consciousness published in 1989 as *Black Lives, White Lives*. By 1979 blacks and whites had come closer together on many issues than they had been in 1968. In the late 1970s and again in the mid-to-late 1980s, both groups were feeling quite pessimistic about the nation's direction. They agreed that America had become a more violent nation and that people were more individualistic and less bound by such traditional values as hard work, personal responsibility, and respect for age and authority. But with this and other convergences, there remained a striking gap in the way European Americans and African Americans evaluated *racial* change. Whites were impressed by the scale of integration, the size of the black middle class, and the extent of demonstrable progress. Blacks were disillusioned with integration, concerned about the people who had been left behind, and much more negative in their overall assessment of change.

In the 1990s this difference in general outlook led to different reactions to specific racial issues. That is what makes the shared revulsion over the Rodney King verdict a significant turning point, perhaps even an opportunity to begin bridging the gap between black and white definitions of the racial situation.

I want to advance the proposition that there are two languages of race in America. I am not talking about black English and standard English, which refer to different structures of grammar and dialect. "Language" here signifies a system of implicit understandings about social reality, and a racial language encompasses a worldview.

Blacks and whites differ on their interpretations of social change from the 1960s through the 1990s because their racial languages define the central terms, especially "racism," differently. Their racial languages incorporate different views of American society itself, especially the question of how central race and racism are to America's very existence, past and present. Blacks believe in this centrality, while most whites, except for the more race-conscious extremists, see race as a peripheral reality. Even successful, middle-class black professionals experience slights and humiliations—incidents when they are stopped by police, regarded suspiciously by clerks while shopping, or mistaken for messengers, drivers, or aides at work—that remind them they have not escaped racism's reach. For whites, race becomes central on exceptional occasions: collective, public moments such as the recent events, when the veil is lifted, and private ones, such as a family's decision to escape urban problems with a move to the suburbs. But most of the time European-Americans are able to view racial issues as aberrations in American life, much as Los Angeles Police Chief Daryl Gates used the term "aberration" to explain his officers' beating of Rodney King in March 1991.

Because of these differences in language and worldview, blacks and whites often talk past one another, just as men and women sometimes do. I first noticed this in my classes, particularly during discussions of racism. Whites locate racism in color consciousness and its absence in color blindness. They regard it as a kind of racism when students of color insistently underscore their sense of difference, their affirmation of ethnic and racial membership, which minority students have increasingly asserted. Many black, and increasingly also Latino and Asian, students cannot understand this reaction. It seems to them misinformed, even ignorant. They in turn sense a kind of racism in the whites' assumption that minorities must assimilate to mainstream values and styles. Then African Americans will posit an idea that many whites find preposterous: Black people, they argue, cannot be racist, because racism is a system of power, and black people as a group do not have power.

In this and many other arenas, a contest rages over the meaning of racism. Racism has become the central term in the language of race. From the 1940s through the 1980s new and multiple meanings of racism have been added to the social science lexicon and public discourse. The 1960s were especially critical for what the English sociologist Robert Miles has called the "inflation" of the term "racism." Blacks tended to embrace the enlarged definitions, whites to resist them. This conflict, in my view, has been at the very center of the racial struggle during the past decade.

THE WIDENING CONCEPTION OF RACISM

The term "racism" was not commonly used in social science or American public life until the 1960s. "Racism" does not appear, for example, in the Swedish economist Gunnar Myrdal's classic 1944 study of American race relations, *An American Dilemma*. But even when the term was not directly used, it is still possible to determine the prevailing understandings of racial oppression.

In the 1940s racism referred to an ideology, an explicit system of beliefs postulating the superiority of whites based on the inherent, biological inferiority of the colored races. Ideological racism was particularly associated with the belief systems of the Deep South and was originally devised as a rationale for slavery. Theories of white supremacy, particularly in their biological versions, lost much of their legitimacy after the Second World War due to their association with Nazism. In recent years cultural explanations of "inferiority" are heard more commonly than biological ones, which today are associated with such extremist "hate groups" as the Ku Klux Klan and the White Aryan Brotherhood.

By the 1950s and early 1960s, with ideological racism discredited, the focus shifted to a more discrete approach to racially invidious attitudes and behavior, expressed in the model of prejudice and discrimination. "Prejudice" referred (and still does) to hostile feelings and beliefs about racial minorities and the web of stereotypes justifying such negative attitudes. "Discrimination" referred to actions meant to harm the members of a racial minority group. The logic of this model was that racism implied a double standard, that is, treating a person of color differently—in mind or action—than one would a member of the majority group.

By the mid-1960s the terms "prejudice" and "discrimination" and the implicit model of racial causation implied by them were seen as too weak to explain the sweep of racial conflict and change, too limited in their analytical power, and for some critics too individualistic in their assumptions. Their original meanings tended to be absorbed by a new, more encompassing idea of racism. During the 1960s the referents of racial oppression moved from individual actions and beliefs to group and institutional processes, from subjective ideas to "objective" structures or results. Instead of intent, there was now an emphasis on process: those more objective social processes of exclusion, exploitation, and discrimination that led to a racially stratified society.

The most notable of these new definitions was "institutional racism." In their 1967 book *Black Power,* Stokely Carmichael and Charles Hamilton stressed how institutional racism was different and more fundamental than individual racism. Racism, in this view, was built into society and scarcely required prejudicial attitudes to maintain racial oppression.

This understanding of racism as pervasive and institutionalized spread from relatively narrow "movement" and academic circles to the larger public with the appearance in 1968 of the report of the commission on the urban riots appointed by President Lyndon Johnson and chaired by Illinois governor Otto Kerner. The Kerner Commission identified "white racism" as a prime reality of American society and the major underlying cause of ghetto unrest. America, in this view, was moving toward two societies, one white and one black (it is not clear where other racial minorities fit in). Although its recommendations were never acted upon politically, the report legitimated the term "white racism" among politicians and opinion leaders as a key to analyzing racial inequality in America.

Another definition of racism, which I would call "racism as atmosphere," also emerged in the 1960s and 1970s. This is the idea that an organization or an environment might be racist because its implicit, unconscious structures were devised for the use and comfort of white people, with the result that people of other races will not feel at home in such settings. Acting on this understanding of racism, many schools and universities, corporations, and other institutions have changed their teaching practices or work environments to encourage a greater diversity in their clientele, students, or work force.

Perhaps the most radical definition of all was the concept of "racism as result" In this sense, an institution or an occupation is racist simply because racial minorities are underrepresented in numbers or in positions of prestige and authority.

Seizing on different conceptions of racism, the blacks and whites I talked to in the late 1970s had come to different conclusions about how far America had moved toward racial justice. Whites tended to adhere to earlier, more limited notions of racism. Blacks for the most part saw the newer meanings as more basic. Thus African Americans did not think racism had been put to rest by civil rights laws, even by the dramatic changes in the South. They felt that it still pervaded American life, indeed, had become more insidious because the subtle forms were harder to combat than old-fashioned exclusion and persecution.

Whites saw racism largely as a thing of the past. They defined it in terms of segregation and lynching, explicit white supremacist beliefs, or double standards in hiring, promotion, and admissions to colleges or other institutions. Except for affirmative action, which seemed the most blatant expression of such double standards, they were positively impressed by racial change. Many saw the relaxed and comfortable relations between whites and blacks as the heart of the matter. More crucial to blacks, on the other hand, were the underlying structures of power and position that continued to provide them with unequal portions of economic opportunity and other possibilities for the good life.

The newer, expanded definitions of racism just do not make much sense to most whites. I have experienced their frustrations directly when I try to explain the concept of institutional racism to white students and popular audiences. The idea of racism as an "impersonal force" loses all but the most theoretically inclined. Whites are more likely than blacks to view racism as a personal issue. Both sensitive to their own possible culpability (if only unconsciously) and angry at the use of the concept of racism by angry minorities, they do not differentiate well between the racism of social structures and the accusation that they as participants in that structure are personally racist.

The new meanings make sense to blacks, who live such experiences in their bones. But by 1979 many of the African Americans in my study, particularly the older activists, were critical of the use of racism as a blanket explanation for all manifestations of racial inequality. Long before similar ideas were voiced by the black conservatives, many blacks sensed that too heavy an emphasis on racism led to the false conclusion that blacks could only progress through a conventional civil rights strategy of fighting prejudice and discrimination. (This strategy, while necessary, had proved very limited.) Overemphasizing racism, they feared, was interfering with the black community's ability to achieve greater self-determination through the politics of self-help. In addition, they told me that the prevailing rhetoric of the 1960s had affected many young blacks. Rather than taking responsibility for their own difficulties, they were now using racism as a "cop-out."

In public life today this analysis is seen as part of the conservative discourse on race. Yet I believe that this position originally was a progressive one, developed out of self-critical reflections on the relative failure of 1960s movements. But perhaps because it did not seem to be "politically correct," the left-liberal community, black as well as white, academic as well as political, has been afraid of embracing such a critique. As a result, the neoconservatives had a clear field to pick up this grass-roots sentiment and to use it to further their view that racism is no longer significant in American life. This is the last thing that my informants and other savvy African Americans close to the pulse of their communities believe.

By the late 1970s the main usage of racism in the mind of the white public had undoubtedly become that of "reverse racism." The primacy of "reverse racism" as "the really important racism" suggests that the conservatives and the liberal-center have, in effect, won the battle over the meaning of racism.

Perhaps this was inevitable because of the long period of backlash against all the progressive movements of the 1960s. But part of the problem may have been the inflation of the idea of racism. While institutional racism exists, such a concept loses practical utility if every thing and every place is racist. In that case, there is effectively nothing to be done about it. And without conceptual tools to distinguish what is important from what is not, we are lost in the confusion of multiple meanings.

BACK TO BASICS

While public discourse was discounting white racism as exaggerated or a thing of the past, the more traditional forms of bigotry, harassment, and violence were unfortunately making a comeback. (This upsurge actually began in the early 1980s but was not well noticed, due to some combination of media inattention and national mood.) What was striking about the Bernhard Goetz subway shootings in New York, the white-on-black racial violence in Howard Beach, the rise of organized hate groups, campus racism, and skinhead violence is that these are all examples of old-fashioned racism. They illustrate the power and persistence of racial prejudices and hate crimes in the tradition of classical lynchings. They are precisely the kind of phenomena that many social analysts expected to diminish, as I did.

If there was one positive effect of this upsurge, it was to alert many whites to the destructive power of racial hatred and division in American life. At the same time, these events also repolarized racial attitudes in America. They have contributed to the anger and alienation of the black middle class and the rapid rise of Afrocentrism, particularly among college students.

As the gap in understanding has widened, several social scientists have proposed restricting the concept of racism to its original, more narrow meaning. However, the efforts of African Americans to enlarge the meaning of racism is part of that group's project to make its view of the world and of American society competitive with the dominant white perspective. In addition, the "inflated" meanings of racism are already too rooted in common speech to be overturned by the advice of experts. And certainly some way is needed to convey the pervasive and systematic character of racial oppression. No other term does this as well as racism.

The question then becomes what to do about these multiple and confusing meanings of racism and their extraordinary personal and political charge. I would begin by honoring both the black and white readings of the term. Such an attitude might help facilitate the interracial dialogue so badly needed and yet so rare today.

Communication can only start from the understandings that people have. While the black understanding of racism is, in some sense, the deeper one, the white views of racism (ideology, double standard) refer to more specific and recognizable beliefs and practices. Since there is also a cross-racial consensus on the immorality of racist ideology and racial discrimination, it makes sense whenever possible to use such a concrete referent as discrimination, rather than the more global concept of racism. And reemphasizing discrimination may help remind the public that racial discrimination is not just a legacy of the past.

The intellectual power of the African American understanding lies in its more critical and encompassing perspective. In the Rodney King events, we have an unparalleled opportunity to bridge the racial gap by pointing out that racism and racial division remain essential features of

American life and that incidents such as police beatings of minority people and stacked juries are not aberrations but part of a larger pattern of
racial abuse and harassment. Without resorting to the overheated rhetoric
that proved counterproductive in the 1960s, it now may be possible to
persuade white Americans that the most important patterns of discrimination and disadvantage are not to be found in the "reverse racism" of
affirmative action but sadly still in the white racism of the dominant social
system. And, when feasible, we need to try to bridge the gap by shifting
from the language of race to that of ethnicity and class.

RACE OR ETHNICITY?

In the American consciousness the imagery of race—especially along the
black–white dimension—tends to be more powerful than that of class or
ethnicity. As a result, legitimate ethnic affiliations are often misunder-
stood to be racial and illegitimate.

Race itself is a confusing concept because of the variance between scientific and common sense definitions of the term. Physical anthropologists
who study the distribution of those characteristics we use to classify
"races" teach us that race is a fiction because all peoples are mixed to various degrees. Sociologists counter that this biological fiction unfortunately remains a sociological reality. People define one another racially,
and thus divide society into racial groups. The "fiction" of race affects
every aspect of peoples' lives, from living standards to landing in jail.

The consciousness of color differences, and the invidious distinctions
based on them, have existed since antiquity and are not limited to any one
corner of the world. And yet the peculiarly modern division of the world
into a discrete number of hierarchically ranked races is a historic product
of Western colonialism. In precolonial Africa the relevant group identities were national, tribal, or linguistic. There was no concept of an African
or black people until this category was created by the combined effects of
slavery, imperialism, and the anticolonial and Pan-African movements.
The legal definitions of blackness and whiteness, which varied from one
society to another in the Western hemisphere, were also crucial for the
construction of modern-day races. Thus race is an essentially political
construct, one that translates our tendency to see people in terms of their
color or other physical attributes into structures that make it likely that
people will act for or against them on such a basis.

The dynamic of ethnicity is different, even though the results at times
may be similar. An ethnic group is a group that shares a belief in its common past. Members of an ethnic group hold a set of common memories
that make them feel that their customs, culture, and outlook are distinc-

tive. In short, they have a sense of peoplehood. Sharing critical experiences and sometimes a belief in their common fate, they feel an affinity for one another, a "comfort zone" that leads to congregating together, even when this is not forced by exclusionary barriers. Thus if race is associated with biology and nature, ethnicity is associated with culture. Like races, ethnic groups arise historically, transform themselves, and sometimes die out.

Much of the popular discourse about rare in America today goes awry because ethnic realities get lost under the racial umbrella. The positive meanings and potential of ethnicity are overlooked, even overrun, by the more inflammatory meanings of race. Thus white students, disturbed when blacks associate with each other, justify their objections through their commitment to *racial* integration. They do not appreciate the ethnic affinities that bring this about, or see the parallels to Jewish students meeting at the campus Hillel Foundation or Italian Americans eating lunch at the Italian house on the Berkeley campus.

When blacks are "being ethnic," whites see them as "being racial." Thus they view the identity politics of students who want to celebrate their blackness, their *chicanismo,* their Asian heritages, and their American Indian roots as racially offensive. Part of this reaction comes from a sincere desire, almost a yearning, of white students for a colorblind society. But because the ethnicity of darker people so often gets lost in our overracialized perceptions, the white students misread the situation. When I point out to my class that whites are talking about race and its dynamics and the students of color are talking about ethnicity and its differing meaning, they can begin to appreciate each other's agendas.

Confounding race and ethnicity is not just limited to the young. The general public, including journalists and other opinion makers, does this regularly, with serious consequences for the clarity of public dialogue and sociological analysis. A clear example comes from the Chicago mayoral election of 1983. The establishment press, including leading liberal columnists, regularly chastised the black electorate for giving virtually all its votes to Harold Washington. Such racial voting was as "racist" as whites voting for the other candidate because they did not want a black mayor. Yet African Americans were voting for ethnic representation just as Irish Americans, Jews, and Italians have always done. Such ethnic politics is considered the American way. What is discriminatory is the double standard that does not confer the same rights on blacks, who were not voting primarily out of fear or hatred as were many whites.

Such confusions between race and ethnicity are exacerbated by the ambiguous sociological status of African Americans. Black Americans are *both* a race and an ethnic group. Unfortunately, part of our heritage of racism has been to deny the ethnicity, the cultural heritage of black Americans. Liberal-minded whites have wanted to see blacks as essentially white people with black skins. Until the 1960s few believed that black culture was a real ethnic culture.

Because our racial language is so deep-seated, the terminology of black and white just seems more "natural" and common-sensical than more ethnic labels like African American or European American. But the shift to the term African American has been a conscious attempt to move the discourse from a language of race to a language of ethnicity. "African American," as Jesse Jackson and others have pointed out, connects the group to its history and culture in a way that the racial designation, black, does not. The new usage parallels terms for other ethnic groups. Many whites tend to dismiss this concern about language as mere sloganeering. But "African American" fits better into the emerging multicultural view of American ethnic and racial arrangements, one more appropriate to our growing diversity. The old race relations model was essentially a view that generalized (often inappropriately) from black–white relations. It can no longer capture—if it ever could—the complexity of a multiracial and multicultural society.

The issue is further complicated by the fact that African Americans are not a homogeneous group. They comprise a variety of distinct ethnicities. There are the West Indians with their long histories in the United States, the darker Puerto Ricans (some of whom identify themselves as black), the more recently arrived Dominicans, Haitians, and immigrants from various African countries, as well as the native-born African Americans, among whom regional distinctions can also take on a quasi-ethnic flavor.

Blacks from the Caribbean are especially likely to identify with their homeland rather than taking on a generic black or even African American identity. While they may resist the dynamic of "racialization" and even feel superior to native blacks, the dynamic is relentless. Their children are likely to see themselves as part of the larger African-American population. And yet many native-born Americans of African descent also resist the term "African American," feeling very little connection to the original homeland. Given the diversity in origin and outlook of America's largest minority, it is inevitable that no single concept can capture its full complexity or satisfy all who fall within its bounds.

For white Americans, race does not overwhelm ethnicity. Whites see the ethnicity of other whites; it is their own whiteness they tend to overlook. But even when race is recognized, it is not conflated with ethnicity. Jews, for example, clearly distinguish their Jewishness from their whiteness. Yet the long-term dynamic still favors the development of a dominant white racial identity. Except for recent immigrants, the various

European ethnic identities have been rapidly weakening. Vital ethnic communities persist in some cities, particularly on the East Coast. But many whites, especially the young, have such diverse ethnic heritages that they have no meaningful ethnic affiliation. In my classes only the Jews among European Americans retain a strong sense of communal origin.

Instead of dampening the ethnic enthusiasms of the racial minorities, perhaps it would better to encourage the revitalization of whites' European heritages. But a problem with this approach is that the relationship between race and ethnicity is more ambiguous for whites than for people of color. Although for many white groups ethnicity has been a stigma, it also has been used to gain advantages that have marginalized blacks and other racial minorities. Particularly for working-class whites today, ethnic community loyalties are often the prism through which they view their whiteness, their superiority.

Thus the line between ethnocentrism and racism is a thin one, easily crossed—as it was by Irish Americans who resisted the integration of South Boston's schools in the 1970s and by many of the Jews and Italians that sociologist Jonathan Rieder describes in his 1985 book *Canarsie*.

White students today complain of a double standard. Many feel that their college administrations sanction organization and identification for people of color, but not for them. If there can be an Asian business organization and a black student union, why can't there be a white business club or a white student alliance? I'd like to explain to them that students of color are organized ethnically, not racially, that whites have Hillel and the Italian theme house. But this makes little practical sense when such loyalties are just not that salient for the vast majority.

Out of this vacuum the emerging identity of "European American" has come into vogue. I interpret the European-American idea as part of a yearning for a usable past. Europe is associated with history and culture. "America" and "American" can no longer be used to connote white people. 'White" itself is a racial term and thereby inevitably associated with our nation's legacy of social injustice.

At various California colleges and high schools, European-American clubs have begun to form, provoking debate about whether it is inherently racist for whites to organize as whites—or as European Americans. Opponents invoke the racial analogy and see such organizations as akin to exclusive white supremacist groups. Their defenders argue from an ethnic model, saying that they are simply looking for a place where they can feel at home and discuss their distinctive personal and career problems. The jury is still out on this new and, I suspect, burgeoning phenomenon. It will take time to discover its actual social impact.

If the European Americans forming their clubs are truly organizing on an ethnic or panethnic rather than a racial model, I would have to support these efforts. Despite all the ambiguities, it seems to me a gain in social awareness when a specific group comes to be seen in ethnic rather than racial terms. During the period of the mass immigration of the late nineteenth century and continuing through the 1920s, Jews, Italians, and other white ethnics were viewed racially. We no longer hear of the "Hebrew race," and it is rare for Jewish distinctiveness to be attributed to biological rather than cultural roots. Of course, the shift from racial to ethnic thinking did not put an end to anti-Semitism in the United States—or to genocide in Germany, where racial imagery was obviously intensified.

It is unrealistic to expect that the racial groupings of American society can be totally "deconstructed," as a number of scholars now are advocating. After all, African-Americans and Native Americans, who were not immigrants, can never be exactly like other ethnic groups. Yet a shift in this direction would begin to move our society from a divisive biracialism to a more inclusive multiculturalism.

To return to the events of spring 1992, I ask what was different about these civil disturbances. Considering the malign neglect of twelve Reagan-Bush years, the almost two decades of economic stagnation, and the retreat of the public from issues of race and poverty, the violent intensity should hardly be astonishing.

More striking was the multiracial character of the response. In the San Francisco Bay area, rioters were as likely to be white as nonwhite. In Los Angeles, Latinos were prominent among both the protesters and the victims. South Central Los Angeles is now more Hispanic than black, and this group suffered perhaps 60 percent of the property damage. The media have focused on the specific grievances of African Americans toward Koreans. But I would guess that those who trashed Korean stores were protesting something larger than even the murder of a fifteen-year-old black girl. Koreans, along with other immigrants, continue to enter the country and in a relatively short time surpass the economic and social position of the black poor. The immigrant advantage is real and deeply resented by African Americans, who see that the two most downtrodden minorities are those that did not enter the country voluntarily.

During the 1960s the police were able to contain riots within the African-American community. This time Los Angeles police were unable to do so. Even though the South Central district suffered most, there was also much destruction in other areas, including Hollywood, downtown, and the San Fernando Valley. In the San Francisco Bay area the violence occurred primarily in the white business sections, not the black neighborhoods of Oakland, San Francisco, or Berkeley. The violence that has spilled out of the inner city is a distillation of all the human misery that a white middle-class society has been trying to contain—albeit unsuccessfully (consider the homeless). As in the case of an untreated infection, the toxic substances finally break out, threatening to contaminate the entire organism.

Will this widened conflict finally lead Americans toward a recognition of our common stake in the health of the inner cities and their citizens, or toward increased fear and division? The Emmett Till lynching in 1955 set the stage for the first mass mobilization of the civil rights movement, the Montgomery bus boycott later that year. Martin Luther King's assassination provided the impetus for the institution of affirmative action and other social programs. The Rodney King verdict and its aftermath must also become not just a psychologically defining moment but an impetus to a new mobilization of political resolve.

14   White Radicals, White Liberals, White People

Rebuilding the Anti-Racist Coalition

In this chapter I focus on the relationship between liberals and radicals in America in an attempt to understand the antagonisms and lack of dialogue between these two political tendencies. For many people, the line separating the more moderate (liberal) from the more extreme (radical) members of the historic Left may be difficult to fathom. In the past two decades, conservatives have succeeded in making the "L word" an epithet that implies an extremity of views beyond the national consensus. Thus, in the public mind the idea of the liberal and the idea of the radical have become confused and confounded, an obfuscation that American radicals are powerless to counter, largely because so few remain.

I write from the radical perspective, out of my own experience of disparaging liberals and their leaders. In 1968 I could not bear to vote for the Democratic Party's candidate, Hubert Humphrey, a prototype of the American "white liberal," because I considered him a weak-willed vacillator without principles. (Vice-President Humphrey had brokered the "compromise" that denied representation to the grass-roots and predominantly black Mississippi Freedom Democratic Party at the 1964 Democratic Convention.) Instead, I voted for the Black Panther Party's Eldridge Cleaver. For many years I considered white liberals to be racist because many of them opposed the goals and tactics of the black militant movement I supported: Black Power, black nationalism, and the revitalization of a black culture. I gave up this belief after years of studying the white interviews from my research project. The data made it clear to me that white liberals, rather than being racist, were defending values and principles that were real and important—even if I didn't share them myself. A similar self-criticism has inspired the present essay.

The immediate stimulus came from sociologist Benjamin Bowser whose anthology *Anti-Racism in World Perspective* reflects an important tendency: instead of emphasizing only the racism of American institutions and the American people, it is now time to acknowledge, and above all, to nurture, our egalitarian, anti-racist potential.

THE TENSIONS between blacks and Jews have been the subject of endless commentary and analysis, in large part because for decades their alliance in the struggle for civil rights had been a bulwark of America's anti-racist coalition. But another split took place in that coalition, also in the late 1960s, that is almost never addressed by social and political analysts. For the last three decades, the antagonisms between American liberals and radicals has inhibited the mobilization of anti-racist coalitions and the participation of most whites in the struggle for racial justice. To me at least, the liberal–radical divide has had a greater impact on American politics than the black–Jewish split.

The terms *liberals* and *radicals* are slippery and difficult to define, but they suggest two important political camps within the white population that have been committed historically to racial justice. Liberals and radicals share—and this distinguishes them from *conservatives*—a commitment to the expansion in practice of the ideals of democracy and equality. They do not characteristically look to the past for their visions of a better society, but to the future. Both liberals and radicals are responsive to the problems of disadvantaged groups and are open to some utilization of the state to intervene in providing a greater measure of economic and social justice. The meaning of liberal, radical, and conservative changes with political circumstances. Who identifies themselves and organizes around liberal, radical, and conservative issues also changes from place to place and through history.

The referents of these terms are contextual and relational rather than absolute. The radical will always be to the "left" of the liberal in that his or her critique of the status quo and political solutions will be more comprehensive, whereas those of the liberal will be more partial, piecemeal, and usually cautious. But the concrete details of specific positions—what distinguishes the two camps at any historical moment—will depend on the contingencies of time and place. Because this is a changing reality, new meanings of who and what is liberal and radical are regularly re-created by new historical circumstances.[1]

The present-day antagonism and lack of dialogue between most white liberals and white radicals is the American equivalent of the fault line between the Social Democratic and Communist movements that evolved in Europe in the years after the Russian Revolution. The inability of socialists and communists to work together is often seen as an important key to the ascendance of fascism in Europe in the 1930s. The liberal–radical split makes it impossible to develop a "united front" with a critical mass of white support against racism in the United States, and racism is America's fascism.

THE CONSEQUENCES OF THE LIBERAL–RADICAL DEMISE

From the Depression of the 1930s through the mid-1960s, liberals and radicals had an uneasy, but a working, relationship—despite their ideological and stylistic differences. True, the anti-Communist hysteria of the immediate post–World War II era, associated with Senator Joseph McCarthy, divided and weakened the American Left. But liberals and radicals tended to be on the same side regarding most of the great issues of social justice and economic change, and were allies especially in the struggle against racial bigotry, prejudice, and discrimination. All of this changed in the 1960s. Liberals and radicals began taking sharply different positions in the charged politics of the time. Race was the primary dividing point. The war in Vietnam and conflicting attitudes toward the increasingly militant protest of white students and youth against the war were also important.

The legacy of this now thirty-year-old split is present in the issues of racial politics that divide America in the 1990s. Most liberals and radicals tend to be on opposite sides of what are today called "the culture wars." The few liberals who still comment on race tend to oppose, either in principle or more often in operation, the present movement toward multiculturalism. They are often ambivalent about organized efforts to diversify the membership and the leadership of social institutions by race, gender, or any other form of social difference. Most of the intellectual arguments against affirmative action have come from white liberals.[2]

In contrast, white radicals have been strong supporters of affirmative action and multiculturalism. Despite the small numbers of radicals in the general population and the greater numbers and influence of liberals, national affirmative action efforts have been sustained as the expressed goals of American businesses, colleges and universities, public associations, and government agencies. Of course, the white Left is not the only group that can take credit for this success. Radicals in alliance with more powerful black and other minority movements, organized feminist groups, and a series of crucial court rulings have upheld the legitimacy of affirmative action.

LANGUAGE AND DISCOURSE

The influence of the white Left, third world, and women's movements has been even greater in the area of language and discourse. Black militants succeeded in changing the term of reference for people of African descent from *Negro* to *black*. Feminists educated the public to refer to women as *women* and not as *girls*. And *racism*, a word favored by white radicals as well as intellectuals and activists of color, replaced the concepts of prejudice and discrimination, terms that liberal whites and moderate blacks were more comfortable with.

The problem is that changes in action and deep belief have not followed changes in the way Americans talk about race. It is an anomalous and an unhealthy political development to have no mass anti-racist movement—today's is weak and almost nonexistent—and at the same time to have anti-racist thought virtually proscribed in everyday language. All indications are that the majority white population is opposed to and resentful of what it perceives as coercive language.

This situation of no anti-racist movement, no coalition between liberals and radicals, plus the use of language far in advance of action, has maintained a white backlash mentality long after the conditions that gave rise to it have passed into history. The discourse of racism predisposes white people to view themselves in terms of a "deficit model," one that focuses on human failings rather than on more positive potentials for growth and change. As with how blacks react to white dialogue about black family, community, and school achievement, the stance of whites in the dialogue of race is also one of defensiveness. The contemporary discourse on white racism is counterproductive for coalition building.

Two things are needed: to describe the role of the Left in the liberal–radical split and to suggest ways to overcome this legacy of the 1960s to begin to heal the breach. I propose a series of arguments aimed at reversing the way Americans conceive of white people, so that it will be possible to look afresh at European Americans and see them in terms of their potentials for overcoming racism and for joining new democratizing movements, rather than continuing to look at them in terms of how racist and irredeemable they are.

HOW LIBERALS AND RADICALS SEPARATED: CONFLICT OVER RACE AND WAR

The history of the radical–liberal demise goes back to the 1950s. After eight years of the Eisenhower administration, Kennedy's election was viewed as a return to the liberal Democratic principles of the Roosevelt-Truman years. Kennedy's narrow victory over Nixon is often attributed to a sizable turnout at the polls of blacks, who were impressed by Kennedy's pre-election gesture of solidarity with an imprisoned Martin Luther King, Jr. Expected to be responsive to their concerns, the new president was disappointing on civil rights issues, spoke out rarely, and, when he did, spoke with great moderation. Above all, he failed to protect the lives of civil rights activists against the racist terror they faced in the South.

The seeds of the radical–liberal tension were sown in the early 1960s, with growing disillusionment over President Kennedy's failure to act decisively in support of civil rights. The 1960s produced a new generation of liberals and radicals who had no experience with the 1930s' social programs, worldwide economic depression, world war, and the slow up-and-down pace of social reforms. The only issues for them were in the present—race, Vietnam, student and youth protest, and the best means of bringing about rapid social change. Women's liberation was also a critical divide for many. The conflicting positions of liberals and radicals became frozen and have remained hardened to this day.

Because Kennedy was viewed as a prototypical white liberal, criticism of this species of political being began to be heard more frequently in the early 1960s. A mistake that third world activists and white radicals made was to generalize legitimate criticisms of Kennedy and other power holders to ordinary rank-and-file liberals. Rank-and-file liberals were still very much a part of the civil rights coalition during the first half of the 1960s.[3]

Rumblings of a liberal–radical break appeared after 1963, as "liberal bashing" was entering the political discourse. Murray Friedman wrote an article, published in 1964, with a prophetic title, "The White Liberal's Retreat." Friedman alleges that white liberals were great at supporting integration as long as the battleground remained in the South. But when the action moved North, and when their own schools, communities, and businesses were affected, their enthusiasm for racial justice weakened.[4]

There is certainly some truth to Friedman's charges. But the same criticisms applied to many radicals who put their personal interests before their commitments to racial justice. If liberals at this point were beginning to be turned off by the black movement—earlier and in larger numbers than radicals would be later—it was largely because the rapidly developing trends in black consciousness and movement strategies thoroughly challenged liberals' fundamental values. The hard edges of militant rhetoric, the undertones of violence, and the threat of violence were being justified by invoking Malcolm X's principle that black people must achieve their freedom by any means necessary. At the same time, a new attitude was growing in the black movement that targeted whites generally and white liberals specifically as the enemy.

The assassination of President John F. Kennedy in November 1963 was a watershed event that would affect the entire decade that followed. Even with his limitations, Kennedy exemplified a youthful energy of hope and optimism. By mid-1963, he seemed to be becoming more committed to the black cause. Kennedy's death served as the backdrop for the anger and alienation—especially among youth—that would mark political life in the late 1960s. The effect of the assassination cannot be overestimated.

But the radicalizing of black civil rights activists that led to rejecting white radical and liberal support and to the demise of the radical–liberal coalition has another more specific source. We must remember that many white radical leaders gained their first social reform experiences during "Freedom Summer" in 1964, when they volunteered to help register black voters in Mississippi. The predominantly black Mississippi Freedom Democratic Party (MFDP) was formed that year as the only political party in the state that included blacks and was based on "one man, one vote." The MFDP went to the Democratic National Convention in Atlantic City fully expecting to be seated as the official state body. But Kennedy's presidential successor, Lyndon B. Johnson, refused to select the MFDP over the all-white "official" state delegates because of his ties to conservative and "Dixiecrat" southerners (all elected without black representation). This betrayal was probably the single most important event that radicalized black civil rights workers and their white allies during the eventful 1960s.[5]

Vice-President Hubert Humphrey, even more the prototypical white liberal than Kennedy, was the architect of a most unsatisfactory compromise offered to the MFDP. As a result, the image of the white liberal in the radical mind sank to a new low. Today, a number of movement veterans, notably Robert Moses, identify this event as precipitating the shift toward Black Power and black nationalism that would soon follow.[6] Had the nation's top liberals not "sold out," had Johnson and Humphrey seated the MFDP, and had they directly challenged the southern power structure, the civil rights movement might have been incorporated into the nation's body politic today. Although other things contributed to militancy, much of the angry, "in your face" separatist rhetoric and style, which alienated the larger white population, might have been avoided.

Vietnam was the other great issue of the 1960s. For radicals, Vietnam was a quintessential liberal war, begun by Kennedy, escalated by Johnson, and run by a cabinet composed of the bulwarks of the Eastern liberal establishment: Robert McNamara, Dean Rusk, McGeorge Bundy, and William Bundy. So it is no surprise that it was primarily white radicals who first mobilized antiwar protest into a serious ongoing movement. An important oversight among radicals is that, within a few years, most rank-and-file liberals also opposed the war, including key members of the Johnson administration—even though this war was originally produced by liberal Democrats.

For many white youth in the 1960s, Vietnam was the key radicalizing experience. Despite the growth in the antiwar movement, many radicals were frustrated at their inability to stop the bloodshed. This led to increasingly aggressive tactics, such as breaking draft and public assembly laws, having violent confrontations with police, and harassing government officials. It was on this question of antiwar strategy that the liberals and radicals finally parted company. Liberals were repulsed by radical extremists, especially those who employed violent methods and were overtly supportive of North Vietnam. In their own opposition to the war, liberals did not want to sacrifice their commitments to due process, free speech and assembly, and civility. These were all values that were becoming more and more fragile during the turbulent 1960s and early 1970s.

Meanwhile, the most visible and vocal young civil rights protesters were continuing to move toward black nationalism, even separatism. Beginning in 1965, white members were dismissed from the Student Nonviolent Coordinating Committee (SNCC) and other militant organizations. In 1966, Stokely Carmichael's call for Black Power signaled the end of the civil rights focus of increasingly radical young blacks, especially those whose focus was moving toward urban economic and political issues. Their new goal was to have black people seek economic and political power on a group level and build autonomous communities of their own.

Most white supporters of civil rights were surprised and puzzled by these developments. Radical whites did not like being told that they could no longer work with their black comrades. They tried to understand the new situation; most, but not all, segments of the radical Left chose to support these new initiatives. White liberals could not. They were committed to interracial, rather than racially defined, organizations and the principle of integration. Central to the liberal tradition is a focus on the individual and the rights of individuals rather than on groups and group rights. Integration made sense to them because blacks and other minorities were to assimilate as individuals rather than as members of an entire group. The call for Black Power turned off white liberals, as did the related tendency of African Americans (and later other third world minorities) to form racially based caucuses within professional and other organizations.

Furthermore, Black Power and black nationalism conflicted with the liberal vision of a colorblind society, where race should be irrelevant, ideally not even noticed, in daily life. Indeed, this liberal response may be faulted for seeing only the racial dimensions of the new black consciousness movements and for minimizing the fact that black nationalism was in large measure a claim for recognition of the ethnic realities of African Americans. But at that time, few people of any political persuasion understood this.

Radicals, white and black, also can be faulted for a hasty and arrogant dismissal of legitimate liberal concerns as "covert" or "objective racism." Just the opposite was the case. In many real-life contexts, a colorblind approach can be rightly criticized as unrealistic, even naive. But the ethic of colorblindness still stems from an outlook that is radically anti-racist in spirit. White liberals were not given sufficient credit for the integrity of their values. Instead, the very term *white liberal* was used with disdain by the mid-1970s.

White radicals need to do some soul searching to acknowledge how we have contributed to the isolation of white liberals from the anti-racist struggle by disparaging their values and underestimating their sincerity. White liberals have often been unfairly stereotyped as a unidimensional political type. Liberals have been viewed as white backlashers par excellence. The liberal backlash is seen by many, especially black radicals, as nothing more than a polite cover for old-fashioned white racism. Liberals were prominent in the backlash against black gains, but for the most part they left the civil rights movement out of principled disagreement with its eventual racial, nationalist vision and physical and verbal violence. The response of the Left was to denigrate all opposition to black militancy as derived from racism and whites' unwillingness to give up racial privileges. It was only through listening carefully to some of the voices in my book, *Black Lives, White Lives* (1989), that I learned that whites were also defending certain values that were meaningful to them and to the society as a whole.

Some Reflections

What lies behind the all-or-nothing approach? The answer is self-righteousness—the belief that we and only we have the correct political line. This position assumes that we know the truth that everyone else, sooner or later, must come to recognize. This righteousness is particularly disruptive in anti-racist politics, which requires a broad coalition of diverse constituencies and can only succeed if it is based on a pluralistic, polycentric tolerance of a wide variety of outlooks.

Most refreshing about the new Left of the 1960s was its new outlook and spontaneity, which manifested itself early on in a rejection of ideology. But its strong passion was also a weakness, making it easier for radicals to dismiss, even demonize, liberals for *their* relative lack of passion and "purity." The new Left was without the old Left's strengths, that penchant for long-term planning, as well as the latter's history of working with liberals that came from a commitment to and experience of building united fronts.

It is time to get rid of our righteousness, to see that the truth is multifaceted and complex, that all political positions, including our own, have blind spots, and that others can contribute important parts of the truth. Liberals and radicals might begin—if they have not already—the process of reevaluating the 1960s and 1970s to understand better what went wrong, how we are still locked in old positions, and what might be done about it.

I propose also to replace righteousness with a spirit of generosity, a willingness to credit and acknowledge the contributions of others, especially where they were right and we were wrong. We radicals, for example, deserve credit for our early, principled, and tenacious opposition to the Vietnam War. Liberals deserve more credit than we give them for their early recognition that there were dangers in Black Power and black nationalism, and that angry anti-white rhetoric would have some negative long-term consequences.

This is not to suggest that mutual criticism should cease. I have already mentioned the difficulty that liberals have in recognizing the cultural distinctiveness of racial minorities. The motivation underlying this may often be benign: perhaps the desire to see nonwhites in terms of their universal human qualities or as American citizens. But such an attitude is too often accompanied by the belief that blacks and other minorities lack rich histories, cultures, and values. This makes it easier for some liberals to dismiss ethnic studies classes as "feel-good" exercises devoid of serious academic content and to oppose multiculturalism in education automatically.

To bridge the gap, we need serious dialogue. Liberals and radicals rarely communicate today. Instead, we perceive each other through off-putting stereotypes. I would like to see radicals make overtures to liberals, setting up conferences and symposia for exchanges on contemporary problems and the history of the 1960s.

ON RACISM AND RACISTS: THE NEED FOR NEW DIALOGUE

In the last chapter I wrote about the changes in the terminology of racial oppression, and how in the 1960s and 1970s the words *racism* and *racist* entered into the nation's common parlance with a vengeance and transformed the way Americans talk about race relations. The Left in the United States—and here I refer to radicals and progressives of all colors and to those intellectuals in and out of universities interested in anti-racism and multiculturalism—seized upon and developed the idea of racism into a master discourse. Racism became the chief weapon in the analysis of American race relations and in efforts to change a racially oppressive system. Now it is part of our general discourse as the politically correct way to talk about racial differences.

Much is positive about this. The discussion of racism has been part of massive public education about the history and present realities of racial oppression, an informal learning process that was initiated by the civil rights movement. *Racism* as a term is much better than previous usages in cutting through obfuscation, especially the American tendency to deny, minimize, or trivialize the pervasive nature of racial oppression. The idea of racism works beautifully as a sensitizing concept, alerting us to the larger social and economic structures and institutional relationships that maintain a society still stratified by color, as well as alerting us to the more subtle interpersonal dynamics of relations across lines of race and color.

But powerful as the idea of racism is, the larger discourse has itself become obfuscating, as well as contentious and politically divisive. With the term being used so broadly to mean everything to everyone, people have absorbed only those meanings with which they feel comfortable. Part of the culture wars is a contest between different groups as to which definition of racism will prevail in the larger society's meaning system. Because these differences are rarely spelled out, the battle over language takes place covertly, and in fact people talk about race past one another, as I elaborated on in the last chapter.

The problem with inflation in the meanings of racism is that the concept loses practical utility as well as believability. If everything and every place is racist, we have no conceptual tools to distinguish what is important from what is not. We are lost in the confusion of multiple meanings. This leads to political pessimism, because if racism is everywhere, then effectively nothing can be done about it.

When college and university students talk about race these days, students of color tend to lead these discussions and whites tend to be relatively quiet. In a sense, this is appropriate. Racial minorities have greater knowledge of the issues involved, both from their life experience and from their studies. They are the experts, although many resent always having to "educate" white students. But a considerable part of the white silence comes from fear, the fear of saying the wrong thing and then being branded a racist. Thus, those whites who do talk tend to express a safe Left-leaning line of thought.

This, of course, is politically correct (PC) language. Many on the Left typically dismiss the PC critique as a red herring, blown up by conservatives who have been using PC as a screen to undermine their real targets: multiculturalism, affirmative action, and larger movements for diversity, inclusion, and social equality. I disassociate myself from such a view, but I have also found in my teaching that today's overheated racism discourse does inhibit openness and freedom of expression. Not only whites but Asians, Latinos, and African Americans have privately expressed to me their frustrations in not being able to share serious reservations, deep feelings, and confusing personal experiences that they might have on the subject of race.

This is a serious matter. Freedom of expression is a basic, indispensable human value, one that supposedly defines American democracy. It is also absolutely essential for anti-racist education. If people cannot speak out, negative feelings and prejudices only harden. For people to gain the kind of personal growth and intellectual development out of which they come to understand and appreciate the experiences of racial others, we must have an atmosphere in which discussion of all views and experiences is possible.

I do not feel that the ambiguities and contradictions inherent in the idea of racism can be fully resolved. Racism by definition has to contain both the potential for divisiveness and the potential for reconciliation and healing. The discourse of racism challenges the basic character of the European-American experience, forcing reevaluation of the historical meaning of being white in America. It implicates most European Americans in the history of colonialism and racial domination, even those whose families have not been in the country long. It therefore will inevitably bring forth resistance and anger. All this is part of the ambiguity and the dilemma we face, that the idea of racism and its larger discourse suggest that the nation has much unfinished business and that we all share a responsibility for the legacy of injustice and present-day inequalities.

In sum, the way we talk about racism more often reinforces the negative, divisive side rather than the positive possibilities for healing that an anti-racist movement must be centered around. People on the Left are often on a "racism alert," exhibiting a compulsive need to show how we have surmounted our own racism. The result is to highlight the racist tendencies of American people, life styles, and institutions, and to cut ourselves off from those ordinary whites to whom racism does not seem pertinent to their everyday lives and who do not want to feel guilty about something over which they feel—rightly or wrongly—they have so little control. At the same time, radicals are neglecting the other pole, the possibilities for supporting and nurturing the inherent democratic anti-racist tendencies that most Americans, regardless of race, have within.

SOME SUGGESTIONS

Radicals have a responsibility in the area of discourse, because we played a major role in creating today's PC language. The discourse on race needs to be loosened and allowed to be more honest. I am not advocating license to use offensive group names and characterizations, but simply suggesting that we stop censoring the use of such commonplace and commonsense terminology as racial prejudice, nonwhite, minority, and even Negro. Indeed, some white radicals today seem reluctant to use the word *black,* feeling that only *African American* has the stamp of approval. The Left's penchant to censor so many words, not just in race but throughout all dimensions of social difference, means that our speech and more of the nation's discourse have become unnatural and cumbersome.

The key term is *racism.* It is so entrenched in common speech that there is no way to eliminate its use or dethrone it from its central place, even if we wanted to. What I advocate instead is to push that word over to the side and make room for the occasional use of some older terms, especially when more precise and less inflammatory language will help begin and maintain dialogue.

Above all, we need to slow down, if not halt entirely, the tendency to call people racists when we do not like their views on racial issues. The escalating tendency of the past few decades to label people and positions racist has become counterproductive. When applied to individuals, the term should be limited to those who overtly advocate white supremacy or disseminate hate-filled characterizations of any racial or ethnic group. Otherwise, we need to give people the benefit of the doubt and assume that most of us are people of good will. Most Americans, whether they were born here or immigrated, inevitably absorb ideas, feelings, and assumptions about the superiority of white Westerners. We all harbor doubts at times about the equality of other races. In reality, we are all in a sense racist.

In addition to the racist in all of us, a resident belief in fairness and in our nation's historic commitment (at least in theory) to democracy exists. With such internal conflicts between racism and equality, the racial thinking of European Americans and people of color is inconsistent. I was continually struck in *Black Lives, White Lives* that the same person would in one breath utter a prejudiced, stereotyped platitude and in the next show a deep commitment to racial justice, a remarkable understanding of the racial politics of the day, or a profound belief in the fair and equal treatment of minority groups. Then would come another idea tinged with bias, distrust, or racial antagonism. Perhaps we need to find ways to encourage the democratic tendency rather than simply hammering away at hidden racist ones.

The issue of labeling particular policies and positions *racist* is more complex. It is important to be careful here, to think a situation through and analyze it before throwing around this double-edged term, which has such a potential to polarize. When charges of racism make sense because they strike a nerve, the ability to educate the public and force a constructive change in policy is also impressive. An example is Jean-Bertrand Aristide's charge that U.S. policy toward Haiti was racist because immigrants who are black were turned back whereas white Cuban immigrants were welcomed, despite fleeing Cuba for many of the same reasons Haitians were fleeing their country.

The trouble with the idea of racism is that it inevitably takes on a personal meaning, even when we try to use it impersonally to connote systems and structures of racial oppression, such as institutionalized racism.

The popular mind does not understand the idea that racism refers to objective or structural realities, the meaning that social scientists and third world activists tend to favor. For most ordinary people, especially European Americans, racism refers to feelings and attitudes and actions. I have tried to explain the larger idea of racism as an impersonal force to popular audiences without success. Many white college students have the same problem and immediately confuse objective with subjective racism. They feel they are being attacked personally as racists, even when that is not the intention.

Many African-American intellectuals and militants have seized upon this objective–subjective distinction to argue that black people cannot be racist because they lack the power to institute or uphold structures of domination. The assumption that black people cannot be racist serves as a green light among some African Americans to legitimate the expression of crude stereotypes and hatreds of ethnic groups (most notably Jews), expressions that would be unacceptable if voiced by whites. I do not think the Left should countenance such attitudes, or defend them. Black anti-Semitism is a form of racism and should be labeled as such.

THE ANTI-RACIST POTENTIAL OF WHITE PEOPLE

As I have suggested throughout this chapter, an anti-racist movement needs wide participation and support from the European-American majority and cannot be successfully developed by people of color or radicals alone. The best strategy for gaining such wide support is to begin viewing white people in terms of their strengths, that is, their possibilities for growth in consciousness and for the transcendence of racism. There have always been white Americans on the frontlines against racism. The anti-racist struggle has never been simply a black-against-white event. Ignorance of this history and of the contemporary reality of principled white opposition to racism is essential to the belief that nothing can be done against racism.

I see two ways to approach this. The first is to emphasize the diversity of the European-American population. Whites should not be viewed monolithically any more than blacks or any other people are. When one looks at whites in their particularity and diversity—rather than globally as "white people"—then one can see that white people in their distinct identities have many positive values. By building upon the strengths specific to a group's character and outlook, we can try to find ways to help its anti-racist possibilities blossom.

In the case of white liberals, I have tried to indicate the positive values in that group's outlook. These include an emphasis on individual rights, a commitment to integration and colorblindness, a strong moral sensitivity to the means of political action and the value of civility, and an abhorrence of violence. Like that of any group, the mentality of the liberal contains blind spots and limitations, some of which I have already alluded to. But for the purpose of nurturing anti-racist potential, the better strategy is to honor liberals' positive virtues, to take their contributions seriously, and to learn from them.

The radical Left as a politically conscious group has its virtues, having made immeasurable contributions to the struggle for racial justice. Because their political work is typically informed by social theory—Marxist or otherwise—radicals often see "the big picture" and are able to place racial phenomena in historical and international contexts. The radical penchant to see race as a structural rather than an individual matter has been illuminating, as well as the related insight that racial and ethnic conflicts need to be examined not only in their own right, but as part of larger systems of economic classes. In this context, the Left's critique of the culture of capitalism is important for anti-racist work, because the capitalist valuing of money, competition, and consumption helps keep racial and other hierarchies entrenched.

Jews are the white ethnic group with the most impressive history of commitment to racial equality. It has been estimated that 50 percent or more of the whites who volunteered to work for civil rights in the South during the 1960s were Jewish Americans. This unique dedication stems from the group's identification as an oppressed minority and from a specific ethnic capacity to identify with "underdogs." Both of these traits have been encouraged and fortified by a religious tradition that strongly emphasizes social justice.

The much discussed Jewish–black conflict stems from recent historical divisions and conflicts of interests, because many Jews occupy positions of authority and privilege that—in perception or reality—block the social and economic advance of African Americans. But part of the conflict is also psychological, in that the Jewish–black alliance was too much of a big brother–little brother relationship, with all the paternalism, resentment, condescension, and envy inherent in such inequality. The key to welcoming greater numbers of Jews back into an anti-racist coalition is to acknowledge the special contributions that this ethnic and religious group has made to civil rights and social justice—in America and around the world—rather than to label it (or any other group) as particularly racist.

Then there are "white ethnics"—collective term that encompasses "hyphenated" Americans who immigrated to the United States from Europe in the late nineteenth and early twentieth centuries. I will leave to others the task of discussing the anti-racist traditions of these groups, and instead say something about a related category that long has been seen as particularly bigoted, the white blue-collar worker. White blue-collar workers have derived such a reputation because of their visibility in attempting to keep blacks out of "their" unions, jobs, and neighborhoods. Unlike middle-class whites, they could not use class privilege to shield themselves from the tensions of racial change. They lived in the neighborhoods and attended the schools facing integration, and worked in the jobs where blacks and other minorities could most easily enter the workforce. All this made the Archie Bunker stereotype plausible, but unjustifiable.

Blue-collar workers actually have been more "multicultural" than the rest of us for many decades. Working closely with people of color on the job, they get to know minorities on a more than superficial level. Because of their own class position, they are often able to identify with the experience of racial oppression. Blue-collar whites are also very job oriented and they judge people on how well they do their work. A strategy for nurturing the anti-racist potential of the white working class is to continue breaking down racial barriers in employment. White workers unlearn their racial stereotypes through equal-status contacts with people on the job. Like all working people, they need a thriving economy and full employment so that economic anxieties and class-based resentments are not channeled toward people of color.

Finally, a category with a particularly strong anti-racist potential is that of young people, including college students. Even though so much racial violence and bigotry has surfaced in the younger generation in recent decades, the anti-racist impulses among white youth and college students are very strong. White youth are like political liberals in their yearning for a colorblind society, and they have a strong desire to get to know people of all kinds. Youth are particularly open to new experiences and ways of seeing the world. They learn from these experiences as well as from books. Thus, it is important that white students at all levels be exposed to outstanding black, Latino, Asian, and Native American instructors, as this in itself is a powerful education in anti-racism. It is essential that our classrooms provide a climate for free and open discussion about race and other sensitive topics.

The development of anti-racist consciousness in white people does not always require direct confrontation with racist beliefs, but is moved by any process that enhances self-knowledge and personal development. Thus, virtually all of today's personal growth, consciousness, self-help, and political movements can be viewed as allies in anti-racist work. Experiences sustained over time and supported by organizational involvement deepen awareness of the range of human feelings and expand consciousness. Whether the internal changes are political, emotional, spiritual, or some combination of the three, they enhance the potential for a greater understanding of racism. Personal racism is based on fear—not simply of the unknown racial other, but also of our own unacceptable feelings and inner complexities.

An example of the type of movement I have in mind would be any of the ubiquitous twelve-step or other recovery movements. The strength of such movements is that they are truly popular and cut across race and class. Directly multiracial experiences are especially valuable for enlarging the human capacity to identify across racial boundaries.

Countless examples could be cited of white people's capacity to "unlearn" racism from life experience simply as part of the process of becoming more fully human. Studs Terkel presents many such cases in *Race*. One of the more dramatic stories is that of C. P. Ellis, a former Klan official, who developed a friendship with a black female political opponent that in time undermined the entire structure of his beliefs.[7] There have been several reports of young White Power activists "seeing the light" and converting to the cause of anti-racism. Lee Mun Wah's documentary film, *The Color of Fear*, depicts the case of David, a white, forty-ish Californian, whose prototypical liberal-conservative viewpoint on race seems invulnerable through most of a weekend of dialogue between men of different races. Despite all his defenses and rationalizations, the stories and feelings of the other men finally get to him. Central to his dramatic transformation is a new ability to listen to the experiences and the pain of men of color. In so doing, the racial other becomes like himself, a fellow human being. Something similar often happens with white college students when they see a documentary such as *Eyes on the Prize* and for the first time begin to understand the historical legacy of racism.

Finally, many white radicals and third world theorists question the anti-racist potential of European Americans, stressing that "white skin privileges" give us an objective interest, a real stake in the continuance of the present system. Almost everyone has some interest in the status quo, if only because we have made some modicum of peace with it. And without doubt, white skin continues to provide many advantages. But whites have an even greater interest in a just society. Given the average person's declining level of economic and social security and relative lack of real power, it is hard to argue that these white privileges can compare in importance with all the pain and loss everyone suffers from living in a society so divided, so lacking in real community, and so rent with underlying hatreds. These losses are political, moral, and spiritual and they are directly related to race. The potential for whites to change exists and must be recognized and worked with. We have no other alternative to reverse the course of racial inequality in the United States and to form the coalitions that will be necessary to change the political and economic direction of this country.

15 Blacks and Jews

A Study in Ambivalence

For most of the twentieth century the bulwark of the America's liberal-Left anti-racist coalition was the alliance between Jews and blacks. Our nation's most visible minorities shared an interest in the elimination of both anti-Semitism and antiblack racism, for in that period the same hardcore extremists tended to hate Jews and blacks with an equal passion. But this alliance broke down during the 1960s for reasons that are analyzed well in Jonathan Kaufmann's excellent study, *Broken Alliance.*[1]

By the 1990s, black anti-Semitism and the relationship between African Americans and Jewish Americans had become one of the hottest topics in the media. In the Crown Heights neighborhood of Brooklyn, where blacks and Hasidic Jews live in an uneasy proximity, tensions had erupted in violence. Louis Farrakhan and other Black Muslim spokesmen influenced audiences with anti-Jewish tirades. A book was published that aimed to prove that Jews had controlled the slave trade that brought Africans to America in the eighteenth and nineteenth centuries. It was even argued that a conspiracy of Jews was behind Martin Luther King, Jr.'s assassination.

My task in this essay is to explain the paradox that the most disturbing—and certainly the noisiest—expressions of anti-Semitism in the 1990s were coming from the most liberal of all American ethnic groups, a group with a long history of political alliance with Jews.

With the economic prosperity of the Clinton era, it is easy for college-age readers to forget that America had a stagnant, no-growth economy for the almost twenty-year period between 1973 and 1992. The economic impasse, marked by high levels of unemployment and a decline in real income because of inflation, was the backdrop for black anti-Semitism, as well as for an upsurge in antiblack racism and increases in violent acts against other vulnerable minorities—Asian Americans, immigrants, and homosexuals. It seems to be the American way for minority groups under economic and social attack to respond by scapegoating one another, rather than entering into coalitions to force reform of the overall power structure.

This chapter was first published in *Tikkun,* a liberal magazine of opinion and the arts. Although *Tikkun's* readership is broad-based, the fact that it is a Jewish-oriented publication explains why my essay ends with a number of suggestions for action that American Jews can take to help resolve the crisis in black–Jewish relations.

This chapter originally appeared as "That Black–Jewish Thing," *Tikkun* 9(5) (September/October 1994), pp. 27–32, 103. Reprinted by permission from *Tikkun: A Bimonthly Jewish Critique of Politics, Culture & Society.*

LATE IN May 1994 at San Francisco State University, in the week before final exams, an African-American artist named Senay Dennis unfurled a mural he had painted to honor Malcolm X and his legacy. The mural was commissioned by the Student Union Governing Board, and the artist was paid $1,500 in student funds. The idea that Malcolm was worthy of a major artistic monument was evidently universally accepted on this very multicultural urban campus, a place that pioneered "third world" or ethnic studies in the late 1960s as well as faculty unionism on the West Coast. What was controversial was the fact that the artist had surrounded the image of black nationalism's patron saint with Stars of David, which were next to dollar signs, skull and crossbones, and the phrase "African Blood."

The artist and his supporters argued that these symbols were anti-Zionist and not anti-Jewish, and that they faithfully reflected Malcolm X's vision. This so incensed an African-American English professor, Lois Lyles, that she got herself arrested in the act of painting "Stop Prejudice" on the mural. Robert Corrigan, the president of S.F. State, was criticized by some for waiting too long before he ordered the mural painted over and by others for a heavy-handed confrontational mode of operation, including "censorship" of a duly commissioned work of art. The president of San Francisco's Hillel Center, David Bergman, supported the idea of honoring Malcolm and therefore regretted that the mural was constructed in such a way that it had to be destroyed in its entirety in order to remove the anti-Semitic symbols. And it seems that most black students at the school were as opposed to Dennis's exploitation of Malcolm X for his own purposes as were white and other students.

The controversy evoked not only storm, but serious discussions of the meaning of multiculturalism and about how racially divided the campus really was. Many felt that the media exacerbated such divisions by portraying the mural story as a reflection of black–Jewish conflict, rather than reflecting only the views of a tiny, die-hard minority.

The S.F. State mural incident is only the latest example of a disturbing pattern of events, in which certain prominent black figures publicly express strong anti-Jewish sentiments. Since black–Jewish tensions were exacerbated three years ago in New York City's Crown Heights, there have been many reports of anti-Semitic utterances, especially in campus appearances by Nation of Islam leader Louis Farrakhan and his former lieutenant Khalid Muhammad. From Professor Leonard Jeffries, Farrakhan, Muhammad, and the students attending their talks have come such assertions as that the Jews controlled the slave trade, that Jews dominate American society today, and perhaps the most outrageous, that Jews killed Martin Luther King, Jr. (the latter reportedly from a recent event at Howard University). And on a number of college campuses, the pressure of black student organizations and the fear of protest and rioting have forced cancellation of scheduled talks by such Jews as Jack Greenberg, the former director of the NAACP's Legal Defense Committee, and the historian David Brion Davis, noted for his writings on racism.

This tendency of some African Americans to target Jews as an especially powerful and racist segment of America has evoked fear, anger, puzzlement, and perhaps above all a sense of betrayal in Jewish Americans. Many Jews have been almost as angry at prominent African Americans who have failed to speak out against black anti-Semitism as they were at the perpetrators. But above all they cannot understand why blacks, of all people, would be turning against them. The historical memory of Jews tends to be well developed, and people know that 50 percent or more of the white volunteers for Mississippi's 1964 Freedom Summer were Jewish, including both of the white martyrs, Andrew Goodman and Michael Schwerner; that Jewish philanthropy made possible the "historically Negro colleges"; and that their group has long been in the vanguard of movements for racial equality. Many of my Jewish students see their group and African Americans as the two most important historically oppressed peoples. With such "similar interests," they feel that today we should be allies rather than antagonists.

Particularly in the aftermath of the Holocaust, Jews are very sensitive to any cues that non-Jews are diminishing the importance of anti-Semitism. Thus, I was disappointed at a recent debate on multiculturalism on the Berkeley campus, when one of the panelists, Ronald Takaki, responded to fellow panelist Nathan Glazer's concerns about the anti-Semitism of Leonard Jeffries's public statements by deeming them "insignificant." Takaki, a professor of ethnic studies, was a major architect of Berkeley's American Cultures requirement, an innovative program exploring the experiences of European-American ethnic groups as well as racial minorities. As a personal friend, I know Takaki's concern about anti-Semitism, especially its impact on young blacks who respond to the statements of Khalid Mohammad and others of his ilk. But because Takaki chose to emphasize the relative insignificance of Jeffries's distortions compared to the pervasive distortion of people of color in conventional scholarship, he missed a chance to denounce anti-Semitism clearly and strongly. As a Jew interested in building bridges between the multicultural movement and European Americans, I keenly regretted that missed opportunity.

Another way that black anti-Semitism can be downplayed is to argue that because such feelings are shared by only a small number of African Americans, the importance of the problem is exaggerated, more a matter of media sensationalism than of substance. In a recent conversation with another friend, the sociologist Hardy Frye, the latter argued that the extremist promoters of anti-Jewish feelings lack substantial following in the black community

While it is true that the media do not give as much attention to the efforts that are being made to restore dialogue and reconciliation between blacks and Jews as they do to provocative statements and divisive conflict, I think Frye is wrong on this point. All indications are that anti-Semitism has increased among African Americans in recent years, especially among the younger generation. And this includes not only streetwise youth of the urban centers, but those college-educated blacks who have been influenced by Afrocentric perspectives. And it is the latter group that will produce many future leaders of the African-American community.

Having said this, I take recent poll data that indicate that African Americans are more likely to be anti-Semitic than other Americans with a grain of salt. It's my hunch that black people tend to feel more strongly about Jews than most other Gentiles do because the histories and fates of the two groups have been so closely intertwined in America. So if there are more African Americans who dislike and resent Jews, there are probably also more who like and admire us. I agree with Cornel West, who implies in his book *Race Matters* that although on the rise recently, anti-Semitism among blacks has been less pronounced in the past than it has been among other non-Jews. But despite the importance of these questions about whether black anti-Semitism has increased and deepened, I don't think they are the most interesting or the most important questions for understanding black–Jewish relations today.

Instead I would pose the following: First, why are the noisiest and most disturbing expressions of anti-Jewish sentiment in the United States today being voiced by some African Americans? Second, why have these attitudes been able to gain *some* legitimacy in their communities? Third, given that recent history makes African Americans particularly ready to scapegoat others for their frustrations, why have *some* selected Jews as the target? And finally, what about Jews? What is our responsibility in this conflict and how can we act constructively today?

The years since the election of Ronald Reagan in 1980 have been a disastrous period for African Americans. Of all ethnic groups, blacks have been most affected by the politics and the culture of conservative retrenchment, a climate in which a selfish mean-spiritedness has replaced social compassion, in which politicians have deserted the interests of civil rights, racial minorities, and the poor. The no-growth economy of the 1970s was an even greater disaster, creating for the 1990s a situation unique in America: one in which the average real income for workers seemed to be in permanent decline; in which the new jobs produced tended to be markedly lower in pay and security than the old jobs lost. As a consequence, the new generations of youth will not, on average, be able to match the living standards of their parents. And yet the rich get richer, while the poor get poorer and the middle classes are increasingly squeezed.

In such a political and economic climate, ethnic and racial antagonisms escalate, given that class struggle is not the American Way. Instead, we scapegoat the most vulnerable groups: new immigrants, Asian Americans, and homosexuals—as well as the two venerable targets of group hatred, black people and Jews.

It is naive to believe that African Americans should be any more immune to the American disease of group-hating-group than any other sector of our society. In the 1960s and 1970s they were promised the freedom and equality for which their people had striven for centuries. But instead, even successful middle-class blacks have been experiencing rising levels of racism (both on an interpersonal level, for example in occupational life, and in the larger society). And for those who are poor or working class, frustrations brought on by the economic situation and the political climate breed anger and a strong sense of betrayal. Hopes have been dashed, people are mad, and they are going to lash out.

And why not lash out at the Jews? Just as most young whites know almost nothing of the nation's history of racism, having been born too late to experience first hand the 1960s civil rights era, young blacks know just as little about the times when Jewish Americans and African Americans were comrades in arms.

Over the long haul, black Americans have been noteworthy—not for their hatred of white people, which would be understandable, considering their historic treatment—but for their ability to transcend hatred and maintain a humanistic belief in the possibilities of change and redemption. And this remains in large part true. But I believe that in recent years the racial hatreds of African Americans, including the recent hatred of Jews, have been given a new legitimacy—perhaps pseudo-legitimacy is a better term—that comes from the Left's "politically correct" discourse on race and racism.

During the 1960s, there was an explosion of new understandings, definitions, and meanings of the term "racism," which soon became the primary expression to denote racial oppression in America. Whereas most white people—aside from a minority of leftists, intellectuals, and academic social scientists—continued to view racism primarily as beliefs, feelings, and actions based on group stereotypes and hatred (that is, in terms of the 1950s model of prejudice and discrimination), many blacks began to see racism as a structural phenomenon. Seizing on a distinction between subjective and objective racism, many blacks argue that although African Americans can be as prejudiced as anyone, they can't be racist because they lack the power to institute or uphold structures of domination or to impose their views on others. I frequently hear this argument in the classroom, and it is a line of thought that is familiar to me because I helped develop and disseminate it and similar ideas in my sociological writings during the late 1960s and 1970s.

Perhaps twenty-five years ago I thought that the kind of distinctions sociologists make would so impress and educate the public that they would readily adopt our understandings and definitions. It hasn't happened. Although we influence, we cannot control the public's use of language. And while racism did replace prejudice as the key term in the language of race, for most people it retains the same "subjective" connotation as does prejudice. Therefore there is something quite disingenuous about those who argue that black people can't be racist, because they know that they are engaged in verbal sleight-of-hand. Even so, this rationalization is useful in dealing with their cognitive dissonance and in serving as a green light among some African Americans to legitimate the expression of crude stereotypes and hatreds of ethnic groups (most notably, but not exclusively, Jews), expressions that would be totally unacceptable if voiced by whites. I do not think the Left should countenance such attitudes, nor such an intellectualized defense of them. Black anti-Semitism is a form of racism and should be labelled as such.

But if the special frustrations of the black population—the combination of economic hardship and the lack of future prospects, especially for the young—help explain this new black anger and need to strike back, we still need to ask, why the Jews? There was plenty of anger in the Black Power era (1965 to 1975), plenty of accusations that some African Americans were engaging in a reverse form of black racism. But then the target was almost always "whitey," "honkey," white folks in general, very rarely Jews or any other specific ethnic group.

The late 1960s was a critical period. The Jewish–black alliance may have already been dead by 1966, when black nationalism and Black Power replaced integration as the major focus of the movement. But three events between 1967 and 1969 can be seen as the nails that sealed its coffin: first, the Six-Day War of 1967, in which black militant leaders sided with Israel's Arab enemies; second, the battle for community control of the schools, especially in Ocean-Hill Brownsville, where the teachers and union leaders who stood in the way of black parents and political organizers were overwhelmingly Jewish; and finally, the institutionalization of affirmative-action programs in 1968 and 1969. Jewish liberals and neo-conservatives took the lead in providing the intellectual and political arguments against these programs, which furthered anti-Jewish sentiment among black Americans.

And yet anti-Semitism per se remained tempered, contained to small circles for many years. Why? I think it's because in the Black Power decade there was still a lively personal and political dialogue between blacks and whites, blacks and Jews. Like other Left-liberal and radical whites, Jews were drawn to groups such as the Black Panthers, who saw the racist, capitalist system, rather than specific ethnic and racial groups, as the enemy. Jews were prominent among white financial supporters of the Panthers, and indeed Huey Newton is reported to have had a Jewish grandfather. (When he took a PLO-sponsored trip to the Middle East in the late 1970s, Newton insisted that his itinerary include Israel, so that he would get both sides of the story.)

Since the 1980s, this heated though rich and honest dialogue between whites and blacks has been largely absent. And during the 1980s and 1990s the leading voices of black nationalism have moved away from the inclusiveness of a latter-day Malcolm X and the Black Panthers. At the same time, main-line civil rights groups and leaders have lost much of their authority. The consequent moral and political vacuum explains the increasingly important role that the Black Muslims and Louis Farrakhan in particular play in providing some ideological direction for black anger and frustration. Combine this paucity of leadership with the economic hopelessness I've already described, and the result is a nihilism and des-peration in black America, which is why so many African Americans are listening to Farrakhan and other anti-Semitic voices in a serious way.

Furthermore, it is only in the case of the African-American minority where we have this peculiar marriage of a nationalist movement associ-ated with Islam, a religion, culture, and politics which is often at war with Judaism and Zionism. In the case of Latinos and Asian Americans, such a "natural" opening to anti-Semitism does not exist.

How ironic that, aside from explicitly neo-Nazi and Aryan "White Power" groups, it is Afro-Americans who are today the primary perpet-uators of Hitler's thought in America. But this is in part because the anti-Semitic discourse that Hitler tapped into and popularized is entrenched in Western culture and deep in the popular psyche. So these archetypal images of the deceitful and all-powerful Jew can be used by any leader when he wants to play demagogue, even leaders of organizations like the Nation of Islam, which otherwise do much that is positive for their mem-bers. Thus the recent allegation that Jews killed Martin Luther King, Jr., echoes the 2,000-year-old belief that Jews killed Jesus, and if, as *The Pro-*

tocols of the Elders of Zion say, Jews have long controlled world finance and economic life, then they must have controlled slavery and the slave trade also.

Jews also became a ready target because we have a special visibility, continuing to stand out through our cultural style, sensibility, and names, if no longer by appearance. And so often Jews just happen to be in those positions where they have some power and control (even if limited) over African Americans. I've mentioned the educational system, the contested terrain during the 1960s. At that time, Jews were still frequently storekeepers in Harlem and other ghettoes. Now Koreans or other Asians, and sometimes Arab Americans occupy such "middle man" positions in urban black neighborhoods, reminding us that Jews are not the only ethnic targets of black anger.

Perhaps anti-Semitism is the underlying motive when Farrakhan and others assert that Jews control the media. But the prominence of Jewish Americans in intellectual and cultural life—in the universities, in Hollywood, in television writing and producing, in book publishing, as owners and editors of such important newspapers as the *New York Times,* as well as our significant role in other journals of opinion—should not be dismissed as unimportant.

In recent years, the racial struggle is being waged more and more on the cultural front. What is at stake is control of those images of black people that the wider public gets from television and film, as well as the control of the interpretations of race relations that are provided by the "opinion leaders" who write books and publish their ideas in newspapers, magazines, and academic journals. African Americans want a greater representation in these positions so that they can determine how their historical and contemporary realities are interpreted—Spike Lee can do only so much.

Consider how many of the writers and critics on jazz and black music are Jewish, how predominant Jews have been among the white experts on black history, black culture, and the sociology of race relations. It matters less today that these Jewish writers have been liberal or radical and black-affirmative; for the Afrocentric movement, all this is a negative situation that needs to be changed.

Finally, I think many blacks have turned against Jews precisely because the two groups have been closely connected in the past. Many people have used the language of family to talk about these ties, which have been described as fraternal or paternal but never as one of equal partners. African Americans have constantly chafed under and worked against the paternalism inherent in this inequality. And since such a relationship cannot easily be reformed, it tends to be ended through abrupt and almost violent rituals of separation, as in the Black Power period when whites (read Jews) were ejected from the Student Nonviolent Coordinating Committee (SNCC) and other civil rights organizations, or as in today's angry anti-Jewish rhetoric.

All this distrust, envy, and hatred is the underside of an African-American identification with and admiration of Jewish Americans. This identification has deep roots in black religion and folk culture. The "Hebrew Children" in the spirituals stood for Africans enslaved in America. Blacks have also admired (and envied) the Jewish capacity for business success, which they see as coming from an ethnic affinity for "sticking together." This is typically contrasted with a characteristic disunity in black communities and seen as the key to the impressive political and cultural power that Jews, a group small in numbers, command. But if the older brother has all the power, he must be using the younger one for his own purposes—enhancing his ego needs through domination, appropriating cultural riches for profit, exploiting black people in countless other ways.

And Jews make an excellent target for charges of racism and exploitation, not because Jews are a particularly racist sector of the white population, but for the very opposite reason. Cornel West points out that blacks have had higher expectations of Jews than they have had of other whites, so that when some Jews become point men in the attack on affirmative action, blacks feel betrayed and unfortunately generalize their anger toward the group as a whole. And from the other side, the strong anti-racism of Jewish Americans makes us more vulnerable to attack, prone to feelings of guilt and responsibility.

Just what is the Jewish role and responsibility in all this? Jewish Americans admire and envy much about African Americans: their rich political history, the profound moral voice of their greatest leaders, the depth and creativity of black culture and art, not to mention the prowess and stylistic flair of black athletes. Jews were among the first whites to "discover" these gifts, to recognize their importance and meaning and to market the African-American aesthetic sensibility to the white American public. During the 1960s, such sponsorship came to be seen as a quasi-colonial appropriation and exploitation of the culture of an indigenous people. This viewpoint remains widely shared today, especially among young blacks and Afrocentric intellectuals.

Just as blacks have often identified with Jews, Jews have gone even further in identifying with blacks—sometimes in ways that seem inappropriate, even ludicrous, to the latter. When we "over-identify" with African Americans and the black experience, the result is a blurring of boundaries and an insensitivity to the other's needs for autonomy and control.

Another result can be an almost pathetic desire to be accepted by black

people, to be looked up to by them, and to be honored for one's unpreju-
diced attitudes. Thus, many Jews feel a nostalgic longing for the days of the
Negro–Jewish alliance. But Golden Ages never return, and the hard fact is
that the "objective conditions" for that historic alliance no longer exist.

It is not just the now-marked gap in economic status and social power
between the two groups. Perhaps even more important, as Julius Lester has
deftly argued, blacks and Jews no longer share a common moral community. "Regardless of how an individual Jew may feel about being a Jew,"
he observes, "the solidity of Jewish history, culture, and religion are incon-
trovertible. It is the very absence of confidence among African Americans
in the solidity of life itself that marks the gulf between Blacks and Jews."
Blacks, Lester suggests, drawing on Laurence Thomas and Orlando Patterson, have "neither equality nor their historical-cultural traditions," and
thus black anti-Semitism may at bottom reflect "envy of the Jewish narrative and the painful longing for a healing narrative of their own."

So I suggest that Jews become sensitive to the pain blacks feel when we
insensitively argue that our shared oppression is more important than our
differences. This means that we Jews should fight racism because it is right
to do so, and it is in the interest of our country as well as our own ethnic
group, but not for the approval of African Americans so that we can
march arm-in-arm once again.

Overidentification can also result in a tendency for Jews to equate slavery and racial oppression in America with their own historic oppression.
Some Jews use the Holocaust as a benchmark to weigh and legitimate the
claims of others to be victims of persecution, a smugness that implies a
belief in a special entitlement to be certified as experts in matters of social
oppression. Such an attitude rankles "many African Americans," who,
according to Walter Fields of the New Jersey NAACP, have the notion
"that somehow Jews have cornered the market on suffering." African
Americans are more likely to feel that "if any group is the American exem-
plar of deprivation and oppression," it is their own or perhaps American
Indians. Farrakhan puts it more strongly: "The holocaust of black people
was 100 times worse than the holocaust of Jews."

The bottom line is that Jews can be as racist as anyone. This is not to deny
that Jews also have demonstrated a unique commitment to social justice,
including racial equality for African Americans, a fact which has not gone
unnoticed by them, even before the recent statement of Urban League
president Hugh Price that no other group of whites has "matched the Jewish community as long-distance runners in the civil rights movement."

Price goes on to suggest that some blacks have been impugning "long-
standing allies" such as the Jews "because of the unconscionable behav-

ior of some of them." It is not clear who he is referring to, but it is certainly true that over the past thirty years, Jews have not been as exclusively Left and liberal-leaning as we once were. Now spread out along the entire political spectrum, Jewish America today produces some of the nation's leading conservative voices, as well as such powerful political players on the Right as Henry Kissinger.

But despite such internal diversity, Jewish Americans as a group, as Michael Lerner points out, consistently support liberal positions on the controversial questions of the day. More than any other group, Jews resisted the swing of white voters to Reagan and Bush and still vote against their (narrowly defined) economic interests in favor of social programs for the poor. This "Jewish exceptionalism" may be waning as the assimilation process continues apace. But because of Judaism's social ethic and a historic tendency to identify with underdogs, Jews are still more likely than other whites to understand that their racial and class privileges pale in significance compared to the costs of racial and economic injustice—the pain and loss we suffer from living in a society so divided, so lacking in real community, and so rent with deep hatreds and alienation.

My arguments are not meant to deny that Jews are, and probably will always be a special minority, with an unparalleled history of persecution that reached its apogee in the Holocaust. Even if we are no longer poor and even if the institutionalized anti-Semitism which once kept Jews from fully participating in American society is largely a thing of the past—in contrast to the depth and subtlety of antiblack racism—we have learned from the experience of Hitler's Germany that economic mobility and cultural assimilation guarantee very little. Jews know that, as a group, they have been offered up as a sacrificial lamb during those periods of history when mankind expresses its darkest impulses. Such expressions of humanity's dark side continue around the world today; because of this, it is not surprising that many Jews persist in feeling a common interest with black Americans in developing an anti-racist politics. And indeed blacks and Jews remain the favorite targets of White Power movements based on hatred and bigotry.

The strains in black–Jewish relations should not be seen in isolation, but rather as one important aspect of the breakdown in the multifaceted civil rights coalition that existed until the mid-1960s. Another important loss for civil rights has been the decline in numbers and social power of organized labor, a fact which has contributed to the conservative drift among white blue-collar workers. Perhaps most pivotal of all—and largely unrecognized—has been the split between white liberals and white radicals that took place in the late 1960s. The mutual antagonism and lack of dialogue between white liberals and white radicals makes it difficult, perhaps impossible, to develop a mass anti-racist movement that would draw upon significant numbers of European Americans.

Without waiting for this to happen, I believe that Jews remain uniquely positioned to play a special role in the fight against racism. If the State of Israel can designate selected Germans and other Europeans as "Righteous Gentiles" because they resisted meaningfully the destruction of the Jews, we could by example encourage others to be Righteous European Americans. We may not be able to give up our class and racial privileges, but we can take the lead, through our actions and our consciousness, in giving up "white" ways of thinking and identifying.

On returning from a visit to Israel, a group of American blacks were puzzled, according to Gerald Early, the chair of the African and Afro-American Studies Department at Washington University, Saint Louis, as to "why Blacks had not done more to embrace the memory of slavery as Jews had the Holocaust." But the memorialization of slavery and racism is not simply the responsibility of African Americans. All of us suffer from the unfinished business of our racial past. The nation as a whole needs to collectively mourn our racial "holocausts"—including the genocide of Native Americans. Indeed, America has probably done less in this regard than Germany has with respect to its own past crimes. Since Jews do have a gift for historical memory and for ritual observance, we could take the lead in insisting that the United States find ways to erect monuments and devise ceremonies that would acknowledge rather than deny the crimes of our racial past. (Parallels that come to mind are the U.S. Holocaust Memorial Museum and the Vietnam War Memorial.)

Of critical importance in my view is the growing movement in favor of some form of "reparations" for African Americans. I would like to see those in progressive Jewish circles support—at least in principle—the idea of reparations. There will certainly be many reasonable reservations, not only about details, but about such larger issues as political impact and economic feasibility. But if reparations were acts of justice in the case of Germany and our own incarceration of Japanese Americans, how can similar redress for African Americans be inappropriate?

Perhaps beginning with this question of reparations, Jewish groups and individuals in various communities can make overtures to African-American groups and individuals for the purpose of forming black–Jewish committees for dialogue and potential cooperation. Such committees were formed in New York City after the Crown Heights disturbances. And after the 1992 riots, blacks and Koreans came together in Los Angeles.

Such "bridging" committees can be a first step toward moving from today's fragmented politics of identity to the building of the more universal and inclusive sense of common purpose that the nation so sorely needs—the heart of a politics of meaning.

16 Race in the 2000 Election

Still the Big News

EARLY IN December 2000, just a few days after George W. Bush became the president-elect, 50 percent of the blacks surveyed in a *CNN–USA Today* opinion poll said that they believed the election had been stolen; only 7 percent thought that Bush had won "fair and square." In the same poll, 54 percent of the whites responded that the outcome had been fair, and a mere 14 percent believed that the election had been stolen.[1] Exit poll data estimated that Vice-President Al Gore received 90 percent of the black vote. The 8 percent that went to Bush was the lowest percentage for a presidential candidate of a major party in recent history. African Americans gave higher percentages of their votes to Ronald Reagan, the elder George Bush, and Bob Dole.[2]

Black voters' identification with the Democratic Party goes back to the Great Depression of the 1930s, when many African Americans gave up a long tradition of loyalty to the party of Abraham Lincoln in order to support Franklin Roosevelt and his New Deal. And despite the fact that for decades American's most vitriolic racists were southern Democrats, blacks continued to vote Democratic, given hope by Harry Truman's order to desegregate the armed forces, John Kennedy's phone call to Martin Luther King, Jr., in a Birmingham jail, and the strong civil rights positions of Lyndon Johnson and his vice-president, Hubert Humphrey. Blacks maintained their allegiance to the Democratic Party through a series of Republican administrations that, except for Jimmy Carter's interregnum, spanned the twenty-four years between 1968 and 1992—administrations that were seen as indifferent, even hostile, to their interests. Then came eight years of Bill Clinton, during which the Democratic Party's hold on the black vote was further consolidated. Despite such questionable policies as welfare reform, Clinton's commitment to civil rights and to his African-American constituents could not be doubted. He was the first American president who could point to a black man as his best friend (Vernon Jordan), who regularly prayed with a black minister (Jesse Jackson), and who made more high-level minority appointments to his administration and to the federal judiciary than any other president. Little wonder then that author Toni Morrison dubbed him "our first black president."[3]

In such a context the fact that in the year 2000 race and ethnicity divided the electorate more than any other demographic category is not surprising.[4] In comparison to other recent Republican candidates, Bush did make more of an effort to cut into the minority vote, surrounding himself with people of color at his nominating convention and leaking to the media before the election his choice of Colin Powell as secretary of state. But despite Bush's impressive record of Latino support in his home state, about two-thirds of the nation's Hispanic population voted Democratic.

In the 2000 election blacks not only voted Democratic, they voted in record numbers. In Missouri, blacks more than doubled their percentage of the electorate (from 5 percent in 1996 to 12 percent in 2000), and their votes were pivotal in electing deceased candidate Mel Carnahan in his Senate race against the ultra-conservative John Ashcroft.[5] In other states too the unexpectedly high turnout of African Americans tipped close races in favor of Democratic candidates, making possible the gains that would result in a deadlock in the U.S. Senate and a narrow Republican majority in the House of Representatives.

The African-American electorate was also the most critical voting bloc in the race for president. Vice-President Gore received more black votes than any candidate in history. African Americans not only were the key group in giving him more than a half-million vote advantage over Bush, they also provided the margin of difference that should have given Gore the electoral college majority that would have made him our forty-third president. In short, blacks elected Gore, but because their votes more than any others were undercounted in the critical state of Florida, we can also say that the black vote—or the right-wing reaction to that vote—also defeated Gore and elected his rival.

The contesting of the results in Florida, which went on for five weeks after the last polling place closed on November 7, was a historic event. But just as historic was the fact that African Americans, who make up 13 percent of Florida's citizenry, represented 15 percent of the state's voters in the November election (an increase from the 10 percent who voted in 1996).[6] Voter turnout rates are always low for people of color and people with low income. To understand why Florida's result in 2000 deviated from the historical pattern, we have to look back to the civil rights movement of the 1960s and its campaigns to enfranchise the disenfranchised in the jim crow South. Those struggles brought about the 1960s civil rights laws outlawing racial discrimination in the electoral process and led to a redistricting of congressional districts that markedly increased the number of blacks in Congress. During the ensuing thirty-five years, the slow but steady increase in education and economic status among minorities has brought about a new level of political interest and sophistication, including an increased propensity to vote. Add to this the Clinton era's tightening of blacks' embrace of the Democratic Party, and the unprecedented and enormously successful get-out-the-vote campaign conducted by the NAACP and organized labor during the 2000 electoral campaign. In the three months before election day, the Reverend Jesse Jackson made more than 300 appearances across the nation; he spent thirteen days in Florida alone and is credited for the fact that in some precincts in that state, 85 percent of eligible black voters went to the polls.[7]

The events in Florida dramatically testify that racial oppression continues to be the big news in American life. What threatens racists to the core is black power and influence. Florida 2000 became a case study in the tug of war between the forces of progressive change that were set in motion by the civil rights movement of the 1960s and the forces that since then have resisted change in order to maintain a social order based on the privileged position of the white rich and the disenfranchisement of poor people and racial minorities.

During November and December 2000 the reactionary forces won the first round in the battle for the White House by undercounting enough of the African-American vote to give Florida's twenty-five electoral votes to Bush, and with them the presidency. This was accomplished through acts of overt racism that recalled the old jim crow South. In some counties police set up roadblocks in front of polling places and intimidated potential voters by demanding to see their identification cards.[8] But even with photo IDs and voter registration cards in hand, scores of students from the historically black Bethune-Cookman College in Daytona Beach, most of them newly registered and eager to vote for the first time, were turned away because their names had been inexplicably removed from the rolls.[9]

With long lines of blacks who had arrived before closing time still waiting to vote, some polling places closed at the appointed time, even though they were legally obliged to accommodate everyone who had queued up in time. Other polling places closed early, also violating the statutes of Florida's voting laws.[10] In one county about 200 Puerto Ricans were denied their vote because they couldn't produce IDs or because they were told that they couldn't understand the ballot.[11] The *New York Times* reported that some Haitian Americans, a heavily Democratic group that was particularly victimized, were saying that it was "worse than an election in Haiti."[12]

In addition to such high-handed and historically familiar acts of oppressive racism, Bush won Florida because of systematic inequities in the machinery of counting votes, inequities that are expressions of institutionalized racism. In contrast to overt racism, institutionalized racism need not be linked to an intent to discriminate or even prejudiced attitudes in order to produce a discriminatory outcome. Because African Americans tend to be poorer than whites, they also are more likely to live in the poorer counties that have the most antiquated machinery for counting votes. According to the *Nation* of December 25, 2000, two-thirds of Florida's black voters resided in counties that used punch-card voting, in contrast to 56 percent of white voters. According to the *Orlando Sun-Sentinel,* counties using the more efficient and modern method, optical scanning, recorded presidential votes on more than 99 percent of the ballots, as compared to only 96.1 percent of punch-card ballots.[13] Although these differences do not seem large, they account for enough votes to reverse the election. Although the spotlight of national attention was on Florida, similar patterns of undercounting the African-American vote were discovered in other states. A *Washington Post* analysis found that "in many black precincts in Chicago, one of every six ballots in the presidential election was thrown out, while almost every vote was counted in some of the city's outer (and mostly white) suburbs."[14]

Another example of institutional racism in the electoral process is the disenfranchisement of people who have committed a felony, whether or not they remain in prison. The great majority of America's four million felons and ex-felons, prohibited from voting in most states, are black and Latino. It is difficult to imagine such a simple, yet effective, reform for rehabilitating prisoners and ex-convicts than reestablishing their right to vote. By providing a sense of citizenship and enhancing involvement in politics and the world, voting could be an important step toward genuine rehabilitation. It is encouraging that the state of Massachussets recently enfranchised this group, but similar changes are unlikely in Republican-controlled states, whose leaders are well aware that Gore would have been elected president had felons and ex-felons voted across the nation.[15]

Sensitive to the fact that the legitimacy of his presidency was in question, especially among blacks, the new president-elect named Colin Powell and Condoleezza Rice as his first major cabinet nominees, almost immediately after the Supreme Court ruled in his favor. That the nation will have its first black secretary of state cannot be discounted. As Powell himself said, his nomination sends a signal to African-American youth that no position is too lofty to aim for and that the corridors of power need not be the turf of white men only. But considering the new president and his policies—best exemplified in tax cuts that would enrich the already wealthy and an almost obscene infatuation with capital punishment, which in his state of Texas (as well as in the nation) primarily kills blacks and Latinos—it is very likely that many, if not most, of America's racial minorities will see the Powell and Rice nominations as window-dressing.

As we begin the second year of the new millennium, racial change in America is marked by ambiguity and paradox. The same tug of war between the progressive forces of equal participation and social justice, exemplified in the historic black turnout in Florida, and the forces of status quo racism, exemplified by that state's undercount, can be seen in every institutional area throughout the nation. A survey of the major social institutions clearly shows that change has been uneven, with some institutions moving effectively toward equality, while others remain stuck in racial oppression and colonial-like patterns. What is not clear as I write this early in 2001 is whether the progressive forces or the retrograde ones will eventually win out.

I consider criminal justice our most backward institutional system; it is one not likely soon to see serious reform, given that the new attorney general, the former Senator Ashcroft, is among the most conservative of President Bush's appointees. The prison system, whose inmates are disproportionately black and Hispanic, can only be called a colonial enclave. The disparity in the arrest and sentencing of the mostly white users of powdered cocaine and the mostly black users of crack cocaine is a legal double standard as egregious as those of the judicial systems of British India and colonial Africa. Perhaps the nature of police work explains the fact that this institution, despite a myriad of sensitivity-training programs, seems less capable than others of checking racist brutality, even in such progressive cities as New York and Los Angeles. Indeed, police officers have become the leading perpetrators of hate crimes. The most notorious recent examples have taken place in New York City: notably the forty-one bullets that killed Amadou Diallo, an unarmed African immigrant, and the sodomizing of Abner Louima, a Haitian suspect, by a number of New York's "finest." In Los Angeles the incidents have not been quite as dramatic, but it is noteworthy that in that city a black chief of police has been unable—or unwilling—to stop a consistent pattern of harassment of minority citizens, carried out by black and Latino officers as well as white ones.

Not surprisingly, in a recent national opinion poll, the widest racial divide was found in attitudes toward the police: 67 percent of blacks but only 25 percent of whites feel that they are not treated equally by law enforcement; 42 percent of the blacks surveyed believe that they have been stopped by police officers because of their race.[16] Now widely publicized as racial profiling, the tendency of police officers to stop black drivers without cause has for many years been known among African Americans as the offense of "driving while black (or brown)." Such perceptions are based on repeated experience and cannot be dismissed as racial paranoia; an internal study of the New Jersey state police conducted in 2000 revealed a consistent pattern of stopping minority motorists. The suppression of this report—as well as its substance—would prove embarrassing for Christine Whitman, who was governor of New Jersey before her nomination as head of the Environmental Protection Agency.

The issue of hate crimes provides an example of the ambiguities and paradoxes of race in America. On the one hand, the number of such crimes, and certainly their sensational character, seems to be on the rise. An unheralded example, reported in a July 2000 *New York Times* article, is the sharp increase in racial harassment cases that have come before the Equal Employment Opportunity Commission (EEOC). The agency received nearly 50,000 such complaints during the 1990s, compared to 10,000 in the 1980s. According to the FBI, the new "hate crime of choice" at the workplace is to leave a drawing of a noose, to symbolize a lynching, at the workstations or lockers of black and other minority employees. The EEOC is at present investigating twenty such cases.[17]

On the other hand, hate crimes evoke considerably more outrage than they did a generation or two ago. Even during the 1960s, the white men who dragged James Byrd to his death tied to the back of a truck would never have been sentenced to death in a small Texas town. It seems to me that the perpetrators of hate crimes are more isolated, with much less mass support for their racial extremism than their predecessors. True, the number of white supremacist Web sites seems to be growing, making communication among hardcore racists easier. Yet I link the desperation and extreme brutality of many hate crimes to this isolation, a hypothesis that recalls a theory of Herbert Blumer that prejudice is most likely to rise when minorities make significant gains in their "group position," thus threatening people who identify themselves through group "superiority."[18]

The modern civil rights movement began in the educational arena with the historic *Brown* decision of 1954. Although the public schools led the way toward racial integration, many of those gains dissipated as whites moved to racially homogenous suburbs or, if they remained in the central cities, placed their children in private schools. The result is that de facto segregation in many school systems is as prevalent today as legal segregation was fifty years ago. In addition, the academic performance of blacks and Latinos lags far behind that of whites and Asians. In higher education, the challenges to affirmative action, and its dismantling at key institutions such as the University of California, threatens to stop the progress of diversity dead in its tracks. Still, the news is not all bad. The institutionalization of black history courses and departments in high schools and colleges is a very significant reform and, unlike affirmative action, most likely a lasting one.

Whenever the question of equality in the economic sphere arises, commentators like to point to the existence and continuing growth of a size-able black middle class. But such optimism must be tempered by the many signs of unhappiness in this stratum—for example, what has been called "black middle-class rage"—and by the fact that even upper-class African Americans continue to face racial barriers in their daily lives. Although income inequality has declined somewhat, alarming racial disparities in wealth remain.[19]

It is certainly a historic change when we can no longer say, as I did in my discussion of the colonial labor principle in Chapter 4, that blacks and other minorities tend to be confined to the unskilled sectors where they do society's "dirty work." But this change come about in part because America now employs immigrants for such work. I have never believed the piety that the black unemployment rate was not worsened by immigration. I suspect that employers and the government fostered Asian and Latino immigration as an alternative to having to train and hire members of the largely black army of the unemployed. In addition to the inroads made by immigrant groups, the decline of basic manufacturing industries has hurt the economic situation of the African-American masses, virtually decimating what was once a large and vigorous black working class. All this has contributed mightily to the very high proportion of black men, many of them Vietnam veterans, in our homeless populations. For the most part, today's largely black "underclass" remains outside the system of opportunity, and as a social-economic grouping, it derived fewer benefits than any other sector from from the growth and prosperity of the 1990s.

Political institutions deserve a slightly better report card. The representation of blacks and Latinos lags in the Senate and the House, as well as in high executive positions on the federal level. The local level has seen more progress in black (and to a lesser degree Latino) political representation. Beginning in the late 1960s, black mayors were elected in virtually every major northern and western city and, beginning in the 1970s, in a significant number of southern cities and small towns. Many of their constituents were disappointed when these mayors were unable to turn around the big city problems of poverty, urban decay, and the flight of jobs and industry to the suburbs. The lack of change dramatized the limits of local power, since real control is held regionally, nationally, and, more and more, globally.

One could argue that the most positive change has occurred in that rather amorphous institutional arena that I can only refer to as culture. The cultural sphere, encompassing entertainment, sports, and the arts, pioneered racial integration long before the modern civil rights movement. For more than a generation now, black stylistic forms in music, sports, fashion, and, above all, language, have provided the most creative and innovative contributions to the larger culture, appealing to Americans of every race and ethnicity, especially the young. The African-American community in recent years has also produced most of the nation's heroes, from Martin Luther King, Jr., and Malcolm X during the 1960s, to the perennially "most-admired American" Bill Cosby, through General Colin Powell during the Gulf War, and Muhammad Ali, honored at the 1996 Olympics. There is something mind boggling about the fact that a dark-skinned protest leader is the only American to have a national holiday all for himself, now that Lincoln and Washington have to share Presidents' Day.

But even in these areas, resistance to racial equality abounds. Blacks may dominate professional sports as players, but except perhaps for the NBA, they continue to be underrepresented in leadership positions, both on the field and in the front office. Many of our heroes may be black men, but at the same time the African-American male is demonized, to the extent that whites will cross the street to avoid passing one. The King holiday is historic, but just as with the media coverage after his assassination (see Chapter 3), it is regularly used to distort the political message of the civil rights martyr. Instead of emphasizing Dr. King's teachings against poverty, war, and racism, his philosophy is portrayed one-dimensionally, as opposition to violence. Even worse, his words have been coopted, out of context, by opponents of affirmative action.[20]

Another paradox that marks contemporary American race relations is that the popular mind continues to focus on the black–white drama at the very moment when both groups have declined as a percentage of the general population. The tension between viewing our racial crisis as binary and seeing it as a multiplicity of "racial and ethnic dilemmas" was played out at the very first meeting of the Advisory Panel of the President's Initiative on Race in 1997. The board's chair, John Hope Franklin, wanted to focus the group's work on the unfinished business of black oppression, while other members wanted the spotlight to include Asians, Latinos, and other new immigrants.[21]

At some point around the middle of the twenty-first century, whites will become a minority in the United States. This will come about because of the rapid growth of two groups that continue to include many immigrants: Asian Americans, the fastest-growing racial group, and Latinos, who will soon surpass African Americans as our largest minority. Both of these growing subsets of the population are extremely diverse, the grab-bag terms Hispanic and Asian masking a variety of national origins. But will these changes put us on the road to a truly multicultural and multiracial society? The big question, whose answer is not easy to forecast, is whether our growing racial and cultural diversity will create the conditions in which cultural differences will become so expected that they will lose their historic association with race, which in the American experience functions as the chief means for ranking one another through invidious comparisons.

The 2000 series on race in the *New York Times* cited abundant journalistic evidence that rich friendships and working relationships across lines of race and color have become almost commonplace. This is certainly a positive development. But the same articles suggest serious limitations to these relations, including the testimony that issues of race are almost never directly addressed out of fear that honest discussions would bring about tension and conflict. This was the case even in such a sophisticated setting as the *Times'* own newsroom.[22]

From my own research I have learned that whites tend to seize upon these (relatively) new relationships and the (again relative) absence of tension as signs of significant progress in race relations. And such progress should not be discounted: The number of people who oppose interracial marriage, for example, is now at an all-time low.[23] The problem is that the decolonization of social and economic institutions, what sociologists call "structural change," has not kept up with changes on the interpersonal and attitudinal levels. In that same research I learned that blacks tend to assess racial progress in terms of structure and institutions, not attitudes and climate, which helps to explain why they continue to be less sanguine than whites about the overall state of racial affairs in the United States.[24]

From the beginning of our nation's history race was the fundamental principle of America's social contract, the criterion that distinguished the condition of freedom from that of bondsman. That may be why it remains the most important of all our measures of status and worth almost 150 years after the end of slavery. Race is unrelenting in its power and persistence, surviving periods in which it appears to be overshadowed by other elements of society's structuring, most often social class; surviving the legions of voices, from neoconservative pundits to social democratic scholars, that assert that its day is passed, and who trumpet triumphantly, but always prematurely, that the new utopia of a colorblind society is at hand.

The idea that race is central to the American experience, pervasive in its impact on every sphere of life, was the core assumption of *Racial Oppression in America*. And of all my assertions in that book, this idea has held up best; race is still central and its effects are still pervasive thirty years later, as the election of 2000 illustrated so dramatically. The gritty old boxer keeps hanging on, as idealistic and hopeful onlookers await that knockout punch. Perhaps by the year 2100, but don't count on it.

Notes

Notes to the Preface

1. Russell Banks, *Cloudsplitter* (New York: HarperCollins, 1998), p. 421.
2. "How Race Is Lived in America," fourteen-part series in the *New York Times,* June 4–July 13, 2000.
3. Charles W. Mills, *The Racial Contract* (Ithaca, N.Y.: Cornell University Press, 1997).
4. Banks, *Cloudsplitter,* pp. 423–24.
5. After drafting this preface, I was pleased to find a kindred soul in political scientist Adolph Reed. Reed also tried to ignore the Simpson trial, seeing it as "a lurid melodrama of celebrity justice—just another instance of the American version of Weimar decadence, in which trash TV provides the basis and frame for collective social experience." Adolph Reed, Jr., *Class Notes* (New York: The Free Press, 2000), p. 29.

Notes to Chapter One

1. Thomas L. Blair, *Retreat to the Ghetto: The End of a Dream?* (New York: Hill & Wang, 1977), pp. 161–62.
2. Gallup poll, September 18, 1968.
3. Harris poll, August 9, 1967.
4. See Jonathan Rieder, *Canarsie: The Jews and Italians of Brooklyn against Liberalism* (Cambridge: Harvard University Press, 1985).

Notes to Chapter Two

1. Harold Cruse, *The Crisis of the Negro Intellectual* (New York: Morrow, 1967).
2. Peter I. Rose, *The Subject Is Race* (New York: Oxford University Press, 1968), pp. 27–66.
3. The publication of Talcott Parsons's *The Structure of Social Action* (New York: McGraw-Hill, 1937) was the most important prewar precursor of this development. More than any other individual, Parsons brought European theory to the forefront of American sociology. In an unreadable, yet somehow influential, article of fifty-three pages on the theory of social stratification, Parsons gave less than two pages to "the ethnic factor": "a secondary basis of modification of the stratification pattern but . . . by no means unimportant." "A Revised Analyt-

ical Approach to the Theory of Social Stratification," in T. Parsons, *Essays in Sociological Theory,* rev. ed. (New York: The Free Press, 1954), pp. 424–25.

4. Simmel also stressed social conflict in his work, and his essay on "the stranger" inspired the notion of "the marginal man" that Park and his students applied to minority relations in the United States.

5. Weber gave some attention to race and ethnicity in his writings; however, these insights were not incorporated into the summaries of his work, which had the most impact on American theory. See Ernst M. Manasse, "Max Weber on Race," *Social Research* 14 (June 1947): 191–221.

6. In the subsequent period, American sociology has not produced an analysis of race comparable in significance to Gunnar Myrdal's *An American Dilemma* (New York: Harper & Row, 1944). Virtually all the new insights about racism and the experience of the oppressed have been provided by writers whose lives and minds were uncluttered by sociological theory.

7. Robert Park, *Race and Culture* (New York: The Free Press, 1950).

8. Louis Wirth, "The Problem of Minority Groups" in Ralph Linton, ed., *The Science of Man in the World Crisis* (New York: Columbia University Press, 1945), pp. 354–64; and Wirth, *The Ghetto* (Chicago: University of Chicago Press, 1928).

9. Milton Gordon, *Assimilation in American Life* (New York: Oxford University Press, 1964); Nathan Glazer and Daniel Patrick Moynihan, *Beyond the Melting Pot* (Cambridge: M.I.T. and Harvard University Press, 1963).

10. William Lloyd Warner, Introduction to Allison Davis, Burleigh Gardner, and Mary Gardner, *Deep South* (Chicago: University of Chicago Press, 1941); and William Lloyd Warner and Leo Srole, *The Social Systems of American Ethnic Groups* (New Haven: Yale University Press, 1945), pp. 284, 295. "Our class system functions for a large proportion of ethnics to destroy the ethnic subsystems and to increase assimilation. . . . The future of American ethnic groups seems to be limited; it is likely that they will be quickly absorbed. When this happens, one of the great epochs of American history will have ended, and another, that of race, will begin."

11. John Dollard, *Caste and Class in a Southern Town* (Garden City, N.Y.: Doubleday, 1957); Davis, Gardner, and Gardner, *Deep South.*

12. Charles Silberman was one of the first white experts to make this point when he wrote in 1964 that "what we are discovering . . . is that the United States—all of it, North as well as South, West as well as East, is a racist society in a sense and to a degree that we have refused so far to admit, much less face." *Crisis in Black and White* (New York: Random House, 1964), pp. 9–10.

13. Myrdal, *An American Dilemma,* p. li: "All our attempts to reach scientific explanations of why the Negroes are what they are and why they live as they do have regularly led to determinants on the white side of the race line. In the practical and political struggles of effecting changes, the views and attitudes of the white Americans are likewise strategic. The Negro's entire life, and, consequently, also his opinions on the Negro problem are, in the main, to be considered as secondary reactions to more primary pressures from the side of the dominant white majority."

14. Herbert Hyman and Paul Sheatsley, "Attitudes Toward Desegregation," *Scientific American* (July 1964), 16–23.

NOTES TO CHAPTER THREE

1. Albert Memmi, *The Colonizer and the Colonized* (Boston: Beacon, 1967), pt. 1.

2. The classic discussion is Memmi's essay "The Colonizer Who Refuses," ibid., pp. 19–44.

3. Michael J. Piore, "Jobs and Training," in Samuel H. Beer and Richard E. Barringer, eds., *The State and the Poor* (Boston: Winthrop, 1970); and Harold Baron, "The Web of Urban Racism," in Louis Knowles and Kenneth Prewitt, eds., *Institutional Racism in America* (Englewood Cliffs, N.J.: Prentice-Hall, 1969), pp. 146–49.

4. Harold Baron, "The Demand for Black Labor: Historical Notes on the Political Economy of Racism," *Radical America* 5 (March–April 1971): esp. 34–38, where he describes the dual labor market. The whole article is extremely important.

5. U.S. Census of Population 1960, Bureau of the Census, Department of Commerce, *Occupational Characteristics,* table 3, pp. 21–30.

6. Ibid.

7. *The Social and Economic Status of Negroes in the United States, 1970,* Current Population Reports, series p-23, no. 38, Bureau of the Census, U.S. Department of Commerce (1970), p. 61.

8. Ibid., p. 67.

9. U.S. Census of Population 1960, Bureau of the Census, Department of Commerce, vol. 1, pt. 1, pp. 544–46.

10. *The Social and Economic Status of Negroes,* p. 61.

11. Lester C. Thurow, *Poverty and Discrimination* (Washington, D.C.: Brookings Institute, 1969), pp. 130–34.

12. The *African Labour Survey* of 1958 cites some typical figures. For Northern Rhodesia in 1956: "in the motor repairing and electrical trades and in the construction industry African wages varied between 5 and 12 percent of European wages for what are nominally the same jobs." International Labour Office, *African Labour Survey* (Geneva, 1958), p. 280. (Calculations from another source suggest that white workers in the same country's mines earned sixteen times as much as African workers. See A. L. Epstein, *Politics in an Urban African Community* [Manchester: Manchester University Press, 1958], p. 102.) In the engineering industry of Southern Rhodesia, African employees' earnings "as late as 1952 . . . were still on the average less than 7 percent [of those] of European employees." And in the mines in the same year the average cash wages for Africans were 6.7 percent of those of whites. In building construction the gap was considerably less. International Labour Office, *African Labour Survey,* p. 281. In Kenya the ratio between average earnings of Europeans, Asians, and Africans in 1957 was 100 to 33.45 to 5.37, respectively, or a European–African ratio of 19 to 1. In the Belgian Congo in 1954 "the average total remuneration of 1,240,000

indigenous wage earners in 1954 equalled roughly the total remuneration of the 32,000 European employees, which represents a ratio of earning per head of 1 to 40." Ibid., p. 284. In the most developed African nation, South Africa, the wages of African men ranged from 20 to 24 percent of those of whites between 1944 and 1954; the overall trend was downward. Ibid., p. 687.

13. Cited in Michael Banton, *Race Relations* (New York: Basic Books, 1967), p. 117.

14. James Baldwin, *Nobody Knows My Name* (New York: Dial, 1969), p. 133: "One cannot afford to lose status on this peculiar ladder, for the prevailing notion of American life seems to involve a kind of rung-by-rung ascension to some hideously desirable state. If this is one's concept of life, obviously one cannot afford to slip back one rung. When one slips, one slips back not a rung but into chaos and no longer knows who he is. And this reason, this fear, suggests to me one of the real reasons for the status of the Negro in this country. In a way, the Negro tells us where the bottom is: *because he is there,* and *where* he is, beneath us, we know where the limits are and how far we must not fall. We must not fall beneath him. We must never allow ourselves to fall that low, and I am not trying to be cynical or sardonic."

15. Everett C. Hughes was one of the first sociologists to emphasize the status aspects of race relations. See E. C. Hughes and Helen M. Hughes, *Where Peoples Meet* (New York: The Free Press, 1952).

16. For convincing reportage on this point from Chicago and Cicero, Illinois, see Gene Marine, "I've Got Nothing Against the Colored, Understand," in Barry N. Schwartz and Robert Disch, eds., *White Racism* (New York: Dell, 1970), pp. 217–28. A particularly sensitive discussion of the importance of home and neighborhood for white ethnic groups is found in Andrew Greeley, *Why Can't They Be Like Us?* (New York: Dutton, 1971), chap. 13.

17. T. H. Marshall, "Citizenship and Social Class," in Marshall, ed., *Class, Citizenship, and Social Development* (Garden City, N.Y.: Doubleday, 1965).

18. This suggests the irrational element in racial labor systems, in comparison with the "rationality" of pure capitalist exploitation—for which the social composition of the industrial labor force is a matter of indifference. Or as Mannoni has expressed it: "North American Negroes may be less well treated than white workers, but it is not because it is more profitable to treat them in this way: in fact they are ill-treated because they are treated *as Negroes,* that is to say in a way which escapes definition in economic terms." O. Mannoni, *Prospero and Caliban: The Psychology of Colonization* (London: Methuen, 1956), p. 32.

19. Harold Cruse, *The Crisis of the Negro Intellectual* (New York: Morrow, 1967).

20. William K. Tabb, *The Political Economy of the Black Ghetto* (New York: Norton, 1970).

21. Michael Reich, "The Economics of Racism," *Upstart* 1 (1971): 57.

22. Sidney M. Willhelm, *Who Needs the Negro?* (Cambridge: Schenkman, 1970).

23. Cruse, *Crisis of the Negro Intellectual.*

24. Reprinted by permission of the publisher from Orlando Patterson, *The*

Sociology of Slavery (London: MacGibon & Kee, 1967), p. 255. Ebo is an alternate spelling of Ibo, a large group of West African peoples from whom many slaves were taken. Guinea was the term for Africa used by the slaves. Kingston is the principal city and capital of Jamaica.

25. Cf. Leon Litwack, *North of Slavery* (Chicago: University of Chicago Press, 1961).

26. Sithole concludes that "no white man in the whole colonial history of Africa was ever sentenced to death for the murder of an African! . . . In perusing the annals of courts in European-ruled Africa, I have failed to discover a single instance where a European was convicted of the murder of an African and sentenced to death, although many cases have been found of Europeans convicted of murder of Europeans and sentenced to death. Many cases of Africans convicted of murder of Europeans and Africans and sentenced to death have also been found." Ndabaningi Sithole, *African Nationalism* (London: Oxford University Press, 1968), p. 139. A similar pattern has existed with respect to other minorities: On the aboriginals of Australia, see A. Grenfell Price, *White Settlers and Native Peoples* (Melbourne: Georgian House, 1949), pp. 107ff.; on American Indians, see W. C. Macleod, *The American Indian Frontier* (London: Routledge & Kegan Paul, 1928); on Mexican-Americans, see Carey McWilliams, *North from Mexico* (Philadelphia: Lippincott, 1949), pp. 112 and 273; and on Chinese, see Thomas Chinn, *A History of the Chinese in California* (San Francisco: Chinese Historical Society, 1969). The black case is so notorious that references seem unnecessary.

Whereas Sithole found no deviant cases, Price mentions that the colonial authorities in 1838 hung seven whites who had perpetrated a mass murder of twenty-eight Native Australians; Chinn quotes a report of the Chinese Six Companies of 1862, which noted that only two whites had been convicted and hung out of at least eighty-eight known cases of murdered Chinese; but these exceptions are hard to find in the literature.

27. This research is summarized in Seymour Martin Lipset and Reinhard Bendix, *Social Mobility in Industrial Society* (Berkeley: University of California Press, 1959).

28. Arnold Toynbee, *A Study in History,* vol. 1 (London: Oxford University Press, 1934), pp. 152–53.

29. In his *Strategy for Labor,* Andre Gorz integrates such human and spiritual needs into an overall Marxian framework (Boston: Beacon, 1967).

NOTES TO CHAPTER FOUR

1. For accounts of this movement at San Francisco State, see James McEvoy and Abraham Miller, eds., *Black Power and Student Rebellion* (Belmont, Calif.: Wadsworth, 1969), especially the chapters by Barlow and Shapiro, Gitlin, Chrisman, and the editors; and Bill Barlow and Peter Shapiro, *An End to Silence* (New York: Pegasus Books, 1971).

2. In addition to its application to white–black relations in the United States—see, for example, Stokely Carmichael and Charles Hamilton, *Black Power*

(New York: Vintage, 1967), esp. chap. 1—the concept of internal colonialism is a leading one for a number of students of Indian–white and Indian–mestizo relations in Latin America. Representative statements are Pablo Gonzalez Casanova, "Internal Colonialism and National Development," *Studies in Comparative International Development,* vol. 1, 1965, no. 4; Rodolfo Stavenhagen, "Classes, Colonialism, and Acculturation," *Studies in Comparative International Development,* vol. 1, 1965, no. 6; and Julio Cotler, "The Mechanics of Internal Domination and Social Change in Peru," *Studies in Comparative International Development,* vol. 3, 1967–1968, no. 12. The Stavenhagen and Cotler papers are found also in Irving L. Horowitz, ed., *Masses in Latin America* (New York: Oxford University Press, 1970). See also André Gunder Frank, *Capitalism and Underdevelopment in Latin America* (New York: Monthly Review Press, 1967); and Eugene Havens and William Flinn, eds., *Internal Colonialism and Structural Change in Colombia* (New York: Praeger, 1970).

3. Gunther Barth, *Bitter Strength, A History of the Chinese in the United States, 1850–1870* (Cambridge: Harvard University Press, 1964).

4. Harry H. L. Kitano, *Japanese-Americans: The Evolution of a Subculture* (Englewood Cliffs, N.J.: Prentice-Hall, 1969).

5. Oscar Handlin, *Boston's Immigrants* (Cambridge: Harvard University Press, 1959), chap. 2.

6. *New York Times Magazine* (September 11, 1966), reprinted in Nathan Glazer, ed., *Cities in Trouble* (Chicago: Quadrangle, 1970), pp. 139–57. Another influential study in this genre is Edward Banfield, *The Unheavenly City* (Boston: Little, Brown, 1970). For a critical discussion of this thesis and the presentation of contrary demographic data, see Karl E. Taueber and Alma F. Taueber, "The Negro as an Immigrant Group: Recent Trends in Racial and Ethnic Segregation in Chicago," *American Journal of Sociology* 69 (1964): 374–82. The Kerner Report also devotes a brief chapter to "Comparing the Immigrant and Negro Experience," *Report of the National Advisory Commission on Civil Disorders* (New York: Bantam, 1968), chap. 9.

7. W. C. Macleod, *The American Indian Frontier* (London: Routledge & Kegan Paul, 1928).

8. For a discussion of these differences in ecological and material circumstances, see Marvin Harris, *Patterns of Race in America* (New York: Walker, 1964), esp. chaps 1–4. Compare also John Collier, *The Indians of the Americas* (New York: Mentor, 1947), pp. 100–103.

9. H. Hoetink, *The Two Variants of Race Relations in the Caribbean* (London: Oxford University Press, 1967), presents a strong argument on this point.

10. For a historical account of this development, see Winthrop Jordan, *White over Black* (Chapel Hill: University of North Carolina Press, 1968), chap. 2.

11. Leonard Pitt, *The Decline of the Californios: A Social History of the Spanish-Speaking Californians, 1846–1890* (Berkeley and Los Angeles: University of California Press, 1970), p. 296.

12. Carey McWilliams, *Factories in the Fields* (Boston: Little, Brown, 1934), and *Ill Fares the Land* (Boston: Little, Brown, 1942). See also McWilliams, *North from Mexico* (Philadelphia: Lippincott, 1948). For papers that apply the colonial

model to Mexican-Americans, see Joan W. Moore, "Colonialism: The Case of the Mexican Americans," *Social Problems* 17 (Spring 1970): 463–72; and Mario Barrera, Carlos Muñoz, and Charles Ornelas, "The Barrio as Internal Colony," in Harlan Hahn, ed., *Urban Affairs Annual Review* 6 (1972).

13. Roger Daniels and Harry Kitano, *American Racism* (Englewood Cliffs, N.J.: Prentice-Hall, 1970), pp. 45–66. See also R. Daniels, *The Politics of Prejudice* (Berkeley and Los Angeles: University of California Press, 1962). The most comprehensive study of American racist attitudes and practices toward the Chinese is Stuart Miller, *The Unwelcome Immigrant: The American Image of the Chinese, 1785–1882* (Berkeley and Los Angeles: University of California Press, 1969).

14. Max Weber, *General Economic History* (New York: The Free Press, 1950), p. 277.

15. John Higham, *Strangers in the Land* (New York: Atheneum, 1969), pp. 45–52.

16. I do not imply a perfect correlation between race and industrial type, only that third world workers have been strikingly overrepresented in the "primary sector" of the economy. Unlike in classical colonialism, white labor has outnumbered colored labor in the United States, and therefore white workers have dominated even such industries as coal mining, nonferrous metals, and midwestern agriculture.

17. Robert Starobin, *Industrial Slavery in the Old South* (New York: Oxford University Press, 1970); and Leon Litwack, *North of Slavery* (Chicago: University of Chicago Press, 1961). For a recent interpretation, see Harold M. Baron, "The Demand for Black Labor: Historical Notes on the Political Economy of Racism," *Radical America* 5 (March–April 1971): 1–46.

18. Of course some Europeans did parallel labor in mining and transportation construction. But since they had the freedom of movement that was denied colored laborers, they could transfer the skills and experience gained to other pursuits.

19. Herman Bloch, *The Circle of Discrimination* (New York: New York University Press, 1969), esp. pp. 34–46. That discrimination in the labor market continues to make a strong contribution to income disparity between white and nonwhite is demonstrated in Lester Thurow's careful study, *Poverty and Discrimination* (Washington, D.C.: Brookings Institute, 1969).

20. As far as I know no study exists that has attempted to analyze industrial and occupational competition among a variety of ethnic and racial groups. Such research would be very valuable. With respect to discrimination against Asians and Mexicans, Pitt, for example, describes how white and European miners were largely successful in driving Chinese and Mexican independent prospectors out of the gold fields. Pitt, *The Decline of the Californios,* chap. 3.

21. Humbert S. Nelli, *Italians in Chicago 1880–1930: A Study in Ethnic Mobility* (New York: Oxford University Press, 1970).

22. Milton Gordon, *Assimilation in American Life* (New York: Oxford University Press, 1964).

23. I do not imply here that African culture was totally eliminated, nor that Afro-Americans have lived in a cultural vacuum. A distinctive black culture emerged during slavery. From the complex vicissitudes of their historical experi-

ence in the United States, Afro-American culture has continued its development and differentiation to the present day, providing an ethnic content to black peoplehood. For a full discussion, see Chapter 7.

24. Collier, *The Indians of the Americas,* pp. 132–42.

25. Pitt, *The Decline of the Californios,* pp. 196–97.

26. Janheinz Jahn, *Muntu* (New York: Grove, n.d.), p. 217:

The peculiar development of African culture in North America began with the loss of the drums. The Protestant, and often Puritan, slave owners interfered much more radically with the personal life of their slaves than did their Catholic colleagues in the West Indies or in South America. . . . And to forbid the drums was to show a keen scent for the essential: for without the drums it was impossible to call the orishas, the ancestors were silent, and the proselytizers seemed to have a free hand. The Baptists and Methodists, whose practical maxims and revivals were sympathetic to African religiosity quickly found masses of adherents.

Thus the long-term interest of many Afro-American youth in the playing of drums, as well as the more recent and general embracing of African and black cultural forms, might be viewed as *the return of the repressed*—to borrow a leading concept from Freudian psychology.

For a discussion of the attack on culture in the context of classical colonialism, see K. M. Panikkar, *Asia and Western Dominance* (New York: Collier, 1969); H. Alan C. Cairns, *The Clash of Cultures: Early Race Relations in Central Africa* (New York: Praeger, 1965).

27. The standard discussion of this phenomenon is Will Herberg, *Protestant-Catholic-Jew* (Garden City, N.Y.: Doubleday, 1955).

28. The ethnic and racially "plural society" is another characteristic colonial phenomenon. See J. S. Furnivall, *Colonial Policy and Practice* (New York: New York University Press, 1956); and M. G. Smith, *The Plural Society in the British West Indies* (Berkeley and Los Angeles: University of California Press, 1965).

29. The connection has been cogently argued by Dale L. Johnson, "On Oppressed Classes and the Role of the Social Scientist in Human Liberation," in Frank Cockcroft and Dale Johnson, eds., *The Political Economy of Underdevelopment in Latin America* (Garden City, N.Y.: Doubleday, 1971); and by William K. Tabb, *The Political Economy of the Black Ghetto* (New York: Norton, 1970), esp. chap. 2.

However, the international perspective on American racial problems is by no means new. W. E. B. Du Bois was one of its early exponents, and Malcolm X placed domestic racism and strategies of liberation in a worldwide context. For a discussion of the internationalizing of Malcolm's politics; see Robert L. Allen, *Black Awakening in Capitalist America* (Garden City, N.Y.: Doubleday, 1969), pp. 31–34.

NOTES TO CHAPTER FIVE

1. This was five years before the publication of *The Crisis of the Negro Intellectual* (New York: Morrow, 1967), which brought Cruse into prominence. Thus,

the 1962 article was not widely read until its reprinting in Cruse's essays, *Rebellion or Revolution* (New York: Morrow, 1968).

2. Kenneth Clark, *Youth in the Ghetto* (New York: Haryou Associates, 1964). Clark dropped the colonial metaphor from his *Dark Ghetto* (New York: Harper & Row, 1965), although much of the data and analysis are the same.

3. Stokely Carmichael and Charles Hamilton, *Black Power* (New York: Random House, 1967).

4. In stressing a general racist dynamic, I do not imply that the specific racial patterns of colonial societies have been identical in all historical and contemporary contexts. In fact, much research on slavery and colonialism has been devoted to the study of differences in the intensity of racial feeling, the definition of the subordinate races, the nature of interracial contacts, and strategies of control between one historical setting and another. Such variation, the importance of which remains a lively area of scholarly debate, has, however, existed within a situation of universal white dominance and belief in European cultural superiority.

For a treatment of this universal aspect, along with an approach to the analysis of variation, see Georges Balandier, "The Colonial Situation: A Theoretical Approach," in Immanuel Wallerstein, ed., *Social Change: The Colonial Situation* (New York: Wiley, 1966), pp. 34–61. Some of the many studies that have focused on comparative patterns of slavery and colonialism include Frank Tannenbaum, *Slave and Citizen* (New York: Knopf, 1947); Stanley M. Elkins, *Slavery* (Chicago: University of Chicago Press, 1959); David B. Davis, *The Problem of Slavery in Western Culture* (Ithaca, N.Y.: Cornell University Press, 1966); Herbert S. Klein, *Slavery in the Americas* (Chicago: University of Chicago Press, 1967); H. Hoetink, *The Two Variants of Race Relations in the Caribbean* (London: Oxford University Press, 1967); J. S. Furnivall, *Colonial Policy and Practice* (New York: New York University Press, 1948); and Immanuel Wallerstein, *Africa, The Politics of Independence* (New York: Random House, 1961).

5. Clark, *Youth in the Ghetto*, pp. 10–11, 79–80.

6. Harold Cruse, "Behind the Black Power Slogan," in Cruse, *Rebellion or Revolution*, pp. 238–39. A business association which primarily serves black communities (The National Association of Market Development) has only 131 black-owned firms out of a total of 407. Andrew Brimmer, "The Negro in the National Economy," in John P. Davis, ed., *The American Negro Reference Book* (Englewood Cliffs, N.J.: Prentice-Hall, 1966), p. 297, as cited in Louis Knowles and Kenneth Prewitt, eds., *Institutional Racism in America* (Englewood Cliffs, N.J.: Prentice-Hall, 1969), p. 16.

For a convincing critique of black capitalism as a strategy for liberation, see Earl Ofari, *The Myth of Black Capitalism* (New York: Monthly Review Press, 1970).

7. Harold M. Baron, "Black Powerlessness in Chicago," *Trans-Action* (November 1968), 27–33.

8. Nathan Glazer and Daniel P. Moynihan, *Beyond the Melting Pot* (Cambridge: M.I.T. and Harvard University Press, 1963), p. 37.

9. "The police function to support and enforce the interests of the dominant political, social, and economic interests of the town" is a statement made by a former police scholar and official, according to A. Neiderhoffer, *Behind the Shield*

(Garden City, N.Y.: Doubleday, 1967), as cited by Gary T. Marx, "Civil Disorder and the Agents of Control," in Marx, ed., *Racial Conflict* (Boston: Little Brown, 1971), pp. 286–306.

10. *Report of the National Advisory Commission on Civil Disorders* (New York: Bantam, 1968), p. 71.

11. This kind of attitude has a long history. During slavery, blacks used the same rationalization to justify stealing from their masters. Appropriating things from the master was viewed as "*taking* part of his property for the benefit of another part"; whereas stealing referred to appropriating something from another slave, an offense that was not condoned. Kenneth Stampp, *The Peculiar Institution* (New York: Vintage, 1956), p. 127.

12. *Report of the National Advisory Commission on Civil Disorders,* p. 178.

13. Frantz Fanon, *Wretched of the Earth* (New York: Grove, 1963); Albert Memmi, *The Colonizer and the Colonized* (Boston: Beacon, 1967).

14. Robert Wood, "Colonialism in Africa and America: Some Conceptual Considerations," unpublished paper (December 1967), Department of Sociology, University of California, Berkeley, California.

15. Frantz Fanon, *Black Skins, White Masks* (New York: Grove, 1967).

16. Memmi, *The Colonizer and the Colonized,* p. 128.

17. During the early civil rights campaigns many whites had the illusion that they could disassociate themselves from racist privilege by participating in the movement for racial equality. Memmi shows how racism is a universal and inevitable part of the mentality of all members of the dominant group in a racially oppressive society. Out of their own experience this understanding came to black activists and led to the position that liberation could only develop out of "a black thing." The black power movement led also to a new reading of American racism as a colonial question. Confronted by this shift in perspective, white activists felt disoriented, left "out in the cold." Many former advocates of "Negro rights" not only turned against the black nationalist trend, but reversed their formerly "positive" orientation toward the Afro-American community as a whole, much in the manner of Memmi's left colonizer's reaction to the "excesses" of the anticolonial struggle. The third world movement seems to have aggravated this response: Black indifference is bad enough, but collective exclusion is intolerable!

18. Ibid., pp. 130, 132, 134.

19. Larry R. Jackson, "Welfare Mothers and Black Liberation," *Black Scholar* 1, no. 5 (April 1970): 35.

20. Memmi, *The Colonizer and the Colonized,* pp. 137–38.

21. Major documents in the school controversy, various viewpoints and analyses are included in Maurice R. Berube and Marilyn Gittell, eds., *Confrontation at Ocean Hill–Brownsville* (New York: Praeger, 1969).

22. This split in the politics and psyche of the black American was poetically described by W. E. B. Du Bois in his *Souls of Black Folk* (New York: Crest, 1972), and more recently analyzed by Harold Cruse in *The Crisis of the Negro Intellectual.*

23. Peter Rossi, et al., "Between Black and White—The Faces of American Institutions in the Ghetto," in *Supplemental Studies for the National Advisory Commission on Civil Disorders* (July 1968), 114.

24. John Hersey, *The Algiers Motel Incident* (New York: Bantam, 1968).

25. "In the Gordon Riots of 1780 demonstrators destroyed property and freed prisoners, but did not seem to kill anyone, while authorities killed several hundred rioters and hung an additional 25. In the Rebellion Riots of the French Revolution, though several hundred rioters were killed, they killed no one. Up to the end of the summer of 1967, this pattern had clearly been repeated, as police, not rioters, were responsible for most of the more than 100 deaths that have occurred. Similarly, in a related context, the more than 100 civil rights murders of recent years have been matched by almost no murders of racist whites." G. Marx, "Civil Disorders and the Agents of Social Control."

26. Jerome H. Skolnick, ed., *The Politics of Protest* (New York: Ballantine, 1969), esp. chap. 7, "The Police in Protest."

27. *San Francisco Sunday Examiner and Chronicle* (May 9, 1971), sec. A, p. 19, summarizing "The Dilemma of the Black Policeman," *Ebony* (May 1971). Comparing the 1971 figures with the 1968 data reported in the Kerner Report (p. 321) shows very little change in the overall pattern. Some cities made absolute and relative gains in police integration; others, including two of the "leaders," Philadelphia and Chicago, lost ground.

That black officers nevertheless would make a difference is suggested by data from one of the supplemental studies to the Kerner Report. They found Negro policemen working in the ghettos considerably more sympathetic to the community and its social problems than their white counterparts. Rossi, et al., "Between Black and White," chap. 6.

28. See, for example, Ofari, *The Myth of Black Capitalism;* Robert Allen, *Black Awakening in Capitalist America* (Garden City, N.Y.: Doubleday, 1969); Martin Oppeneheimer, *The Urban Guerilla* (Chicago: Quadrangle, 1969); William K. Tabb, *The Political Economy of the Black Ghetto* (New York: Norton, 1970); and Jan Dizard and David Wellman, "I Love Ralph Bunche But I Can't Eat Him for Lunch: Corporate Liberalism, Racism, and Reform—Emerging Strategies for Ghetto Control," *Leviathan* 1 (Summer 1969): 46–53.

29. Franz Schurmann, "System, Contradictions, and Revolution in America," in Roderick Aya and Norman Miller, eds., *The New American Revolution* (New York: The Free Press, 1971).

30. On the network of interests in the ghetto, see Harold Baron, "The Web of Urban Racism," in Knowles and Prewitt, eds., *Institutional Racism.*

31. *Report of the National Advisory Commission on Civil Disorders,* pp. 253–56.

32. Lee Rainwater, "The Revolt of the Dirty-Workers," *Trans-Action* 5, no. 1 (November 1967): 2, 64.

NOTES TO CHAPTER SIX

1. George Orwell's character Ellis, in his novel *Burmese Days,* is an excellent depiction of this mentality (1934; reprint ed., New York: New American Library, 1963).

2. K. M. Panikkar, *Asia and Western Dominance* (London: Allen & Unwin, 1953).

3. H. Alan C. Cairns, *The Clash of Cultures: Early Race Relations in Central Africa* (New York: Praeger, 1965), pp. 176–78.

4. The best study of the moral arrogance of Europeans in relation to non-Western societies is V. G. Kiernan, *The Lords of Human Kind* (London: Weidenfeld and Nicholson, 1969).

5. Cairns, *The Clash of Cultures*, pp. 77–79.

6. Ibid., p. 78.

7. "The purchase of slaves called for a business sense and shrewd discrimination. An Angolan Negro was proverbial for worthlessness; Coromantines (Ashantis) from the Gold Coast were good workers but too rebellious; Mandingoes (Senegal) were too prone to theft; the Eboes (Nigeria) were timid and despondent; the Pawpaws or Whydahs (Dahomey) were the most docile and best-disposed." Eric Williams, *Capitalism and Slavery* (New York: Russell, 1961), pp. 37–38. See also Stanley Stein, *Vassouras* (Cambridge: Harvard University Press, 1957), pp. 70–71.

8. See Eugene D. Genovese, "The Treatment of Slaves in Different Countries: Problems in the Application of the Comparative Method," in Laura Foner and E. Genovese, *Slavery in the New World* (Englewood Cliffs, N.J.: Prentice-Hall, 1969), pp. 202–10, for a general discussion of these differences. On Brazil, see David B. Davis, *The Problem of Slavery in Western Culture* (Ithaca, N.Y.: Cornell University Press, 1966), chap. 8, and Stein, *Vassouras.*) The significance of African ethnicity until late in the nineteenth century is discussed in Stein, ibid., for Brazil, and by Orlando Patterson in *The Sociology of Slavery* (London: MacGibbon & Kee, 1967) for Jamaica. Stein notes that the contraband slave trade continued to supply Brazil through the 1860s; and Patterson calculates that almost a quarter of Jamaican slaves were African born at the time of emancipation (1838).

9. Ndabaningi Sithole, *African Nationalism* (London: Oxford University Press, 1968), p. 68.

10. Ibid.

11. Some general works on colonialism and plural societies that discuss these issues are Rupert Emerson, *From Empire to Nation* (Boston: Beacon, 1962); Stewart Easton, *The Rise and Fall of Western Colonialism* (New York: Praeger, 1964); J. S. Furnivall, *Colonial Policy and Practice* (New York: New York University Press, 1956); Immanuel Wallerstein, *Social Change: The Colonial Situation* (New York: Wiley, 1966), and *Africa, The Politics of Independence* (New York: Random House, 1961); and M. G. Smith, *The Plural Society in the British West Indies.*

12. Examples of such prepolitical or protopolitical movements are the Ghost Dance religions of the North Americans Indians, the Ethiopian and Messianistic Churches in South and Central Africa, the Ras Tafari movement in Jamaica, Pentecostalism among Mexicans in the U.S. Southwest, and the famous Cargo Cults of Melanesia.

13. The concepts of new societies and fragmentation are borrowed from Louis Hartz, *The Founding of New Societies* (New York: Harcourt Brace Jovanovich, 1964).

14. Winthrop Jordan, *White over Black* (Chapel Hill: University of North

Carolina Press, 1968), and Lewis Copeland, "The Negro as a Contrast Conception," in Edgar T. Thompson, ed., *Race Relations and the Race Problem* (Durham, N.C.: Duke University Press, 1939), pp. 152–79.

15. Joel Kovel, *White Racism: A Psychohistory* (New York: Random House, 1970).

NOTES TO CHAPTER SEVEN

1. Gunnar Myrdal, *An American Dilemma* (New York: Harper & Row, 1944).

2. Ibid., pp. 927–30.

3. Nathan Glazer and Daniel P. Moynihan, *Beyond the Melting Pot* (Cambridge: M.I.T. and Harvard University Press, 1963), p. 53. Glazer, it is true, views Negroes as an ethnic group rather than simply a racial category. But for him the contents of black ethnicity are only common interests and social problems. His account of black New York ignores the existence of a collective ethos, community social structure, and group institutions.

4. M. Herskovits, *The Myth of the Negro Past* (New York: Harper & Row, 1941).

5. E. Franklin Frazier, *The Negro in the United States,* rev. ed. (New York: Macmillan, 1957), pp. 680–81. For a later statement, see Frazier, *The Negro Church in America* (New York: Schocken, 1964), chap. 1.

6. For example, Charles S. Johnson, *Shadow of the Plantation* (Chicago: University of Chicago Press, 1934); St. Clair Drake and Horace Cayton, *Black Metropolis* (New York: Harcourt Brace Jovanovich, 1945); and Hylan Lewis, *Blackways of Kent* (Chapel Hill: University of North Carolina Press, 1955). The distinctive culture of Harlem is emphasized in the writings of James Baldwin, and in Claude Brown, *Manchild in the Promised Land* (New York: Macmillan, 1956), though not in the scholarly study of Kenneth Clark, *Dark Ghetto* (New York: Harper & Row, 1965).

7. Charles Keil, *Urban Blues* (Chicago: University of Chicago Press, 1966), p. 170.

8. Bennett M. Berger, "Soul Searching," *Trans-Action* (June 1967): 54–57. This review also appears under the title of "Black Culture or Lower-Class Culture," in Lee Rainwater, ed., *Soul* (Chicago: Trans-Action Books, Aldine, 1970), along with an earlier version of the present essay.

9. Kenneth Stampp, *The Peculiar Institution* (New York: Random House, 1956), p. vii.

10. Janheinz Jahn, *Muntu* (New York: Grove, n.d.), p. 225.

11. Howard Brotz, *The Black Jews of Harlem* (New York: The Free Press, 1964), pp. 129–30.

12. Will Herberg, *Protestant-Catholic-Jew* (Garden City: N.Y.: Doubleday, 1956).

13. L. Singer, "Ethno-genesis and Negro Americans Today," *Social Research* 29, no. 4 (Winter 1962): 419–32.

14. Jahn, *Muntu,* pp. 18–19.

15. Melvin B. Tolson, *Harlem Gallery* (New York: Twayne, 1965), pp. 75. Reprinted with permission of the University Press of Virginia.

16. Ibid., p. 94. Reprinted with permission of the University of Press of Virginia.

17. On African philosophy and aesthetics, see Placide Tempels, *Bantu Philosophy* (Paris: Présence Africaine, 1959); and Jahn, *Muntu,* as well as the considerable literature on *négritude.* These findings can be compared with the discussions of Soul and Afro-American aesthetics in LeRoi Jones, *Blues People* (New York: Morrow, 1963); Keil, *Urban Blues;* and Vernon J. Dixon and Badi Foster, eds., *Beyond Black or White* (Boston: Little, Brown, 1970), esp. chaps. 2 and 4. For another approach to African culture, see W. E. Abraham, *The Mind of Africa* (Chicago: Phoenix, 1966).

18. Arnold J. Toynbee, *A Study of History,* vol. 1 (London: Oxford University Press, 1934), pp. 429–30. His discussion converges with Herskovits's observation that "Africanisms" in religious beliefs were stronger than those in the sphere of economics and politics; it also suggests a new light on the Black Panther slogan, attributed to Huey Newton, that "the spirit of the people is greater than the man's technology."

19. On the African bases of Afro-American culture, the most comprehensive scholarship has taken place in the area of music. See Jones, *Blues People;* Paul Oliver, *Savannah Syncopators: African Retentions in the Blues* (New York: Stein & Day, 1970); Gunther Schuller, *Early Jazz: Its Roots and Musical Development* (New York: Oxford University Press, 1968), chap. 1; Richard A. Waterman, "African Influence on the Music of the Americas," in Sol Tax, ed., *Acculturation in the Americas* (Chicago: University of Chicago Press, 1952); Ralph H. Metcalfe, Jr., "The Western African Roots of Afro-American Music," *Black Scholar* 1 (June 1970): 16–25; Lawrence W. Levine, "Slave Songs and Slave Consciousness: An Exploration in Neglected Sources," in Tamara Hareven, ed., *Anonymous Americans* (Englewood Cliffs, N.J.: Prentice-Hall, 1971), pp. 99–130; Alan Lomax, "The Homogeneity of African-Afro-American Musical Style," in Norman E. Whitten, Jr., and John F. Szwed, eds., *Afro-American Anthropology* (New York: The Free Press, 1970), pp. 181–201; and John F. Szwed, "Afro-American Musical Adaptation," in Whitten and Szwed, *Afro-American-Anthropology,* pp. 219–28.

On language and folklore, see J. L. Dillard, "Non-standard Negro Dialects: Convergence or Divergence," in Whitten and Szwed, *Afro-American-Anthropology,* pp. 119–27; Raven I. McDavid, Jr., and Virginia Glenn McDavid, "The Relationship of the Speech of American Negroes to the Speech of Whites," *American Speech* 26 (February 1951): 3–17; William A. Stewart, *Non-Standard Speech and the Teaching of English* (Washington, D.C.: Center for Applied Linguistics, 1964); Richard A. Waterman and William R. Bascom, "African and New World Negro Folklore," Maria Leach, ed., *Standard Dictionary of Folklore, Mythology and Legend,* vol. 1 (New York: Funk & Wagnalls, 1949), pp. 18–24; and Daniel J. Crowley, "Negro Folklore: An Africanist's View," *Texas Quarterly* 5 (Autumn 1962): 65–71. Aside from the question of African roots, the literature on black English is enormous. An exemplary case of research and interpretation is William

Labov's "The Logic on Non-Standard English," in Alfred C. Aarons, Barbara Y. Gordon, and William A. Stewart, eds., "Linguistic-Cultural Differences and American Education," in the *Florida FL Reporter* 7 (Spring–Summer 1969): 60–74, 169.

20. Omnipresent racism notwithstanding, the West has generally appreciated the cultures of Asia more than those of Africa. Even Toynbee omits African societies from the civilizations he interprets in his eleven-volume *Study of History*. The same practice is continued in one of the more recent syntheses of world history, William H. McNeill's *The Rise of the West: A History of the Human Community* (Chicago: University of Chicago Press, 1963), which discusses Africa only marginally. The neglect is apparently justified by a view that this continent was peripheral to the mainstream of cultural and political developments from ancient times to the modern period!

21. Thomas Hodgkin, *Nationalism in Colonial Africa* (London: Frederick Muller, 1956), esp. pp. 172–77. The author notes that until recently the view prevailed "that any remarkable work of art or architecture discovered in Africa south of the Sahara must have been produced by non-Africans—Arabs, perhaps, probably Portuguese—since Africans were by definition incapable of this level of achievement. This was the only way in which Europeans could account for the sculptures of Ife and Benin, the castles of Gondar, the fortifications of Zimbabwe, without disturbing their preconceptions."

22. See Harold Isaacs, *The New World of Negro Americans* (New York: Viking, 1964), pt. 3, pp. 105–322, for an excellent treatment of attitudes toward Africa.

23. Leslie W. Dunbar, "The Changing Mind of the South," in Avery Leiserson, ed., *The American South in the 1960's* (New York: Praeger, 1966), p. 4. "Only Lillian Smith had the greatness to wrestle with what the others saw, but passed by, and that was the centrality of race to the southern self-consciousness."

24. Blacks also assimilated some of the values and styles of the southern ruling classes, though they were not always in a position to emulate them. Ellison has attributed the general aristocratic flavor of ghetto life styles to this origin, as well as the American Negro's apparent lack of passion for business entrepreneurship. Interview with Ralph Ellison, in Robert Penn Warren, *Who Speaks for the Negro?* (New York: Random House, 1965), pp. 334–36. See also the stimulating and surprisingly neglected collection of essays by Calvin Hernton, *White Papers for White Americans* (Garden City, N.Y.: Doubleday, 1965). In his *Manchild in the Promised Land,* Claude Brown emphasizes the cultural conflict between the traditional "down home" (southern) older generation and their more modern urban-oriented Harlem offspring. As a youth, Brown was sent South for a year to live with relatives; this is a fairly common pattern among American blacks. For another instance, see Henry Williamson, *Hustler!,* ed. R. L. Keiser (Garden City, N.Y.: Doubleday, 1965).

25. See Stampp, *The Peculiar Institution,* for historical evidence on this point.

26. Norman Podhoretz, "My Negro Problem—And Ours," in Bernard E. Segal, ed., *Racial and Ethnic Relations* (New York: Crowell, 1966), p. 250.

27. Ernest Gaine's novel *The Autobiography of Miss Jane Pittman* (New York: Dial, 1971) gives an excellent sense of this movement.

28. On the long-term function of the immigrant ghetto, see Oscar Handlin, *The Uprooted* (Boston: Little, Brown, 1951). For the vibrancy of cultural development in the Jewish ghetto, see Hutchins Hapgood, *The Spirit of the Ghetto* (New York: Funk & Wagnalls, 1902).

29. For historical accounts of the development of ethnic institutions and associations in the two largest northern black communities, see Gilbert Osofsky, *Harlem: The Making of a Ghetto* (New York: Harper & Row, 1965); and Allan H. Spear, *Black Chicago* (Chicago: University of Chicago Press, 1967). A more detailed analysis of cultural developments in Harlem in the twentieth century is found in Harold Cruse, *The Crisis of the Negro Intellectual* (New York: Morrow, 1967).

30. The most recent and influential statement (actually a perversion) of this position is Edward Banfield's *The Unheavenly City* (Boston: Little, Brown, 1970), which defines social class in terms of values related to achievement and planning, rather than seeing subcultural orientations as a consequence of objective economic and social circumstances. The latter, more usual treatment is argued by Elliot Liebow in his valuable study of streetcorner men in Washington, D.C., *Tally's Corner* (Boston: Little, Brown, 1967). Liebow argues explicitly that cultural traditions have little relevance in this community. For a criticism of his book on this score see Douglas Davidson, "Black Culture and Liberal Sociology," *Berkeley Journal of Sociology* 14 (1969): 164–83.

31. Berger, "Soul Searching," p. 56.

32. Among the many examples that might be cited are Brown, *Manchild in the Promised Land; The Autobiography of Malcolm X* (New York: Grove, 1965); Iceberg Slim, *Pimp: The Story of My Life* (Los Angeles: Holloway, 1969); and Leonard H. Robinson, "Negro Street Society: A Study of Racial Adjustment in Two Southern Urban Communities," Doctoral dissertation, Department of Sociology, Ohio State University (1950).

33. Johnneta B. Cole identifies style and soul as the most consistent and important themes in black American life. "Culture: Negro, Black, Nigger," *Black Scholar* 1 (June 1970): 40–44.

34. Hortense Powdermaker, *After Freedom* (New York: Viking, 1939), pp. 259–60.

35. The persistence of racial oppression from slavery to the present has solidified the continuity of the Afro-American experience and its traditions. Only this can explain the remarkable fact that the major types of orientations of slaves to the white man's system that Kenneth Stampp identified in his historical study—the cooperative or "white folks Negro," the rebel or "bad nigger," and the clever, crafty "smart nigger"—were the same dominant social types discovered by Samuel Strong in the Chicago ghetto a generation ago. Stampp, *The Peculiar Institution,* esp. chaps. 3, 4, and 8; and Samuel Strong, "Social Types in the Negro Community of Chicago: An Example of Social Type Method," Doctoral dissertation, Department of Sociology, University of Chicago (1940).

36. James Baldwin, *Notes of a Native Son* (Boston: Beacon, 1955); William M. Kelley, *A Different Drummer* (Garden City, N.Y.: Doubleday, 1962).

37. Keil, *Urban Blues,* p. 152.

38. Oscar Lewis, *La Vida* (New York: Random House, 1967), pp. xlvii–xlviii.

39. On the middle-class rejection of black ethnicity, see Jones, *Blues People;* E. F. Frazier, *Black Bourgeoisie* (New York: The Free Press, 1957); and Nathan Hare, *The Black Anglo-Saxons* (New York: Marzani, 1965).

40. Berger, "Soul Searching," p. 54.

41. Cruse, *The Crisis of the Negro Intellectual.*

NOTES TO CHAPTER EIGHT

1. *The Chicago Commission on Race Relations* (Chicago: University of Chicago Press, 1922).

2. Charles S. Johnson, *Shadow of the Plantation* (Chicago: University of Chicago Press, 1934), and *Growing Up in the Black Belt* (Washington, D.C.: American Council on Education, 1941).

3. *Violence in the City—An End or a Beginning?* Report by the Governor's Commission on the Los Angeles Riots (December 2, 1965).

4. Ibid., pp. 87–88.

5. Ibid.

6. Ibid., p. 4. Quotations from the McCone Report are cited hereafter in the text by page number.

7. During the riots Parker stated to the Watts population, "We're on top, you're on the bottom." He said the rioters were behaving like "monkeys in the zoo." Anthony Oberschall, "The Los Angeles Riot of August 1965," in James Geschwender, ed., *The Black Revolt* (Englewood Cliffs, N.J.: Prentice-Hall, 1971), p. 266.

8. Professional social workers as well as delinquent youth concurred on many points of fact with respect to the police presence. Officers were overconcentrated in the ghetto, children felt themselves under constant police surveillance, youths were frequently stopped for questioning even when there had been no apparent wrongdoing, and many instances in which innocent bystanders or observers of fights and disturbances were arrested along with or instead of the guilty parties were cited. True, the police were aware of their "negative image," a number of officers were undoubtedly trying to do a difficult job in a spirit of justice and fairness, and a minority of the sample felt that they were doing a good job. But unfortunately more typical appraisals were those of the public welfare director and the "well-adjusted" nondelinquent Negro youth in the twelfth grade quoted below:

The attitude of the authorities toward the youth of this area is brutal and oppressive for the most part. The police were afraid, to a certain extent, of the Negro population. There is a tremendous tension between the police and the Negro community.

When you come up in Watts, you can live practically any place because you know that if you're around, whatever happens when the police get there, you know they're going to take you even though you didn't do anything. Say, for instance, if you were coming home from the store, and there was a fight across the street, and you . . . stayed to watch it, the police come by, and they'll grab you.

Youth Opportunities Board of Greater Los Angeles, *First Interim Report on the Area Survey in South Central Los Angeles: A Working Document* (June 1963).

9. The UCLA survey seems to confirm this point. Forty-five percent of the sample said they had personal experience with nonviolent police malpractice: insulting language, stopping and searching cars, unnecessary frisking. The proportions who reported experiencing or witnessing more violent forms were much smaller: 13 percent for unnecessary force in arrests, 1 percent for beating people in custody, 6 percent for unnecessary home searches. However, 65 to 70 percent believed that the latter practices occurred; the same proportion felt that the less violent behaviors were common. Nathan Cohen, ed., *The Los Angeles Riots: A Socio-Psychological Study* (New York: Praeger, 1970), p. 11.

10. That the character of the outbreak is a difficult and real question is suggested by the debate within the black community as to the appropriate term of reference. Many people felt that the automatic reflex use by the media of *riots* as the label of designation missed the essence of what had happened and thus subtly distorted the issues. A preference for the word *revolt* and other similar terms was often expressed, though unfortunately we do not know how widespread these usages became.

11. Bayard Rustin, "The Watts Manifesto," *New America*, September 17, 1965, p. 7.

12. *Los Angeles Times,* August 14, 1965, p. 2.

13. Frantz Fanon, *The Wretched of the Earth* (New York: Grove, 1968). On this point see also Jean-Paul Sartre's preface.

14. Rustin, "The Watts Manifesto," pp. 7, 8.

15. *New York Times* (November 7, 1965) reported more than 100 organizations established in the Los Angeles ghetto since the riots.

16. Shana Alexander, "My Friend in Watts," *Life,* August 27, 1965, p. 18.

17. R. M. Fogelson and R. B. Hill, "Who Riots? A Study of Participation in the 1967 Riots," *Supplemental Studies for the National Advisory Commission on Civil Disorders* (Washington, D.C., 1968). See also David O. Sears and T. M. Tomlinson, "Riot Ideology in Los Angeles: A Study of Negro Attitudes," in Geschwender, ed., *The Black Revolt,* pp. 375–88; and Nathan Caplan, "Identity in Transition," in Roderick Aya and Norman Miller, eds., *The New American Revolution* (New York: The Free Press, 1971).

18. Cohen, *The Los Angeles Riots,* pp. 3, 140–257.

19. Caplan, "Identity in Transition."

20. Cohen, *The Los Angeles Riots,* p. 3. Other similar estimates of riot participation appear in the articles collected in Geschwender, *The Black Revolt,* and in Allen D. Grimshaw, ed., *Racial Violence in the United States* (Chicago: Aldine, 1969).

21. Cohen, *The Los Angeles Riots,* pp. 2–3.

22. Sears and Tomlinson, "Riot Ideology in Los Angeles."

23. *Report of the National Advisory Commission on Civil Disorders,* with an introduction by Tom Wicker (New York: Bantam Books, 1968).

24. There have been many critiques of the Kerner Report. Symposium on "The Kerner Report, Social Scientists, and the American Public," six essays, *The Social Science Quarterly* 49, no. 3 (December 1968): 433–73. See also Gary T. Marx, "Two Cheers for the Riot Commission Report," *Harvard Review,* 4 (Summer 1968): 3–14; Amitai Etzioni, "Making Riots mandatory," *Psychiatry and Social Science Review* (May 1968); and Tom Christoffel, "Black Power and Corporate Capitalism," in Barry N. Schwartz and Robert Disch, eds., *White Racism* (New York: Dell, 1970), pp. 333–40. On the politics of riot commissions, see Robert M. Fogelson, *Violence as Protest* (Garden City, N.Y.: Doubleday, 1971); and Michael Lipsky and David J. Olson, "Riot Commission Politics," *Trans-Action* (July–August 1969): 9–21.

NOTES TO CHAPTER NINE

1. A number of books have been devoted in full or in part to the Newton trial. For an unusually sensitive personal perspective, see Gilbert Moore, *A Special Rage* (New York: Harper & Row, 1971). For the account by a defense attorney, including the court transcript of significant testimony, see Edward Keating, *Free Huey* (New York: Dell, 1971). Discussion of the trial appears also in Reginald Major, *A Panther Is a Black Cat* (New York: Morrow, 1971), pp. 179–81, 215–38; Gene Marine, *The Black Panthers* (New York: New American Library, 1969), chap. 9; and Bobby Seale, *Seize the Time* (New York: Random House, 1970), pp. 201–54. See also Kathy Mulherin, "Stalking the Panthers," in Barry N. Schwartz and Robert Disch, eds., *White Racism* (New York: Dell, 1970), pp. 240–51.

2. *Minimizing Racism in Jury Trials,* ed. Ann Fagan Ginger (Berkeley: National Lawyers Guild, 1969), was prepared as a manual to inform other attorneys about Garry's method of handling the voir dire. The book contains a list of the questions Garry asked related to race, 120 pages of extracts from the transcript of the voir dire, a preface by the chief attorney, and the appellate brief to the higher courts on jury selection prepared by his chief associate Fay Stender. The present chapter also appeared in a slightly different version in *Minimizing Racism.*

3. Hans Zeisel, *Some Data on Juror Attitudes Towards Capital Punishment* (Chicago: Center for the Study of Criminal Justice, University of Chicago, 1968). With Harry Kalven, Jr., Zeisel coauthored *The American Jury* (Boston: Little, Brown, 1966).

4. For a defense of this position, see Editorial Board, Yale Law Review, "The Case for Black Juries," *Yale Law Journal* 79, no. 3 (January 1970): 531–51.

5. Many of these issues are discussed, with abundant citations from case law, in Jennie Rhine, "The Jury: A Reflection of the Prejudices of the Community," *Hastings Law Journal* 20 (May 1969): 1417–45.

NOTES TO CHAPTER TEN

1. The immigrants interviewed by Manuel Gamio during the 1920s were striking in their loyalty to Mexico and in their critical attitude toward U.S. cultural values and treatment of Mexicans. An aversion to the idea of U.S. citizen-

ship was almost universal. Manuel Gamio, *The Mexican Immigrant: His Life Story* (Chicago: University of Chicago Press, 1931).

2. This tendency may be weaker in Texas, where anti-Mexican prejudice has been particularly vicious, and in New Mexico where Mexican-Americans retained a numerical majority until well into the twentieth century. Yet recent students at the University of New Mexico inform me that they have observed this phenomenon in the white movement there. It is no accident that the two major studies of Mexican-Americans written by Chicanos up to 1970 bear the title and subtitle, respectively: *Forgotten People* and *Forgotten Americans*. George I. Sanchez, *Forgotten People* (Albuquerque: University of New Mexico Press, 1940), and Julian Samora, ed., *La Raza: Forgotten Americans* (Notre Dame, Ind.: University of Notre Dame Press, 1966).

Joan Moore remarks, "Of the half-dozen texts on minorities on my shelf only one contains more than a paragraph on Mexican-Americans." Moore, "Political and Ethical Problems in a Large-Scale Study of a Minority Population," in Gideon Sjoberg, ed., *Ethics, Politics, and Social Research* (Cambridge: Schenkman, 1967), p. 227.

3. This reluctance to cooperate with Anglo investigators is at least a hundred years old. The pioneer historian of California and the West, H. H. Bancroft, reported that he and his research assistants were plagued by the "feeble memories," "lack of time," "evasion and lies," and outright refusal to be interviewed on the part of many of the leading Californios they sought as informants. Leonard Pitt, *The Decline of the Californios* (Berkeley and Los Angeles: University of California Press, 1966 and 1970), pp. 280–81.

4. O. Romano, "Minorities, History, and the Cultural Mystique," *El Grito* 1 (Fall 1967): 7.

5. O. Romano, "The Anthropology and Sociology of the Mexican-Americans," *El Grito* 2 (Fall 1968): 13–26. See also Nick Vaca, "The Mexican-American in the Social Sciences: 1920–1970," pt. 1, *El Grito* 3 (Spring 1970); 3–24; pt. 2, *El Grito* 4 (Fall 1970): 17–51.

6. For critiques of the Department of Labor Report: *The Negro Family in America* by D. P. Moynihan, see Lee Rainwater and William Yancey, *The Moynihan Report and the Politics of Controversy* (Cambridge: M.I.T. University Press, 1967). For reactions to *The Confessions of Nat Turner* by William Styron, see John H. Clarke, ed., *William Styron's Nat Turner: Ten Black Writers Respond* (Boston: Beacon, 1969).

7. The bibliographies consulted were *The Mexican American—A Selected and Annotated Bibliography* (Palo Alto: Stanford University Press, 1969); *The Mexican American—A New Focus on Opportunity* (The Inter-Agency Committee on Mexican-American Affairs, March, 1969); and Leo Grebler, Joan Moore, and Ralph Guzman, *The Mexican American People* (New York: The Free Press, 1970), pp. 677–741. For purposes of calculating percentages, works authored by institutions rather than individuals were discounted; materials prepared by a mixed team of Anglo and Spanish-surnamed authors were figured as one-half Chicano. There were no appreciable differences among the categories into which the bibliographies were subdivided, that is, among books, journal articles, and dissertations.

8. Some indication of a possible change is suggested by an analysis of the books

that have appeared since 1969, when the three bibliographies were assembled. Ten of the twenty-three new books I have located are authored by Mexican-Americans.

9. Gunnar Myrdal, *An American Dilemma* (New York: Harper & Row, 1944), pp. 1144–80. Omitted for the purpose of calculation were foreign and institutional authors, books about race relations outside the United States, general books about the South, studies of ethnic groups other than blacks, fiction, and autobiography. When the books were coauthored, the race of the first author was used. The result was a sample of 130 books where I was reasonably certain of the author's race; twenty-one titles could not be classified, because of uncertainty.

10. E. Franklin Frazier, *The Negro in the United States,* rev. ed. (New York: Macmillan, 1957), pp. 715–48. The method employed was similar to that described for Myrdal. See note 9. Frazier's bibliography is divided into five categories. I did not analyze the first, "The Negro Under the Slave Regime," because the historians listed were overwhelmingly white. After the elimination of duplication, the result was forty-six black authors, fifty-three white, four racially mixed, and twenty-six unknown or unidentifiable.

11. Elizabeth W. Miller, *The Negro in America: A Bibliography* (Cambridge: Harvard University Press, 1966), pp. 1–68. Calculating books only, in Miller's first five most general sections, the result was one hundred eight white authors, fifty-three black, one other nonwhite, and twenty unidentifiable.

12. "Starting with a language difference and moving on to cultural values of all types, La Raza is even less 'American' than black people in the United States. The villages of Northern New Mexico . . . seem more than any black ghetto to be of another country. . . . The weight and intricacy of family and other relationships, with roots that are centuries old, create a Raza society in which layer after layer of truth can be peeled away—still leaving an outside observer with the feeling that the fundamental has yet to be grasped." Elizabeth Martinez, "An Exchange on La Raza," *New York Review of Books,* February 12, 1970.

13. This relative underrepresentation of Mexican-Americans is true of other institutions committed to integration in recent years. An ethnic survey of San Francisco's public schools in October 1970 revealed that only 3 percent of teachers and administrators were Spanish speaking—compared with almost 14 percent of the students. Blacks were seriously under-represented also but the 1 to 3 ratio between 28 percent of the pupils and 9 percent of the teachers and 8 percent of the administrators was smaller than the corresponding Chicano–Latino ratio. Chinese underrepresentation was about the same as for blacks, that of Filipinos (1 to 4) closer to the Spanish-speaking. The total picture: 35 percent of the pupils were white compared with 80 percent of the teachers and administrators. *San Francisco Chronicle,* May 8, 1971, p. 2.

NOTES TO CHAPTER ELEVEN

1. It appears as if the Latin American and North American theories developed for the most part independently of one another. See Pablo Gonzalez Casanova, *Internal Colonialism and National Development* (St. Louis: Washington University Monograph Series, Studies in Comparative International Develop-

ment, I, no. 4, 1965), and Rodolpho Stavenhagen, "Classes, Colonialism and Acculuration," *Studies in Comparative International Development* 1, no. 6 (1965). For a statement similar in outlook to the present essay, see Stavenhagen, "Decolonizing Applied Social Sciences," *Human Organization* 30, no. 4 (Winter 1971): 333–57. For discussions of internal colonialism in the United States, see Harold Cruse, *Rebellion or Revolution* (New York: William Morrow, 1968); Stokely Carmichael and Charles Hamilton, *Black Power* (New York: Vintage Books, 1967); Robert Allen, *Black Awakening in Capitalist America* (Garden City, N.Y.: Doubleday, 1969); Robert Blauner, "Internal Colonialism and Ghetto Revolt," *Social Problems* 16, no. 4 (Spring 1969); and Mario Barrera, Carlos Muñoz, and Charles Ornelas, "The Barrio as Internal Colony," in Harlan Hahn, ed., *Urban Affairs Annual Review*, vol. 6 (1972).

2. In the United States the most strategic expression of this clash took place in the community and academic response to the "Moynihan Report." In Latin America the pivotal case of research serving American imperialism was Project Camelot, a Defense Department–financed study of internal conflict that was attacked as a counterinsurgency operation. On the relatively more complete research colonialism in the study of Mexican-Americans as compared to Afro-Americans, see Chapter 10 above.

3. An upsurge of critical questioning of the social scientist's ethical and political role in the mid-1960s is indicated in the publication of *Ethics, Politics, and Social Research,* ed. Gideon Sjoberg (Cambridge, Mass.: Schenkman Publishing Co., 1967).

4. For searching insights into the dynamics of this situation, we recommend Albert Memmi's *The Colonizer and the Colonized* (Boston: Beacon Press, 1967). Franz Fanon's "Medicine and Colonialism" in *Studies in a Dying Colonialism* also speaks to the fundamental irrelevance of the manifest purpose and professional goals of the colonizer in the colonial situation. Even though the French doctor in Algeria was committed to the cure of his patient, the structural and cultural conflict made it inevitable that the colonized Arab would react to him as an alien and an enemy.

5. Of course there is nothing new in this critique of standard research qualifications. The idea of using "indigenous" community people in research is part of the widespread subprofessional or paraprofessional movement, sometimes formulated as "new careers for the poor."

6. For example, some of our respondents had participated in riots in the Bay Area. When researchers arrived to study these events and wanted to look at our interviews, our staff decided against opening our interviews to them.

NOTES TO CHAPTER TWELVE

1. Ronald Takaki, *From Different Shores: Perspectives on Race and Ethnicity in America* (New York: Oxford University Press, 1987).

2. For an earlier brief comment on "the declining significance of race" and the class-race issue, see Bob Blauner, *Black Lives, White Lives: Three Decades of Race Relations in America* (Berkeley: University of California Press, 1989), p. 170.

3. I suspect that the absence of a felt place for white males in the "identity politics" that so dominates liberal and progressive circles is one reason for the emergence of a men's movement in the past few years. Despite obvious differences, there's a parallel to the women's movement's emergence in the late 1960s and 1970s, when (mostly) white women developed feminism after the nationalism of the civil rights movement and the sexism of the antiwar movement left them without a political home.

NOTES TO CHAPTER FOURTEEN

1. It also depends on whose perceptions we are talking about. Many Rightwing Republicans, as well as many in the general public, see liberals as far out and radical, lumping together the two segments of the Left. In the media today, *liberal* encompasses the entire range of Left politics. The word *radical* is rarely heard, as if this political species became extinct when the movements of the 1960s died out. Even radicals contribute to the blurring of the liberal-radical distinction in the public mind when they refer to political groupings as "liberals and progressives" in an attempt to court respectability. Perhaps the idea of liberal and radical became so blurred because conservative Republicans (above all, Ronald Reagan) were successful in portraying the liberal wing of the Democratic Party as far-out radicals who destroyed America's economy by giving us the welfare state and weakened our culture by encouraging the ethos of permissiveness and the victim mentality.

2. For example, Nathan Glazer in his *Affirmative Discrimination: Ethnic Inequality and Public Policy* (New York: Basic Books, 1975). Yet this example also shows how fluid the labels are. It was largely in opposing affirmative action that a number of leading American liberals—including Irving Kristol, Norman Podhoretz, and Glazer—staked out the political worldview that has been called *neoconservatism.*

3. Rank-and-file liberals probably made up the bulk of the whites who thronged to the 1963 March on Washington. Many liberal white college students volunteered for the Mississippi Freedom Summer in 1964 and returned North newly radicalized. See Douglas McAdam, *Freedom Summer* (New York: Oxford University Press, 1988).

4. Murray Friedman, "The White Liberal's Retreat," in Allen Westin, ed. *Freedom Now* (New York: Basic Books), pp. 320–28.

5. McAdam, *Freedom Summer.*

6. Robert Allen, *Black Awakening in Capitalist America* (Garden City, N.Y.: Doubleday, 1969).

7. Studs Terkel, *Race: How Black and Whites Think and Feel about the American Obsession* (New York: New Press, 1992).

NOTE TO CHAPTER FIFTEEN

1. Jonathan Kaufmann, *Broken Alliance: The Turbulent Times between Blacks and Jews in America* (New York: Scribner's, 1988).

NOTES TO CHAPTER SIXTEEN

1. Broadcast on Cable News Network (CNN), December 19, 2000.

2. Marjorie Connelly, "Who Voted: A Portrait of American Politics, 1976–2000," *New York Times*, November 12, 2000, p. 4.

3. Jack E. White, "The Real Winners: Black Voters," *Time*, vol. 156, no. 22, November 27, 2000, p. 60, praises the Clinton administration for its "track record of defending affirmative action, reducing black unemployment to an all-time low, and appointing the most diverse cabinet in history."

4. *New York Times*, "Who Voted."

5. White, "The Real Winners."

6. Ibid.

7. Ibid.

8. Ibid.

9. Don Van Natta, Jr., "Democrats Tell of Problems at the Polls Across Florida," *New York Times*, November 10, 2000, p. A24.

10. David Gonzalez, "Blacks Citing Flaws Seek Inquiry into Florida Vote," *New York Times*, November 11, 2000, p. A11.

11. David Gonzalez, "Some Say They Were Denied a Chance to Vote," *New York Times*, November 12, 2000, p. A24.

12. Van Natta, Jr., "Democrats Tell of Problems." These are just a sample of the many and varied practices, either clearly illegal or highly questionable, that could be cited. My summary omits two important examples, either of which in itself could have swung such a close election: the confusing "butterfly ballot" in Palm Beach County, which almost certainly caused large numbers of black and Jewish Gore voters to record an unintended vote for Reform Party candidate Patrick Buchanan; and second, the Duval County Democratic Party workers who told people to punch a hole on every page, resulting in the disqualification of many Gore ballots.

13. The *Orlando Sun-Sentinel* data are cited in that same *Nation* article: David Corn, "The Unscanned Majority," *Nation*, vol. 271, no. 21, December 25, 2000, p. 5.

14. John Mintz and Don Keating, "High Rate of Disqualified Ballots in Chicago's Black Precincts," *Washington Post*, reprinted in the *San Francisco Chronicle*, December 27, 2000, p. A5.

15. Alex Keyssar, "Fractured Franchise," *Nation*, vol. 271, no. 19, December 11, 2000, p. 19, cites the four million figure and the Massachusetts example.

16. Kevin Sack and Janet Elder, "Poll Finds Optimistic Outlook, But Enduring Racial Division," *New York Times*, July 11, 2000, pp. 1, A23.

17. Sana Siwolop, "Noose, Symbol of Race Hatred, at Center of Work Place Lawsuits," *New York Times*, July 10, 2000, pp. 1, A16.

18. Herbert Blumer, "Race Prejudice as a Sense of Group Position," *Pacific Sociological Review* 1, no. 1 (Spring 1958): 3–7.

19. Melvin L. Oliver and Thomas M. Shapiro, *Black Wealth, White Wealth* (New York: Routledge, 1995).

20. See Michael Dyson, *I May Not Get There with You: The True Martin Luther King, Jr.* (New York: Free Press, 2000).

21. Michael Omi, "The Changing Meaning of Race," paper presented at the National Research Council Conference on Racial Trends, National Academy of Sciences, Washington, D.C., October 15–16, 1998.

22. *New York Times,* "How Race Is Lived in America," a series of fourteen front-page articles, June 4 through July 13, 2000, plus the *New York Times Magazine,* July 16, 2000, and promotional materials.

23. Sack and Elder, "Polls Finds Optimistic Outlook."

24. Bob Blauner, *Black Lives, White Lives: Three Decades of Rate Relations in America* (Berkeley: University of California Press, 1989); and Sack and Elder, "Poll Finds Optimistic Outlook."